In Dedication

*As as a spiritual and cultural legacy
to my children and grandchildren:*

Richard and Julie Soderquist, Hannah and Rachael,
Jon and Karen Zull, Jacob and Sarah.

CONTENTS

Introduction — 7

Part One
Perspective on the Origin of Our Republic

Chapter 1 — *Western Civilization, the Guardian of Liberty* — 13
Chapter 2 — *The transition of Western Civilization* — 31
Chapter 3 — *Two Paths for Modern Republics* — 35

Part Two
Discovering Republicanism in Bible Law

Chapter 4 — *The Author of Liberty* — 45
Chapter 5 — *Twin Principles of Liberty and Equality* — 53

Part Three
The Hebrew Constitution

Chapter 6 — *A Federal System of Republics* — 65
Chapter 7 — *Local Judicial Power and Due Process of Law* — 81
Chapter 8 — *The National Government* — 87

Part Four
The American Republic

Chapter 9 — *The Future Depends on Understanding the Lessons of the Past* — 107
Chapter 10 — *Maintaining National Liberty* — 113
Chapter 11 — *Maintaining National Unity* — 123
Chapter 12 — *Conclusion* — 133

Epilogue — 141
Appendices — 147
Bibliography — 169
About the Author — 171

Introduction

The word *republic* is derived from the Latin word *respublica*, and refers to representative government. If one breaks down the word, the syllable *res* means concerns, and *publica* means of the people. Such a government forms as a social contract, or covenantal system, and sometimes is referred to as a commonwealth. But this form of government was not the invention (as often claimed) of the Romans or even the Greeks. This inquiry will show that God, through his chosen nation Israel, introduced mankind to the first covenantal republic at Mount Sinai in 1446 BC.[1] That rule of law was further defined through a series of speeches made by Moses and compiled in the Book of Deuteronomy. When the rule of law laid out by Moses was followed to the letter, it made Israel the most free and justly ruled people of all history before the time of Christ. But Israel slowly began to compromise the constitution of Moses by a series of efforts to be like other nations, and it declined in its glory and finally fell to outside foreign empires. A major turning point in that decline began in 1050 BC when Israel adopted human monarchy, and it became a total collapse in 586 BC with the destruction of Jerusalem by Babylon.

Governments and cultures tend to be copied by other neighbor nation-states for many and varied reasons. After 586 BC, while Israel was under imperial domination by four Gentile empires in succession,[2] her cultural and historical writings became widely available for others to examine. There is much evidence that Babylonian and Persian cultures tended to learn from those they conquered and to preserve their writings in libraries. Both the ancient writings of Moses and the then-contemporary writings of captive Hebrew prophets were preserved and were available for study in the time of the successive rise of Babylon's and Susa's hegemony.

Interestingly, the last two Jewish colonial rulers (Greece and Rome) had early histories (between 594 and 49 BC) as less successful, but great, ancient republics. Even before they overthrew Persia, the Greeks commonly visited the Middle East and even voluntarily enlisted in the service of Persian emperors. The Hebrew commonwealth had been in decline for hundreds of years, but between 640 and 609 BC, the constitution of Moses was under re-examination by King Josiah of Judah. This was only 15 years before Athens would begin developing her own republican institutions. Several Greek city-state republics would develop between 594 and 338 BC. I suggest that it is reasonable to assume that a Jewish/Greek intercultural connection evolved in those ancient times. The Roman Republic rose and declined in slow progression between 509 and 49 BC. I will connect the dots between these overlapping international developments in Part One of this book.

It is often suggested by historians that conquerors sometimes end up the conquered as they adopt the superior cultures of those they take over. Certainly Greek culture dominated in the Roman Empire, and even earlier the Greeks adopted many ideas from the Middle Eastern nations with whom they had traded and later would rule. Throughout history, the exchange of ideas has been a more important effect of open trade between nations than the exchange of goods.

Republics have historically been difficult to sustain. As with the Hebrew commonwealth, which started out as a free republic and declined

---

1. See Appendix 7 and the key to the Biblical foundation of dates used in this book.
2. Babylon of the Chaldeans, Susa of Persia, Alexandria of Ptolemy (Greek) Egypt, and the Roman Empire all dominated the "Holy Land" in succession.

into an absolute monarchy, so the Greco-Roman republics also declined in succession into absolute rule by one. Free Greece fell to the absolutism of Alexander, and free Rome fell to the absolutism of Augustus Caesar

To picture the progression of republics in history, I have designed what I call a Liberty Time Wheel.[3] You will note that I have divided this wheel into 400-year benchmark eras. Each era is represented by dates printed in red on the outside of the circle. This allows me to more accurately place the other dates on the inside of the circle in correct proximity to one another, creating an even-ruler effect for measurement of time. The four hundred years between each benchmark do not always fit perfectly as turning points in history, but they do fall in amazingly close proximity to important turning points in the progression of history I am covering.

In the history before the time of Christ, the half circle starts with the year 1446 BC and ends at 246 BC. **1446** BC was the year of the Exodus and birth of the Hebrew republic, under the leadership of Moses. Four hundred years later, **1046** BC was during the reign of Saul, the first king of Israel. The period between 1050 and 930 BC turned out to be both the time of Israel's greatness among nations and the beginning of the decline of her freedoms. Again, four hundred years later, **646** BC falls right between the time of the reformations of Hezekiah and Josiah, as kings of Judah.[4] These kings tried to bring back the whole republican assembly and to reunite the split Kingdoms of Judah and Israel during specific celebrations of the Passover in Jerusalem. Between Hezekiah and Josiah came the King Manasseh (679-42 BC), an evil ruler. Almost as an omen, it is recorded that:

the king of Assyria took Manasseh prisoner, put a hook in his nose, bound him with bronze shackles, and led him to Babylon. In his distress he sought the favor of the Lord his God . . . and thus he was brought back to his kingdom.[5]

Later, after the reign of King Josiah, it was only 23 years before Jerusalem was sacked by Babylon. In the meantime, the Greeks had an opportunity to copy Israel's ideas regarding republican government, and Rome took advantage of the opportunity to copy the Greeks. An exchange of ideas through reading the literature of each other's writings in this ancient time could not help but expose the Greeks to Moses and his law. By **246** BC, even these free western republics had already failed or were failing. This 400-year benchmark was during the time of the First Punic War conducted by Carthage against Rome. The decline of the Roman Republic began with this war and a series of others following it. Rome more and more turned to generals and less and less to elected heads of state. The date 49 BC was the year Julius Caesar proclaimed himself dictator for life. Assassins, who were trying to save the Roman Republic, cut Julius Caesar's life short. But, despite this, the life of the Roman republic was not to survive this turning point in history.

The next 1117 years on the circular timeline should be viewed as if it were a compressed intermediate era. Right at the height of the democratic-republic of Rome it entered a period of empire building conflicts called the Punic Wars between 264 and 146 BC. Then from 107 to 49 BC Rome was engulfed in recurrent civil wars ending up under permanent dictatorship. Therefore, between 246 BC and 871 AD, it was a time in which the knowledge of God-given freedom was hidden from nations for the most part. For 920 years following 49 BC Roman Emperors and then the Roman Papacy dominated Western Civilization and

---

3. View the Liberty Time Wheel located in Appendix 1 of the Appendix, where it can be folded out to the side for reference as you read through the Introduction.

4. Second Chronicles Chapters 30 and 34.

5. Second Chronicles 33: 10-17.

Introduction

republican freedoms were generally nonexistent. But Christian monks in isolated monasteries, by God's providence, kept making copies of the ancient Jewish and Christian texts, as well as copies of ancient Greek and Roman texts. These texts were just waiting for someone in a position of significance to rediscover them.

In **871** AD, Alfred the Great of England rediscovered the God-given rule of liberty under the law as he read the Bible in Latin. He was the first king of England to begin a process of molding a national common law based on Biblical teaching. As a result, English common law became an influence that limited the power of England's future kings. Four hundred years later, in **1271** AD, was the year before the rise of King Edward the First. The rule of Edward the First from 1272-1307 was indeed a benchmark era in English common law. Before the rule of King Edward, a series of baronial rebellions against absolute monarchy had occurred, lasting from 1215 to 1295. In 1215 King John of England was forced to sign the Great Charter (*Magna Charta*), but it took 80 years of civil war for the *Magna Charta* to really produce a settled place in English government for parliament. King Edward the First, though a tyrant in his own right, wisely instituted what became known as the *Model Parliament.* Again, 400 years after the start of Edward the First's reign, shortly after **1671** AD, a parliamentary republic was formed in England. This occurred just 18 years after 1671, but was driven by more civil war that produced a Puritan commonwealth, followed by a very limited restoration of the monarchy (all between 1628 and 1689). This new republican government was patterned directly after that of the ancient Hebrew republic. Overlapping this Bible-based English republic there also arose several English-American colonial republics that drew on the long history of common law. Actually, the American and English republics have been even more successful than the Hebrew republic of ancient history. Throughout the 19th and 20th centuries AD, various nations all over the earth have copied the English-speaking republics, in some fashion, as their despotic governments have been overthrown as the result of great revolutions and wars in those centuries.

Like the dawn of every day, with its darkness dissipating into light, each succeeding era of Western history since the birth of Christianity has seemed to enter a transition from tyranny to free republican government.[6] The resulting modern era of Western Civilization is all about the twin effect of a growing church and a growth of liberty within governments influenced by the church. My objective in this book is to demonstrate to you this premise: that all free republics had their origin in the Bible, and that freedom cannot survive outside the influence of Judeo-Christian principles.

In fact, the ideals of freedom and justice without a national unity centered in submission to God's Law could not be sustained in ancient Israel and cannot be sustained in America. All ancient and modern experiments with republican government that have tried to maintain themselves apart from God's Law have failed or are in the process of failing. In Chapters Two and Three of Part One, I will explain how the modern republics of Western Civilization have taken two separate paths, one Christian and more stable, and the other secular and less stable. At that point, I will demonstrate the unique character of Protestant Christianity that is based on individual accountability. The maintenance of individual spiritual accountability under God, as opposed to a forced democratic collectivist accountability under a godless human authority, is the only secure foundation for a truly free republic.

An unknown author, often quoted, said that "there is a natural cycle in the rise and fall of republics: 1) from bondage to spiritual faith, 2) from spiritual faith to great courage, 3) from courage to

---
6. For example: the fall of absolute monarchies throughout Europe culminating finally in WWI, and the more recent results of WWII, as well as the fall of Soviet Communism.

liberty, 4) from liberty to abundance, 5) from abundance to complacency, 6) from complacency to apathy, 7) from apathy to dependence, and 8) from dependence back to bondage." Indeed, our own republic was born out of a spiritual revival called the Reformation, and may have advanced to stage six or seven in our own time. Does that mean we must move into a death spiral and end up again under bondage as a people? No, we do not have to move into stage eight. I am hopeful that this book (and many other current efforts by Christian movements taking place in America) will help us recover our moral compass and that we will demonstrate it is possible for a nation to learn from history.

I make no apology for drawing some of my research from the books of Moses and from the writers of ancient Israel's Biblical history. If your historical studies have never taken you to that source, let me be the first to introduce that knowledge to you. My own knowledge of the history of Western Civilization also will be woven into this inquiry. Having a master's degree in political science, having taught both European/American history and government in public schools for 37 years, and having been a student of the Bible from the time I was in high school to now my 70th year of life, I am convinced that I am prepared to address this thesis. I am not the first to do so, however. Other scholars who have held the same opinion will be quoted at times in this book. Sadly, the trend today in many colleges and high schools is to abandon the teaching of Western Civilization and to teach multiculturalism in its place. I do not advocate that schools not teach about other cultures, but I do object that it is being done at the expense of an in-depth look into the exceptional influence Western Civilization has had on all nations. I never taught the direct tie between Moses and our Western Civilization when I was in the classroom, but I did teach about the separate grandeur of Western Judeo-Christian culture in history. It is time for me to make the case now for the direct correlation between Moses and our republic.

I hope everyone interested in freedom will read my book, but my writing probably will appeal mainly to Biblical and secular history buffs, and to teachers. This audience likely will find it easiest to follow the sweeping nature of my text. I hope you will discover, as I have, the amazing correlation between the Mosaic covenantal constitution and the modern concepts of republican government[7]

For the skeptics who begin with the presupposition that the Bible is just myth, and to whom God plays no personal role within their worldview, my thesis will at times seem sermonic in nature. This is an academic exercise, but in my zeal for the subject I hope the reader will accept the now and then exposure of my faith that undergirds all I expound upon. I am of the opinion, that God is personally involved in history, but also that not everything that has occurred in history was his will. I only ask the skeptics to at least open the doors of their minds to the objective evidence in the Bible regarding a recorded history of the Jews and the connection to Western Civilization's concepts of freedom and justice. If you just go that far, I believe you will find that this book makes a sound argument for how the roots of our republic are indeed Biblical.

Under the glory of the Old Covenant, mankind was given a perfect foundation for just and righteous government. But humanity could not overcome its sinful nature and ended up under absolute tyranny. However, under the glory of the New Covenant, victory was won against sin and death; if a nation submits to Christ, it escapes the tyranny of the "Man of Sin" for the freedom of the "Spirit." First, victory occurs within a succession of individuals, then, as a leading remnant of the nation walks in the Spirit, victory can occur nationally. "Now the Lord is the Spirit, and where the Spirit of the Lord is, there is freedom."[8]

---

7. [8]Biblical history and law is profitable for both individual and societal reformation; but today many overlook the redemptive implications for society in the Holy Bible.

8. Second Corinthians 3:17.

Part One
Perspective on the Origin of Our Republic

THIS IS WHAT THE LORD SAYS:
Stand at the crossroads and look;
Ask for the ancient paths,
Ask where the good way is, and
walk ye in it,
and you will find rest for your souls.

But you said, "We will not walk in it."
I appointed watchmen over you and said,
Listen to the sound of the trumpet!
But you said, we will not listen.

Therefore hear, O nations,
Observe, O witnesses,
what will happen to them. Hear, O earth:
I am bringing disaster on this people,
the fruit of their schemes,
because they have not listened to my words,
and have rejected my law.

Jeremiah 6: 16-19

Chapter 1

Western Civilization, the Guardian of Liberty

"The God who made the world and everything in it is the Lord of heaven and earth, . . . From one man [Noah] he made every nation of men, that they should inhabit the whole earth, and he determined the times set for them and the exact places where they should live. God did this so that men would seek him and perhaps reach out for him and find him, though he is not far from each one of us."[1]

The Old Testament Book of Genesis explains the origin of nations. From it we learn that all nations are descended from the three sons of Noah: Shem, Ham, and Japheth. The posterity of the nations of Shem are modern nations predominantly founded in the Middle East. Prominent among them is Israel.[2] The posterity of the nations of Ham are modern nations founded from Afro-Asian language groups. The posterity of the nations of Japheth are modern nations founded from Indo-European language groups. The birthplace of civilization is the *Middle* East, from which all nations migrated outward in all directions. The nations to the west, which began their cultural development in Greece, then Italy, and then all of Europe, are the western civilizations of history. Our particular interest in this inquiry will be about how, in God's providence, Western Civilization has inherited from Israel the guardianship of the great principles of republican government.

What is there about the development of nation-states that would cause men to seek God? Could it be that the tendency of governments to enslave humanity draws men to God? The theme of this book is, "Now the Lord is the Spirit, and where the Spirit of the Lord is, there is freedom."[3] All good things come from God, including freedom. Why would God choose one nation and take such great pains to tell it how it should be governed? The answer is, freedom is not natural in this world. Tyranny is the natural order of things if man is left to his own devices. Moses was God's ideal nation builder for his chosen nation, Israel. God gave Moses not only the direct revelation of his Creation, the Fall of Man, and the Great Flood preceding the rise of nations, but also divine wisdom regarding the art of governing a nation. The first five books of the Bible were written by Moses and contain all the foundational knowledge through which men can build a free state.

The corruption of all human government is but a reflection of the fallen nature of mankind. Since the nature of man is sinful, it is my contention that without the truth revealed to Moses, as God's builder of his chosen nation, no people throughout history would have discovered the rule of law necessary to experience justice and freedom.[4]

---

1. Acts 17:24-27.

2. Shem is the origin of the term Semitic people, which include Hebraic, Aramaic and Arabic language groups.

3. Second Corinthians 3: 17.

4. The most fundamental purpose of God's chosen nation

In an overly simplified outline, the Bible is the story of God's Creation of a perfect world, how it went bad, was then destroyed by a universal flood, was given an opportunity for redemption, and still awaits an ultimate triumph on God's terms. With the fall of Adam and Eve, paradise was lost, and over time violence and corruption so ruled mankind that it was necessary for God to wipe out the world in a watery judgment. It would have been the same after the Flood had not God forced the confusion of tongues and thus established nations. The introduction of cultural/national divisions in human history became a deterrent to worldwide centralized and wicked tyranny. In God's plan, wicked nations would rise up against each other and thus create a kind of balance of power to prevent unified and worldwide corruption from occurring again. Then, by the introduction of God's chosen nation to be an example of how to govern with justice and freedom, mankind also had a template for good government that checks the sinful nature of people. I will examine this template in Parts Two and Three of this book. First, however, I need to make the connections in historical progression of how Western Civilization has been the inheritor and guardian of free government. Part One is a survey of my Liberty Time Wheel, which traces the history of republics from Israel to the United States of America.[5] Finally, Part Four will bring us back to America's present state of affairs as either the latest best hope for freedom and justice or the next in line to fail and pass this providential baton on to another nation.

For allegorical purposes, consider this circular timeline like it was a clock. Let us imagine that after God ordained the birth of nation-states, as a result of the experience at Babel, he then established his own special nation-state, Israel, and set it down in history as a fully wound-up clock.[6] Israel was to be the best example of good government if it would be obedient to the Law and constitution[7] given by God through Moses. Man himself was, and is, in a fallen state and unable to govern righteously. Therefore, man could only maintain this best of governments if he had a means of confession and repentance for his sins, through religious ceremonies under God's ordained priesthood. If the true role of the priesthood ever broke down, so too would the clock slowly wind down and lead to a corrupted form of the good government, or even its demise. Some in Israel almost immediately became disobedient, but God was patient and, like a father, continually put them under severe discipline. If Israel's sins became willful, and it remained unrepentant long enough, God's judgment would no longer be withheld and his chosen people would lose all of their freedom. But the seed of freedom planted by Israel under the leadership of Moses would not die. It would be transplanted into a series of nations to be called Western Civilization.

God's providential order is not directed by an inherited instinctual goodness within human nature, but rather is one of inherited law and personal responsibility, resulting in either blessings, based on obedience, or curses, based on disobedience. Only if this chosen people were seeking after God and consensually striving to be obedient

---

was to prepare humanity, in general, for a Savior, who would be a son of Israel, to bring redemption for our fallen nature. But this chosen nation also would introduce to any society seeking freedom from tyranny the possibility of salvation socially and politically.

5. See Appendix 1 and unfold the circular timeline so, as you read this section of Part One, you can observe the progression of dates and time.

6. Lest one think that I am coming from a Deist point of view, let me firmly assert that this is more in line with what is called the Christian Reconstructionist point of view. See my epilogue at the end of Part Four for a detailed explanation.

7. As I refer to the Law of Israel, it will mean the Mosaic Covenant; but when I use the term constitution, it will mean the system of institutional centers of authority meant to uphold the Law of Israel.

to God's Law would they be able to maintain their free constitution.

The federal republic of Israel will be defined in Part Two and Part Three of this book. In this first chapter, I will provide only a brief outline of Israel's history between 1446 and 586 BC. Israel was governed by an assembly (which I will call a states-general) and by a national judge, without a capital city, between 1446 and 1050 BC. However, most secular governing was the responsibility of elected princes within each tribal territory, and elected magistrates within every city of each tribe. This republic had its problems, but didn't really begin to crumble until the last 57 years of its existence. Israel didn't adopt rule by a monarchy until 1050 BC. Ironically, Israel's Golden Age came under her early kings, David and Solomon, between 1010 and 930 BC. In the early monarchy, between 1050 and 930 BC, kings were elected and answered to the national states-general by means of a constitutional contract. Her former national judges became national prophets to hold the king accountable to God's Covenant. Under Kings David and Solomon, Israel's wealth, creativity, and beautiful architecture in her capital city, Jerusalem, was the envy of the world.

To some limited extent, Israel's republican forms and her Law continued to have power over the nation all through the monarchy era. However, after 930 BC, the nation split and the states-general faded away in both the northern and southern kingdoms. The maintenance of the Rule of Law after 930 BC was upheld, on a irregular basis, by prophets who would confront the kings at given times. Also, at least in the southern kingdom's capital, Jerusalem, the concept of constitutional monarchy was put in place and enforced by the high priest.[8] Despite this, the people themselves, after 930 BC, copied nations around them and quickly submitted to rule by absolute kings, who were not elected. The northern kingdom was so corrupted in its disobedience to the Law that it finally fell, under God's judgment, to the conquest of Assyrian kings. The southern kingdom was called Judah because it was still ruled from Jerusalem by kings who inherited the throne as descendents of King David. Judah had a mix of both evil and good kings. Good rulers led the people in submission to God.

Evil Empire Threatens the Survival of Human Freedom[9]

The Hebrews living through the years between 726 and 586 BC witnessed the "last gasping breath" of a dying constitutional monarchy for ancient Israel/Judah. The northern kingdom, ruled from Samaria, would perish quickly in 722, while the southern kingdom, ruled from Jerusalem, would "catch its breath," so to speak, and under reformation kings would almost revive its republican foundations. Almost, but it was not to be. A cruel absolutism was sweeping through the whole Middle East, led by the Assyrians, and quickly followed by a neo-Babylonian tyranny.

A truly threatening world empire, in the vein of Nimrod of the Tower of Babel, was forming again, in this time of Israel's final collapse. But, as referenced at the start of this chapter, God had raised up nation-states as a deterrent to the absolutism of empires. At this moment in time, Hebrew history helps us see an example of how God's purpose for nation-states works. Out of the absolutism of the powerful Egyptian state had come the first free republic of history, the Hebrew commonwealth. Egypt had been held in check by an equally powerful nation called the Hittites. Neither Egypt nor the Hittites could create an empire

---

8. See Second Kings Chapter 11, but especially verse 17. A constitutional monarchy implies a legal contract, in this case a contract between God, the king, and the people.

9. Again and again in history, evil empires have threatened the survival of freedom, but freedom survives in God's providence. Modern examples are the outcome of World War II, and the fall of the Soviet Empire.

on a very effective level. Even small states play a role in this scheme that maintains a balance of power to hold back absolute world tyranny. The small state of Phoenicia learned to mind her own business when it benefited her and to make and switch alliances when it served her best. At different times Phoenicia and even Syria could be allies or enemies with the Hebrew states. But at the very moment Israel and Judah were ripe for God's judgment, there arose a real terrifying and growing Assyrian hegemony that threatened to wipe out all states that stood in the way of its conquest. The great powers still standing in the way of Assyria were the Nubian Pharaohs of Egypt[10] and the northern and southern kingdoms of the Hebrews. Damascus (Syria) had been at war with Samaria (Israel), with Assyria benefiting by waiting and watching as one weakened the other, all the while planning on coming in to take over both. Phoenicia was playing it cool trying to stay neutral.

The balance of power described above could be superimposed on almost any other era of world history following this ancient one, even to our own time, but, of course, with different players, while still producing the same effect. The effect was always the erosion and demise of human attempts to build and maintain world empires.

Biblical history reveals the key role played by Judah in holding back the Assyrian hegemony. But interestingly, between 726 and 586 BC, the Biblical record reveals how God directed the outcome. God's role in this regard throughout all history is usually only apparent in hindsight. The reformation king of Judah, Hezekiah, reigned from 726 to 697. It is recorded:

Hezekiah ... in the first month and the first year of his reign ... opened the doors of the Temple of the Lord ... and said, "Listen to me Levites! Consecrate yourselves now and consecrate the Temple of the Lord, the God of your fathers. Remove all defilements from the sanctuary. Our fathers were unfaithful they did evil in the eyes of the Lord ... and turned their backs on him. They shut the doors of the portico and put out the lamps ... This is why our fathers have fallen by the sword and why our sons and daughters and our wives are [taken and will be taken] in captivity. Now I intend to make a covenant with the Lord, the God of Israel, so his fierce anger will turn away from us ... So the service of the Temple of the Lord was reestablished ... Hezekiah sent word to all Israel and Judah and also wrote letters to Ephraim and Manasseh, inviting them to come ... [to] Jerusalem and celebrate the Passover ... The plan seemed right both to the king and the whole assembly [as many as they could assemble of the old states-general]. They decided to send a proclamation throughout Israel from Beersheba to Dan ... The couriers went from town to town in Ephraim and Manasseh, as far as Zebulun, but the people scorned and ridiculed them. Nevertheless, some men of Asher, Manasseh, and Zebulun humbled themselves and went to Jerusalem. Also in Judah the hand of God was on the people to give them unity of mind to carry out what the king and the officials had ordered." [11]

Samaria had not yet come under the direct rule of the Assyrians, and it had a very weak king. Observe how the king of Judah reached out to the tribes of Israel, who were then under the tyranny of having to pay tribute to Nineveh.

The king of Samaria was Hoshea, and he was fearful of a takeover by the Assyrians and, if not by them, then by Judah. Note the lack of popular support for the spiritual revival in the northern tribes, when asked by Hezekiah to come to Jerusalem to celebrate the Passover. The Biblical record

---

10. 750- 670 BC was the time of Egypt's black kings from Cush/Nubia (today's Sudan).

11. Second Chronicles, quoting parts of Chapters 29 and 30.

claims that this was the cause of God's judgment that fell on Samaria in just four years.

> In King Hezekiah's fourth year, which was the seventh year of Hoshea . . . king of Israel, Shalmaneser, king of Assyria marched on Samaria and laid siege to it [722 BC] . . . The king of Assyria deported [many in] Israel to Assyria [as slaves] . . . This happened because they had not obeyed the Lord their God, but had violated his Covenant . . . .[12]

The reformation under King Hezekiah was mainly spiritual, but a later reformation would be more social and political in nature. First hearts must be made right and then God can bestow the gifts of justice and freedom to any nation submitting to him. The northern kingdom (Israel) had already become a vassal state of Assyria, even before the fall of Samaria. Its last king Hoshea, sought an alliance with Egypt and refused to pay the tribute required by Assyria. Then the Assyrians sacked Samaria. King Hezekiah of Judah had opened the door, so to speak, to reunite all of Israel, but the invasion of the Assyrians would postpone that goal. After the sacking of Samaria, Hezekiah was forced into a war with Assyria for the rest of his reign.

The Assyrian Shalmaneser the fifth and Sargon the second Co-Kingship only lasted from 727 to 705 BC. But Hezekiah would still be king of Judah into the first eight years of the next ruler of Assyria, known as King Sennacherib. Reacting to Hezekiah's earlier attempt to reunite Israel and Judah the new Assyrian king took the war to Jerusalem and Judah. Sennacherib ruled the Assyrian Empire from 705 to 681. In 701, King Hezekiah's Kingdom of Judah was invaded by Assyria. Sennacherib's huge army immediately captured the northern frontier cities, including Lachish. Interestingly, this Assyrian king's own recorded history helps verify the accuracy of Jewish Biblical history or, as some may prefer, Jewish Biblical history helps verify the accuracy and inaccuracy of Assyrian recorded history.[13]

Hezekiah's reaction was varied. On the one hand, when he learned about Sennacherib's plans to sack Jerusalem, he tried to bribe his way out of trouble by paying a tribute that included 30 talents of gold taken from the overlay of the Temple doors.[14] Almost immediately following the above action, Hezekiah became deathly sick. During the illness, he called on the prophet Isaiah, who gave him advice and also healed him. Immediately upon King Hezekiah's recovery, either at his invitation or out of the self-interest of the rebel king in Babylon (we are not told), envoys of the king of Babylon visited the king of Judah, who showed them all the treasures in the temple.[15] Again, we are not told why King Hezekiah did this, but it would seem it was to curry an alliance with Babylon against Assyria. The Bible helps us gain many inside details of this war, not otherwise available to us in secular history.

As regards the war itself, it is recorded that Hezekiah boldly stood up to the Assyrians after Isaiah prophesized that the armies of Assyria would not shoot one arrow or even build siege ramps against Jerusalem, and that Sennacherib would himself leave suddenly and be killed in his own capital shortly after returning home.[16] Both the Bible and Sennacherib's own historical record

---

12. Second Kings 18: 9-12. This is Shalmaneser 5 whose Co-Rex, Sargon 2, also took over Babylon. Sargon 2 is better known as an Assyrian king than Shalmaneser 5. From 722 to 625 BC, Nineveh dominated Babylon, but Nineveh was destroyed by Babylon in 625.

13. The detailed Biblical record is found in 2 Kings 18-20, 2 Chronicles 29-32, and Isaiah 36-39.

14. An amount exactly verified by Sennacherib's chronicles, today preserved at the Chicago Oriental Institute as the so-called Taylor Prism.

15. Isaiah questions the wisdom of this and prophesizes that Babylon will come back later and extract all of the Temple treasures and take Hebrew sons captive to Babylon. (39: 5-7).

16. Isaiah 37: 33-38.

show that the invading king split his army into two forces at Lachish, and that the king of Assyria then led half the army down to Egypt because he had received a report that Egypt was marching out to defend Judah. Both historical accounts also record that another force was led by Sennacherib's field commander to approach Jerusalem and taunt the residents with the hopelessness of resisting an Assyrian army that thus far had destroyed all enemies. The outcome as recorded in Sennacherib's chronicles was that he defeated both Egypt and Judah; in his own words, he said this of Hezekiah:

> *I shut him up in Jerusalem, his capital city, like a bird in a cage, building towers round the city to hem him in, and raising banks of earth against the gates, so as to prevent escape . . . Then upon Hezekiah there fell the fear of the power of arms, and he sent out to me the elders of Jerusalem with 30 talents of gold . . . and diverse treasures. All these things were brought to Nineveh.*[17]

The truth of the matter is that both Egypt's and Judah's histories say Sennacherib left in a hurry, and without raising any assault against Egypt or Jerusalem.[18] Further, the next Assyrian king's historical scribe recorded that Sennacherib died at the hands of his own sons in Nineveh very shortly after returning home, thus also confirming the Biblical record.

The Assyrians left in disgrace, but after Hezekiah the next king of Judah, Manasseh, led his people in idolatry, and even was taken prisoner by Assyria for a short time. Then an opportunity arose again in all the land of Israel for a king in Jerusalem to try and finish what Hezekiah had started. This would be the last good king of Judah. His name was Josiah and he boldly invited those under oppression as far north as the tribal territory of Naphtali, as well as Manasseh and Ephraim, to repent of their idolatry, along with all of Judah. But the biggest part of this reformation took place because the priests rediscovered the Book of the Law, and read it to the king, who then tried to reestablish the states-general of Israel and, most likely, the republican principles of justice found in the book.[19]

The reign of Josiah was between 640 and 609 BC and could not have gone unnoticed by the surrounding nations, especially Athens, Greece, which, 15 short years later, was undergoing its own reformation in order to save the city-state from economic collapse and stop a class rebellion by lower-level citizens deeply in debt and under the threat of becoming permanent slaves of the richer classes. Athens adopted a republican constitution under the leadership of Solon in 594 BC. It is more than mere coincidence that Solon's constitution included reforms like the concept of bankruptcy, jury trials, and equal justice under the law, without privileged classes. All these concepts were open to discovery by King Josiah and anyone else at that very time in history, in the Book of the Law, written centuries before, in the time of Moses.[20] But despite these late attempts at revival, Judah fell 23 years after the death of King Josiah because of the succeeding weak kings and the people's continued willful and widespread disobedience to the Law.

However, nothing in God's timing is wasted. As the Jews came under judgment because of

---

17. See footnote 14.

18. The writer of 2 Kings 19 says an angel of the Lord went out and put to death 185,000 men in the Assyrian camp that surrounded Jerusalem, so Sennacherib's forces broke camp and withdrew. As regards Egypt, the Greek historian Herodotus wrote, in his *Histories* ca. 450, a story based on Egyptian records from the time of Sennacherib, that a witness spying on Sennacherib's encampment outside the gates of Egypt saw a multitude of field mice invade the camp at night and eat up all the bow strings and thongs by which a shield is held, and thus the army left the next morning without a fight.

19. Second Chronicles 34–35.

20. See Appendix 9. (In Hebrew, Deuteronomy means repetition of the Law).

their sins, the Book of the Law containing the promise of justice under republican government became available as a template for Western Civilization to examine. In the 182 years between the rise of the reformation king, Josiah of Judah (640 BC), and the revival of a limited Jewish home rule under Ezra (458 BC), the Athenian Republic and the Roman Republic would both burst onto the world stage. In Parts Two and Three I will again and again compare and contrast these later republics with that of Moses' republic.

In God's plan to restrain worldwide tyranny, he always puts down empire builders throughout history by turning nations against each other.[21] In 625 BC, Nabapolassar of Babylon destroyed Nineveh and the Assyrian Empire and the last kings of Judah were made his vassals. Nation rising against nation had once again held back worldwide tyranny. Finally in 586 BC, Jerusalem was destroyed and sacked by a new Babylonian king, Nebuchadnezzar. This Neo-Babylonian empire lasted only 89 years (625-536 BC). It fell to the Medes and Persians. While most of the Hebrews remained in their homeland under a series of successive foreign governments for about 400 years, for the first 70 years (606-536 BC) her brightest and most skilled lived in forced exile in Babylon.[22]

It was 536 BC when Cyrus, king of the Medes and Persians, agreed to permit the Jews in Babylon to return to the homeland.[23] Under the leadership of Zerubbabel, a few would leave Babylon in that year, but bigger migrations took place later under other Persian emperors. While the Persians were establishing an empire in the Middle East, the Greeks also were beginning an impressive rise as a civilization to the west. Before and during the exile in Babylon, four significant prophets of Israel: Isaiah, Jeremiah, Ezekiel, and Daniel helped prepare the Jewish exiles for their return and a future transition, under a promised Messiah, to a New Covenant.[24] It was under the high priest, Ezra, that the Jews would rebuild the Temple in Jerusalem, and in 458 BC he led another rededication to the Law and constitution of Moses.[25] It is recorded in Ezra Chapter 10, and expounded upon in the Babylonian Talmud, that Ezra became the first high priest of the revived Council of 70 referred to as the Great Assembly (Knesset Gedolah).[26] This Great Assembly is believed to have put together the first canon of books making up today's Old Testament. Jewish colonial self-government slowly evolved under Ezra's contemporary, Nehemiah, who was appointed by the Persian emperor, Artaxerxes, to be governor of the renewed Jewish homeland. Nehemiah promoted a written and binding constitution holding all priests and other leaders of the people accountable to it.

> *All these* [the priests and leaders and by inference all the Jewish people they represent] *now join . . . and bind themselves with a curse and an oath to follow the Law of God given through Moses.*[27]

As governor, Nehemiah directly promoted public service in the common interest and confronted governmental officials that "lorded it

---

21. As examples, note the ultimate failure of the Mongols, the Moors, the Ottomans, the Spanish, the English, the Germans and Japanese, and the Soviet Communists.

22. See Exhibit B, Appendix 4. The prophet Daniel predicted this whole succession of empire builders and the coming "Kingdom of God" through which true spiritual and social justice could finally be rebuilt.

23. Most think the first exiles, which included Daniel, were taken to Babylon in 606 BC before the total destruction of Jerusalem. Jeremiah prophesied the Jews would be in exile 70 years and then begin to return home. This would place the first return to the homeland in 536 BC.

24. See Exhibit B, Appendix 4.

25. See Nehemiah Chapter 8, Deuteronomy 16: 13-20, and Ezra 7: 25-28.

26. Adin Steinsaltz, *The Essential Talmud* (London, England: Weidenfeld and Nicolson, 1976), 14.

27. See Nehemiah 9: 38 and 10: 29.

over the people."[28] This Great Assembly later became known as the national Sanhedrin. But under the influence of the Greeks, who became the next masters of the revived republic of Judah, this home-rule of the Jews was greatly compromised. The Sanhedrin would become more like an aristocratic senate than a representative body held accountable to the people.

Significantly, Ezra's life was contemporary with the Golden Age of Athens under her leader Pericles between 461-429 BC. Preceding this Golden Age, the Greek-Persian War (499-480 BC) positioned Athens to lead a defensive alliance of most of the Greek city-states. The unsuccessful invasion of Greece by the Persian Emperor Xerxes propelled Athens to a place of dominance in the western world. What followed was called the Age of Pericles. From that Golden Age on into the time of Alexander the Great, the Greeks were heavily involved in the trade of goods and ideas in the world around them. The Persians and Greeks were destined to participate in an unprecedented integration of cultures and to compete for hegemony in the world. Under Alexander the Great, the Greeks finally overthrew the Persian Empire. A Greek imperialistic empire arose and, though it made the claim that it ruled the world, it would fall finally to a close neighbor Rome.

How could it not be in God's providence that the concepts of freedom and republican government would pass from the Jews to Greece, and then to Rome? As early as 594 BC (within 15 years of King Josiah's attempted reinstitution of Israel's Council of 70), the Solon Constitution of Athens created an elected council of 400 to make the laws and elect magistrates, and also instituted citizen juries to be picked by lot to administer justice. The Jewish restoration of home rule between 536 BC (Zerubbabel) and 432 BC (Nehemiah) overlapped the rise of Greek and Roman republics. The Roman Republic was instituted in 509 BC. By 508 BC, under the leadership of Clisthenes, Athens had become a direct democracy ruled by a citizen assembly and would encourage the development of the arts, drama, academic freedom, and magnificent architecture. Her Golden Age under the leadership of Pericles overlapped the time of Ezra's rediscovery of the Book of the Law, as he and Nehemiah began the process of nation building for the Jews. While the Jews were rebuilding a national government of limited independence in the Persian empire, and rediscovering the Law of Moses, Greek city-states (especially Athens) were also in the process of developing their republican governments. It is my purpose, in Part Two and Three of this book, to help you discover how representative government and justice by jury trials all had their origin in the more ancient Mosaic commonwealth, not in Athens.

In the meantime, at the moment Athens was becoming a democracy (by ancient standards) in 509 BC, there was the overthrow of the Etruscan monarchy and the birth of the Roman Republic. Roman republican government copied Athens, but Rome's constitution was more stable and her freedom was more limited. Because of the human inclination to tyranny, Rome's chief magistrates were two elected Consuls with only one-year terms. Each Consul had veto power over the other as they administered policy. Rome had a hereditary aristocratic Senate, and elected Tribunes of its lower classes who could check the Senate by demanding a popular plebiscite vote on issues affecting the masses (called the plebeians). Her system of justice was not by juries but by impartial judges, who were elected as experts in the law.

Greek republican rule ended with the rise of Alexander the Great, shortly after 338 BC, and Greek despots ruled Hellenistic empires in the Middle East until overthrown by Rome in 146 BC. Rome became a constitutional monarchy under Augustus in 27 BC. Much as the forms of the Hebrew republic survived into its early

---

28. See Nehemiah 5: 15.

constitutional monarchy, the Roman adversarial system of justice, which was reserved for her citizens, would survive even after the fall of its republic. In Parts Two and Three, I will explain how all the above protections of personal liberty really had their origin hundreds of years earlier in the Hebrew republic.

The Spiritual Battle between Good and Evil

Having given these very brief descriptions of the Greek and Roman republics of pre-Christian history, let me now reveal an even more ancient connection between Greece and the earliest Hebrew national origins. Both Athens and Rome had become magnificent centers of beautiful temples where Western man worshiped pagan idols backed up by a common ancient mythology. The Parthenon temple in Athens was the first to be built and was the starting point for this western mythology. It was still standing in all its beauty at the time of Christ. Interestingly, Robert Bowie Johnson, Jr. recently documented a direct connection between the Book of Genesis, written by Moses, and Greek mythology. Until this scholarly work, no one could explain the origin of ancient Western mythology.

Everyone has always recognized that Greek myth and Greek art are inseparable. Greek art depicts the myth and Greek myth explains the art. But the one place it all came together was on the acropolis, in the Parthenon temple, above ancient Athens. Johnson calls this connection the Parthenon Code. He says:

> The Parthenon Code is a simple method of expression devised by ancient Greek artists to communicate religious ideas and historical information to their fellow countrymen. The artists' painted and sculpted declarations were very simple and far less abstract than writing. We can compare them to other types of visual language such as stained glass windows in medieval times, and even comic strip panels and storyboards for television in our own day. I call it the Parthenon Code because it was on Athena's Temple that this artistic communication reached its height, and in many ways its most straightforward and simple form. The seven sculptural themes on the outside of the temple, and Athena's gold and ivory idol-image on the inside, portrayed interconnected truths about Greek origins. These historical and religious truths all appeared in similar ways on vase-paintings or on other temple sculptures, or on both.[29]

To truly grasp who Athena was and what Greek artists were trying to say with their temple code, we need a frame of reference outside of Greek myth. That all-important frame of reference is the Book of Genesis. The story of the Garden of Eden, the Great Flood, as well as the Nimrod rebellion after the flood, are all told again by Greek mythology, except from an opposite point of view. I refer you to the book *The Parthenon Code* itself for the pictures and images, because here I can only relate a summary of the story being told. Athena is the new Eve of the Greek age, the one honored and worshiped for bringing the Serpent's enlightenment in the Garden of Eden back to mankind after the Flood. Athena stands 42 feet tall in the center of the temple, and beside her is a sculpture of a serpent rising to a striking pose almost 15 feet high. In her right hand rests the 6-foot figure of Nike, signifying victory. Contrary to the story in Genesis where the Serpent is condemned to crawl on its belly, and Eve and all humankind descended from her are condemned to experience death, Athena claims victory over death, and the serpent stands erect.

In Greek Myth the gods are all men and women who, having lived a bigger-than-life exis-

---

29. Robert Bowie Johnson Jr., *The Parthenon Code* (Annapolis, Maryland: Solving Light Books, 2004), 5.

tence, have earned eternal life as additions to the pantheon of all gods, who live in heaven while observing mortal humans on earth. In this religious myth, Zeus and Hera are the first humans on earth (Adam and Eve). Hera is the goddess of childbirth and marriage. All the gods and all mortal men sprang forth from this first couple. There is no transcendent god above creation, like St Paul is introducing to the Athenians in the quote at the start of this chapter. But the serpent is everywhere in Greek art as a back stage performer. Perhaps the expression "as wise as a serpent" comes from the Greeks. Greek mythology promotes the wisdom of the serpent (Satan) as enlightenment. Hephaestus (Cain), the first born of Zeus and Hera, becomes a rival to his brother, Ares (Seth). Homer, a great poet of ancient Greece, refers to Ares (Seth) as the *bane of mortals*. The competition of the ancestral line of Hephaestus (Cain) and Ares (Seth) spills over into history after the Great Flood. Ares' greatest descendent is Nereus (Noah) who is found numerous times in ancient Greek vase art, and always as an adversary. The Great Flood wipes out the entire ancestral line of Hephaestus (Cain), and Nereus (Noah) is blamed for this. Only Nereus, his wife, and his three sons and their wives are left to repopulate the earth. Then once again some men desire to know the wisdom of the serpent.

The entire Greek myth, or Zeus religion, was summarized in sculptures of figures on the back (west) pediment and front (east) pediment of the temple that remains today in ruins on the acropolis above Athens, Greece. This beautiful temple and wonder of ancient history was built under the direction of Pericles and completed in the year 432 BC, but the myth it was built to portray had its origin much earlier in history. The temple remained in continuous use for about a thousand years. Christianity made idolatry unpopular in the fifth and sixth centuries AD, and the temple was defaced. Later in history at least twice, it experienced wartime destruction, which caused much of its idolatrous art to crumble. Today most of its art and even its structure is lost or held in various museums. Drawings made before any destruction, and an examination of artifacts and ancient texts, have made it possible to piece together the myth. My summary is a review of Robert Bowie Johnson's work.

The temple is called the Parthenon of Athena, which means the shrine of the virgin Athena. The west pediment once made the Noah and Genesis connection. In the center stood Athena and Poseidon. According to the myth, Poseidon, god of the power of the sea, slowly took the power of Nereus (Noah) away, and is here recognizing Athena as the leader of a new age. The evidence for this is revealed in vase art in a very compelling manner, and documented with pictures in Johnson's book. The Myth goes on to explain that Zeus (Adam), who had become a god, gave birth shortly after the Flood to Athena, a fully grown women who burst forth out of his head. Like Eve of Genesis, she was begotten out of man and not born of a woman. She would never marry and would prepare Greece for future greatness. As depicted on the west pediment of the temple, Athena was holding on to an olive tree growing out of the acropolis. This represented the source of the olive tree leaf, which was brought back by the dove to Nereus (Noah) in the ark as a sign that the Flood had abated. On the other side of Poseidon stood Amphitrite, his wife, and a daughter of Nereus. This marriage represented the beginning of a revenge for the pre Flood era when the sons of Ares (Seth) saw that the daughters of Hephaestus (Cain) were beautiful and took them for wives. The offspring of these kidnapped wives were giants.[30] According to the Zeus religion, Nereus' many daughters, born after the Flood, were taken by force to marry those in rebellion against the God of Nereus (Noah). Greek Myth took the mystery of the antediluvian world and pictured it with strange symbols of creatures

---
30. Genesis 6: 1-4.

unknown to mankind after the victory of Athena. Nereus was pictured as half man and half fish. The sons of Nereus and their pre Flood Sethite ancestors are pictured as Centaurs, half man and half horse. The Greeks borrowed such half-man half-animal images from Babylon after the Flood. According to the myth, it was in Babylon that Hermes (Cush, son of Ham, son of Noah) began the religion of Zeus, and from there it spread to various cultures, including Greece.

The east pediment, or front of the temple, celebrated the victory of Athena. In the center stood Zeus (Adam), the supreme god of heaven, with a lighting bolt in his right hand. To his right stood Athena, and to his left stood Hera (Eve). The figures to Zeus' right all represented the rise of Zeus' religious origin out of Babylon. To Zeus' far right was Helios, driving his chariot forward out of the waters of the flood toward Athena. Helios was the sun god and herald of a new age (day). Before him sat Hercules (Nimrod of Genesis), ready to set up an empire at Babylon, and to do battle with the Centaurs (half man half horse) and the three bodied monster representing the three sons of Nereus. From Babylon the religion of Zeus moved west to Pergamum (in Asia Minor, or Turkey today), and from Pergamum finally to Athens. Between Hercules and Athena were the three fates representing birth, longevity, and death, and also Nike pushing back against the fate of death, in front of Athena. To the left of Hera stood Hephaestus (Cain), her first son, whose revenge for being wiped out by the Flood is made by Hermes, who stood just left of Hephaestus. Then to the left of Hermes (Cush) is the figure of Atlas who is pushing back the heavens, and with it the God of the heavens. Atlas allows the exposure of the paradise of Eden where the figures of Hesperides sit inviting man to enter the garden and taste of its fruit. The tree of knowledge in the garden is represented behind the Hesperides figures entwined with the serpent and holding the golden apples of wisdom. Contrast this sculptured scene with the Hebrew genesis story of God's angel guarding the entrance to Eden so as to keep man from coming back in and taking of its fruit. Finally, the pre Flood era from which this ancient history has its origin is represented by the sculptured figure of Nyx (god of darkness) driving his chariot left into the secrets of the darkness. Who has a better explanation of the Parthenon east pediment sculptures than that of Robert Bowie Johnson?

Archaeologists may have failed to find the Ark of Noah in Turkey, but in ancient Greece Johnson has found Noah. Archaeologists have also found sculpted on the temple alter of Zeus in ancient Pergamum, Turkey, a more detailed story of Greek myth regarding Nereus. The Zeus religion relegated the Supreme God of scripture to the status of a nonentity and elevated the Serpent (Satan) and humanity to supreme heights. The Greek myth of Zeus elevates the way of Cain, while the Hebrew faith elevates the way of Seth. It should not surprise us that the true Messiah, Jesus, had this to say from his heavenly throne about the Church of Pergamum.

> *To the angel of the Church in Pergamum write: These are the words of him who has the sharp double-edged sword. I know where you live, where Satan has his throne* [The Temple of Zeus]. *Yet, you remain true to my name. You did not renounce your faith in me, even in the days of Anita's, my faithful witness, who was put to death in your city, where Satan lives."*[31]

Zeus (Adam) and Hera (Eve) once kicked out of the Garden of Eden, eventually (during the antediluvian era) became adversaries of God, according to Greek myth.

After the Great Flood, the migration of mankind westward from the land of Shinar (Mesopotamia) to Athens brought a powerful story of the

---
31. Revelation 2: 13.

origin of humanity straight out of Biblical history. Truly Greek myth was a lie, but it had a memory of a beginning like that found in the first book of the Bible. As nations spread out in all directions of the map from Babylon, they all took with them some memory of the Great Flood, and thus the many flood myths that have been discovered in civilizations spread far and wide around the globe.

There were about 2,000 years between Babel and the founding of the nation of Israel under Moses, but Israel still had the historical records going all the way back to Adam. Like the delay in the development of a comprehensive story of the genesis of human history finally written by Moses, a real comprehensive written story of Greek civilization didn't emerge developing the Zeus myth and city-state form of republican government until 850 years after the Hebrew exodus from Egypt. The forefathers of the Greek Golden Age had plenty of time to have picked up the history written in Genesis before migrating finally to Greece.[32] But since the libertarian ideas adopted by the Greco-Roman governments did not include the Law of God and obedient surrender to his sovereignty, these republics were a greater failure in the end.

The common thread in this history is consistent with the opening Biblical quote at the start of this chapter. God is sovereign in history, setting up nation-states at his will and taking them down as well when their cup of iniquity is full. Consider the rise and fall of Athens and Rome as an example of how God uses nations to both preserve important heritages and to bring judgment on other nations. God's judgment may come from the hands of one evil nation against another evil nation, or from a righteous disciplinary cause led by good men against evil men. Thus nation-states are instruments of God to prevent total chaos and worldwide tyranny over all mankind. God's purpose being fulfilled as humanity seeks him and longs for his justice, peace and security. Not even Rome could conquer the whole world, and it was brought down by corruption within, as well as by barbarian German nations. But ironically, both Greece and Rome picked up concepts of freedom and justice from Israel in their infancy and passed it on further to the German barbarians. I suggest that this was one way God's own chosen nation, Israel, was to be a priest to the other nations.[33]

The Rise of Christianity and its Influence

Finally, in the fullness of time, God sent his Son, and with the birth of Christianity, Western Civilization would slowly be remade in the image of the template left by Moses. In 70 AD, the Jewish Temple of the Old Covenant was destroyed, and in 135 AD the Jews were once again scattered all over the world and their homeland became known as Palestine. A post temple Jewish culture became interspersed throughout Europe. At the same time, the followers of Christ began to grow in numbers and take over the culture of an evolving Western Civilization. This civilization would be Judeo-Christian in nature as Christians kept the Old Testament writings of Moses and the prophets and attached to it the New Testament writings of the Apostles as one holy Bible. After Christ was crucified and arose from the grave to ascend to heaven as head of the church, he commissioned the children of God to go to all nations and make disciples. Some converts were Jews, but most were Gentiles. Now the New Covenant was set in place.[34] The first 300 years were years of great tribulation for the church. But, as has often been noted by historians, the blood of the martyrs

---

32. The Dorian invasion (1150 BC) caused a Mycenaean flight to western Asia Minor (Ionia), and a renaissance, stimulated by interaction with Phoenician culture present in Ionia. The Phoenician civilization had a long-standing interaction with the Hebrews. Miletus of Ionia became a kind of sister polis to Athens in the time of Homer.

33. Exodus 19: 5-6.
34. See Exhibit B, Appendix 4.

became the seed of a harvest of believers that by the fourth century constituted a population that could no longer be treated as outlaws in the Roman Empire.

Not only would the church bring the hope of salvation to all of humankind, but it also would naturally make reformation in society wherever it spread. If you would, imagine (in a metaphorical way) that the cross of Christ was like a key put in the clock of the Liberty Time Wheel we have pictured, so as to wind it up again. The effect was to create a new chosen nation within existing nation-states to make reformation from within.

> *You are a chosen people, a royal priesthood, a holy nation, a people belonging to God, that you may declare the praises of him who called you out of darkness into his wonderful light. Once you were not a people, but now you are the people of God, once you had not received mercy, but now you have received mercy. Dear friends [says the Apostle Peter] I urge you, as aliens and strangers in this world, to abstain from sinful desires, which war against your soul. Live such good lives among the pagans that, though they accuse you of doing wrong, they may see your good works and glorify God.*[35]

This passage goes on to urge the people of God to obey and submit to the governments of the nations they live in, and to make such an impact as to bring in the "Kingdom of God." In God's providence, this "Kingdom of God" would slowly remake the world, one nation at a time. It should not be confused with human government, but should be thought of as individual godly self-government that makes less human government necessary. The point is, the "Kingdom of God", promoted by the church within nation-states did make reformation, and even changed the nature of human governments. I will now proceed to show how in fact this did occur, and urge the reader to bravely again take Christian dominion in our own time.

It didn't take long before the Roman Catholic Church was organized and Christianity became the sanctioned religion of the Western World. By 324 AD, the Emperor Constantine, a converted Christian, witnessed such a growth of the "Kingdom of God" within the empire that he was able to successfully call a church-council together at Nicea to form a unified doctrinal creed of Christianity and end its persecution by the state. But sadly the Roman Church became so corrupted with pagan adaptations that it produced more human tyranny than godly freedom in Western Civilization. What was missing was a popular understanding of the teaching of the Bible. For a very long time the only Bible the Christian people had was written in Latin, a language most couldn't read. Church attendance was a ritual, and very little teaching from the Bible ever took place. The church became more about collecting guilt offerings to build St. Peters Cathedral and for enriching the papacy in Rome than about redemption of the soul from the bondage of sin. The Roman Church itself slowly became a tyranny[36]

Finally, in a moment of significance, Biblical, Judeo-Christian justice and freedom were rediscovered by a Saxon king of England, Alfred the Great.[37] He is the only English king ever given the title "The Great" and is credited with the start of what became known as English common law. This Saxon ruler educated himself to read Latin and studied the Bible. Then he created a legal code of

---

35. 1 Peter 2:9-12.

36. Remember, my purpose is to show the correlation between the development of Judeo-Christianity and free republican government. Many true believers will always live in tyranny, but if the mature fruits of the Spirit develop in the hearts of leaders it can become a seed that grows into true national republican freedom.

37. Again, be sure to fold out the Liberty Time Wheel from Appendix 1 to follow the progression of dates in English and American history that complete the contents of Chapter One.

law right out of the Ten Commandments and the Sermon on the Mount. From this beginning, England developed a constitutional monarchy with limited authority. The whole of Saxon Britain, and even all of pagan Viking Europe, witnessed his good Christian works, all to the glory of God and the bringing in of "His Kingdom."

Kings and great generals come and go in history. Most of them leave only tyranny and destruction in their paths, despite the short time of honor attributed to them in their lifetime. A few actually create a lasting legacy as culture builders. King Alfred of English fame, who ruled from 871 to 899 AD, was the founder of Judeo-Christian culture that extended itself all the way through the development of English and American history. Sir Winston Churchill and other historians have credited Alfred the Great with three foundational contributions upon which Western Civilization has been built, right up to and including the founding of our American Republic.

First, like Christians in Eastern Europe had to be saved from the Mongol barbarians, Christians in Western Europe had to be saved from the Norsemen or Viking barbarians.[38] The pagan Viking culture was taking over all of northern Britain until only Wessex England, protected by young prince Alfred, stood in their way. Just as Prime Minister Churchill, alone, stood in the way of the German Nazi onslaught in our time, so Alfred the Great, alone, stood in the way of the evil onslaught against Christianity by the Vikings in 878 AD. The Battle of Edington was a decisive victory for England and Western Civilization. Thereupon, Alfred established the naval supremacy policy of England and dispersed the invaders, allowing only those who would peacefully convert to Christianity to stay in the British Isles. Without this victory, the future of both France and England may have been quite different. Alfred was a nationalist like Moses, and not an imperialist. That is, he was a nation builder, but prepared to defend his nation against all enemies. Like Moses, he offered his enemies peace first, but if they rejected his terms of peace he would smite them brutally, not leaving anyone alive to corrupt his people.[39]

Second, Alfred the Great promoted a national education system once he was crowned king. The Vikings had burned down monastery libraries. The king had them restored, and invited internationally famous scholars to come and teach in his schools. He had the Bible, written in Latin, made available all over England. He especially made sure his people learned and applied the Law of Moses to all policy when possible. Alfred the Great established his legal Code of Law right out of the Ten Commandments and case law of Moses. This became the foundation for what England would call her common law.[40] Alfred's Code was known as his "Doom Book". Doom is a Saxon word for judgment. Quoting from Leviticus 19: 15, one line reads, " Do not doom one doom to the rich and another to the poor; nor doom one doom to your friend and another to your foe."

Third, King Alfred established the importance of local government within his kingdom. This advice he took from Deuteronomy.[41] He saw the wisdom of limited national government, as opposed to absolute monarchy, which has been so prevalent in history. He established England's system of shires (later called counties by the Norman kings). The shire was administered by a sheriff, who was appointed by the king. The office of sheriff was a combination of tax collector and enforcer of the law. A shire was divided into "hundreds," later

---

38. Actually, before the Mongol invasion of Eastern Europe, the Ukrainian Byzantine state had already Christianized the Norsemen; but the Viking culture was much more threatening to Christian England than it had been to Christian Eastern Europe.

---

39. See Deuteronomy 20:10-20.

40. See Appendix 9, Exhibit A.

41. See Deuteronomy 1: 9-18.

called townships. Each township was made up of 10 "tithings" and each "tithing" was made up of 10 households. All households were entitled to their own private property plot, called a "hide." A "hide" was 15 to 30 acres; thus a shire could be up to 30,000 acres. Each "hundred" (or township) elected judges to sit as fact finders and preside over trials. Again, like Moses, King Alfred could sit as the court of last resort, and he often gathered a "Witenagemot," or assembly of lords, to assist him in deciding cases.

The next major development of English common law came in 1100 AD when the Norman King Henry the First reaffirmed Saxon law with his Charter of Liberties. A governmental separation of powers was established between an independent church and a free nobility class under the monarchy. Then, in 1154, Henry the Second added to the Charter trial by jury, taken from the Book of Deuteronomy.[42] But in 1215, King John ignored the common law and governed with absolute authority. This resulted in a rebellion by the nobility, who commissioned Archbishop Langton to draw up what became known as the Magna Charta, reaffirming the rights of the nobility and the church and adding the right of free republican government in the cities.[43] The most famous declaration in the Magna Charta became the line, "there shall be no taxation without representation." King John lost that power struggle, but Henry the Third, his successor, again ignored the Magna Charta, and once more the nobles rebelled. Drawing up the Oxford Charter in 1258, they demanded that the king call a parliament to advise him, and that it act as a supreme court with veto power over the king. This time the king was prepared and a civil war erupted. The freedom fighters led by Lord Simon de Montfort, were defeated in battle. But the next king, Edward the First, wisely allowed a "model parliament" to form, which included representatives of the cities, as well as the nobility and clergy. Such parliaments were always subject to the call of the king and did not sit continuously as a branch of government. But from this point on, English taxation without a parliamentary vote of consent would be considered a violation of her constitutional government.[44]

While western European civilization was dividing into many nation-states, in Rome the papacy was trying to maintain a loose Holy Roman Empire that could still exercise authority over kings.[45] But within Europe there was a growing rebellion led by lower members of the clergy, and later joined by princes and kings. One early Reformation priest/monk was the Englishman John Wycliffe. In 1384 he produced the first English version of the Bible so as to educate his fellow countrymen on the differences between the teaching of Rome and the actual teaching of the Bible. He was considered an enemy by the Roman Church, but was protected in England by powerful nobles at a time when England's king, Richard the Second, was a youth and never very powerful. Wycliffe's Lollard priests were sent out two by two into all of England to preach the Gospel, despite the objections of the archbishop. England was, at that time, still under the absolutism of Christendom. One quote attributed to Wycliffe was "the Bible is profitable for preserving government of, by, and for the people."[46] The adaptation of that quote by later advocates of republican government has become "democracy is government of, by and for the people." Even before this first English

---

42. See Appendix 9 Exhibit B, #7.

43. Of course Archbishop Langton and these nobles were all still part of Roman Catholic Christendom.

44. The Biblical origin of no taxation without consent is found in 1 Kings 12.

45. This Papal dominion was called Christendom. Keep in mind that this work is not claiming that government-forced Christianity produces freedom, but that true Christian influence in a nation will likely oppose tyranny and encourage the evolution of a free constitutional system.

46. Rousas John Rushdoony, *The Institutes of Biblical Law* (Phillipsburg, NJ: The Presbyterian and Reformed Publishing Co., 1973), 1.

Bible could be produced, the Wycliffe message of freedom in Christ caused a peasant revolt in 1381, resulting in the assassination of the archbishop. Despite the rebellion, the peasants lost their fight for freedom. Wycliffe was opposed to the violence, but could not control it. Later in the 16th century, Germany had a very similar experience led by Martin Luther.

In the 100 years between Wycliffe's introduction of his English Bible and the rise of the 16th century German Reformation, England had evolved, once again, into an absolute monarchy. But in 1525, William Tyndale put out another English language Bible for the people, only to be imprisoned, convicted of heresy, and burned at the stake under the absolute power of the Tudor dynasty. Interestingly, Henry the Eighth, a Tudor papal defender, joined the Protestant movement when the pope denied him a divorce. He broke with Rome and declared himself head of the Church of England. Later, under Elizabeth Tudor, England developed into a Protestant state. At this time the growing popularity of the Presbyterians and Puritans, as new Protestant groups, even began to turn on the Church of England as not being Protestant enough. The Church of England for them was still Catholic, despite its independence from Rome.

When Elizabeth the First left no heir to the throne, a new Stuart dynasty took over the government. An English Protestant Reformation broke out as fierce as the German Reformation led by Martin Luther had been in the last century. At the time of these Stuart kings, Calvinists, who wanted to copy the Mosaic constitution of government found in the Bible, were pushing for republican rule. Their favorite Bible was the Geneva Bible, printed in 1599, with its notes by John Calvin. King James, the first of the Stuart kings, claimed absolute power by divine right, as head of the Church of England. Trying to divert the English people's interest in the Geneva Bible and its notes, the king commissioned what became the printing of the King James Bible in 1611. Many began to leave England for America, taking with them the Geneva Bible and their ideas of republican government. Little did King James the First know that he was aiding republican opposition to the monarchy by introducing what later became one of the most loved of English, Bibles.

In 1620, William Bradford, pastor of a dissenting Protestant church, sailed for the new world with his congregation and made a covenant with God upon arrival at Plymouth. Named after the vessel they sailed in, the covenant was called the Mayflower Compact. It called for representative government under the Law of God. In the meantime, back in England, a great civil war was in the making. A Puritan, Edward Coke, along with other Protestants who were members of The House of Commons, drew up the Petition of Rights in 1628. This was an act of interposition much like that of the ancient Hebrews who overthrew King Rehaboam.[47] This Petition of Rights became the origin of the American concept of the right of lesser representatives of the people to petition higher government for redress of grievances. In this petition they were reclaiming all the common law long abandoned in England. When King Charles the First refused to accept the petition and jailed Coke and others, the English Civil War broke out, led by the Puritan Oliver Cromwell, in 1641. The king was defeated and beheaded for treason. In the meantime, people were continuing to leave England for the American colonies. While chaos reined in England, Thomas Hooker, a Congregationalist, moved his church into what he called Connecticut and established a full-blown republic in 1638. There he commissioned Roger Ludlow to lead in the development of a complete Constitution, establishing republican governing institu-

---

47. Second Chronicles 10 covers an act of interposition by the elders, as representatives of the tribes, regarding the taxation policy of this king.

tions, their limited powers, and the rights of the people. It was the first complete written Constitution of modern history.[48] To this day Connecticut calls itself the Constitution State.

In 1689 England finally completed its transformation into a republic. This was called the Glorious Revolution. In a bloodless reform, parliament drew up the English Bill of Rights. A new king, William the Third, agreed to a government in which parliament and the monarchy would jointly rule, with a clear separation of powers equally divided between the House of Commons, the House of Lords, and the monarchy. Soon prime ministers, picked from parliament by the king, were the acting head of government. Later, kings actually became figureheads without power to even veto an act of parliament.[49]

In 1776, the United States of America was born as an independent nation state, claiming her rights came from God and the people and not from a king or parliament. After a war for independence, the American Constitutional Convention of 1787, copying the experience of nearly 200 years of colonial history, created the first modern federal republic of history, modeled after the ancient Hebrew Republic and the common law history of England. In 1791, the American Bill of Rights was added to the Constitution, reserving rights to the people and the individual states of the union. The eventual addition of rights abolishing slavery (1865) and granting women the right to vote (1920) made America a truly democratic republic. A new standard of democracy would now of necessity always include the right to vote by women, and no barrier to suffrage based on race.

As a result of British/American history, many nations have yearned for freedom in the 20th and 21st Century like no other time in history. Others will make it work only as long as the growth of Christianity also expands within such nations. On the other hand, as Christianity declines within America, or any nation in which it has been planted, so too will freedom decline. As one of America's great statesmen, Noah Webster (1758-1842), said,

> The Bible is the chief moral cause of all that is good, and the best book for regulating the concerns of men. The principles of . . . liberty, of wise laws, and administration, are to be drawn from the Bible and sustained by its authority. The man, therefore, who weakens or destroys the divine authority of that Book may be accessory to all the public disorders which society is doomed to suffer . . .[50]

The world owes most of the above outline of Western Civilization's preservation of republican concepts of government to its author, Moses. In the above record of dates outlining milestones in English common law, the most important foundation was the rediscovery of the Bible. Kings first and then the common people themselves learned to read and apply the principles in the Bible to re-order their lives not only spiritually, but also socially and politically.

---

48. It has become appropriate to capitalize the word constitution when one is referring to a single written document that defines a government's powers and the people's rights. This practice has only been applied since the American revolution.

49. Beginning with George the First the veto power of the English monarchy ended and Prime Ministers became head of the government.

---

50. Noah Webster quotes (1758-1843), www.thinkexist.com/authors.

CHAPTER 2

THE TRANSITION OF WESTERN CIVILIZATION

If we want to truly understand the roots of the founding of the American republic, we must return to history as it was taught during the first generations of this nation. Today's teachers of our youth are telling a different story. History textbooks today teach that the American and French Revolutions were essentially the same revolution, and that is simply not true. American history texts once began with the Reformation history in Europe and the struggle for freedom of religion. Now textbooks hardly mention this influence and take the student directly to what were called the Philosophes[1] of the Enlightenment to find the cause of the rise of the American republic. Both the Reformation and the Enlightenment arose between 1500 and 1800 AD.[2] These two movements, though overlapping in time, are in many ways opposed to one another, as I will show. It is at this point in Western history that a major challenge is made to the claim that the origin of our liberty is in God.

But before looking at these overlapping philosophical movements, let us take a larger view of Western Civilization between the Middle Ages and modern history. It was a period driven by four overlapping trends: 1) It was a transition from feudalism to absolute monarchy, moving from a very decentralized society to one of highly centralized states. 2) It was a renaissance of large commercial cities governed as free local republics. Free enterprise was becoming the source of the new wealth of nations. 3) It was a Reformation that diversified Christianity, helping develop nation-states and ending Roman Christendom. The new Christians collectively were called Protestants, and they led rebellions against not only the papacy, but also against divine right kings who made themselves heads of state churches. And 4) It was a time of growing Western dominance of the world through competing colonial empires based on the Great Commission of Christianity and the Western control of naval power that monopolized ocean trade routes.

The significance of the transition from feudalism to absolutism is that the Reformation still saw value in the former and the Enlightenment was tied to the latter. The American Revolution was building on the value of separation of powers, and checks and balances, both of which were intrinsic to feudalism. Federalism, or the maintenance of local government authority while also embracing the strength of a limited central government, is nothing more than a modern adaptation of the old-age feudal system. The French Revolution was all about the elimination of powerful local interests like bishops and lords, and bringing about centralization of all authority. These revolutionaries wanted to develop the state as the absolute authority without competition.

---

1. French for secular philosophers, who were usually atheists or deists.

2. See Appendix 2.

The second transition was an economic change with governmental implications. A new middle class, made up mainly of Protestant capitalists of revived and new cities, was replacing the landed aristocracy as the national source of wealth. These cities tended to be locally governed as republics, and they naturally demanded representation in the national councils of the king, who was eager to tax them. The capital and commercial interests tended to move to nations where the king was open to reform. Capitalism ultimately led to republican revolutions on a national scale. It also led to the shrinking of serfdom, and a growing middle class. The French Revolution was motivated by class hatred between the commons and the aristocracy, but the American Revolution was motivated by equal opportunity, which allowed peasants to rise rapidly from serfdom to middle class.

The third transition was centered in Christian reformation. Religious issues dominated the three centuries between the Middle Ages and modern times. The Reformation, driven by Protestants, was the reason for the rise of all early colonies in North America. The American colonies became havens for the freedom to experiment with new forms of government developing out of diverse Christian denominations. Thus, the American Revolution grew out of a search for Biblically based economic and governing principles upon which to build a Christian nation. In contrast, on the European continent, bloody religious wars were pushing toward revolution of a different sort. The middle class Protestants of Europe became advisers to kings and queens when they could, and otherwise became adversaries of rulers by calling for representative government. European religious wars had turned many intellectuals against Christianity in general. Some of the new middle class group of advisers to kings called themselves the Philosophes. They hated the church and were open atheists. Not believing in freedom under God, which Protestants were espousing, they turned to the idea of a secular state as the protector of freedom. Since all states were ruled by absolute monarchy, they tried to make kings what they called "enlightened despots". This led to the French Revolution.

The fourth transition was the rise of Western dominance worldwide. It was in the interests of both the French Revolution and the American Revolution. For the secularists colonialism was all about the glory and gain of the state, and not so much a matter of concern about spreading the Gospel. Not that those who were supposed to be about fulfilling the Great Commission of Christianity did not sometimes yield to the temptations of greed over Gospel. However, the universal church, both Protestant and Catholic, saw the spread of colonialism as their supreme opportunity to spread the Gospel of Christ. Despite some modern revisionist history today, the primary motivation driving Columbus was that of taking the Gospel to the heathen. It was the Hidalgos (Spanish aristocrats) that subverted Columbus' intentions and slaughtered the natives of the New World. After America won its independence, George Washington urged in his farewell address that we not become entangled in international empire building. Of course, the Monroe Doctrine later also tried to protect the Western Hemisphere from continued colonization. The American Revolution was anti-colonial and pro free and independent states in the Western Hemisphere.[3]

The *ends* of both the French Revolution and the American Revolution and their combined impact on all of Western Civilization was that of creating elected representative governments to displace the absolute monarchies of Europe. The process was slow but steady and was climaxed in what we

---

3. Study the Appendix 2 timeline by looking for contemporary events in Europe and in America, and then proceed with a closer comparison of the overlapping Reformation and Enlightenment.

call World War I. The *means* to the end, however, was not the same for the French Revolution and American Revolution. The French influence on all of Europe helped produce absolute national democracies and preserve powerful centralized nation-states. Kings were made figureheads or totally removed from government, but *stateism* remained intact. The American influence was a creative decentralized union of powerful local States within a limited but sovereign national republic. The European modern republics would be known as parliamentary democracies. The American modern republic would be a unique system of separation of powers and checks and balances. Absolutism remained the "hallmark" of European secular states. Limited government, under God and Constitution, became the "hallmark" of the United States of America.

Chapter 3

Two Paths for Modern Republics

The brief snapshot of history in Chapter Two was designed to show the wider perspective of the centuries between 1500 and 1800 AD. It is not my intention to present a detailed history in this book, but rather to outline the philosophy that shaped our nation's origin. The 300 years of transition for Western Civilization between 1500 and 1800 set the stage for two very different republican revolutions. I will now outline the differences between the Reformation that shaped the American Revolution, and the Enlightenment that shaped the French Revolution.

The Reformation

You may be familiar with Martin Luther and the German Reformation, and you may associate it only with the rise of Protestantism. But the effects of the rise of Protestantism were far wider than doctrinal divisions within Christianity. The Romanization of the church in the Middle Ages had created something called Christendom throughout Europe. The papacy in Rome, at the very height of Christendom, had enough power over kings to enlist them to lead military crusades designed to take Jerusalem back from the Muslims. All secular authority was subject to the pope. Kings and princes had to be ordained in a church ceremony of investiture. Ideally, kings were crowned by popes and lords answered to bishops. But actually, from the beginning, there developed an investiture controversy and increasingly secular rulers began to rebel against Christendom. More and more, Roman Catholic Christendom had become corrupt and national secular rulers sometimes appointed their own church bishops. In 1517, when Luther challenged the authority of policies of the papacy, he found ready allies among German princes who resented the power of Rome over them but didn't want to be perceived as anti-Christian.

The effect was that northern German principalities within central Europe fought for independence from what had been called the Holy Roman Empire. Northern German states were actually granted independence from Rome under the Treaty of Augsburg in 1555. Also, as early as 1529, Henry the Eighth of England broke with Christendom. In both Germany and England, Reformation leaders helped develop national written languages, thereby giving the people Bibles in languages they could learn to read. This helped nations break the power of Rome over the church and produced a foundation of Biblical common law that eventually evolved into Constitutionalism.[1] The traditional absolute rule of man was slowly being replaced by a rule of Christian law. Now even secular rulers, especially in England, came under a commonly understood rule of Biblical law, due to a growing mass literacy among Protestants and the availability of printed Bibles.

---

1. Constitutionalism (or reference to the Constitution) implies a written document fully defining the powers of government and its limited authority, whereas the common law implies an established system of evolving governmental authority under the law.

Supreme rulers, however, seldom surrender easily to a rule of law. The Reformation had begun with the people fighting the papal system, but now kings made themselves rulers by divine right, exchanging the absolutism of the pope for their own absolutism as heads of Protestant national churches. The Reformation then continued with the people, led by lay ministers, rebelling against divine right kings. The Reformation creating a popular principle of government under God and his law could not be stopped. Thus, the Reformation became the foundation of what later would be called limited government under a written Constitution.

Effectively, the main leaders of Protestantism that influenced the American Revolution were the Calvinists. John Calvin looked to Biblical law to form institutions for governing a nation or city. In Geneva, Switzerland, Calvin established a Biblical republic. He had been forced to flee France for Switzerland, but left behind the Huguenot movement, which would end up softening the French position of intolerance toward Protestants. This occurred without Calvin's leadership between 1555 and 1610 and could be called the French Reformation. Like all national reformations, this was a civil war against the crown, but this time it was more a victory for the Catholics, then for the Protestants. Following the St. Bartholomew Day Massacre in 1572, France made a peace of toleration with the Huguenots. They could ill afford to have these Protestants flee the country. When Protestants left a country it was a drain on the nation's economy. Protestants made up almost all the capitalist entrepreneur population in that era. Catholics, on the other hand, tended to hold on to preserving serfdom and aristocratic control of society. These fleeing Huguenots were heading for South Africa to join a Dutch Reform colony, and also were going to the American colonies.

Further, men like Richard Hakluyt and Edwin Sandy, both of whom were Calvinists of the Puritan variety, shaped America's beginnings. They were advisers to Queen Elizabeth the First and James the First, whose contributions led to republicanism in Virginia and New England. Later in the 1640s, England itself experienced a civil war led by Calvinists like Oliver Cromwell and Edward Coke that gave parliament a continuous and permanent role in the government. Again, Calvinism produced men like William of Orange who fought for the independence of Holland from Spain in 1581. This independence, however, was not fully recognized until after the Thirty Years War ending in 1648. This William preceded by two generations the William of Orange who would become king of England and Holland in 1689, during the Glorious Revolution. Exactly 100 years before George Washington would be sworn in as president of the new American republic, the United Kingdom had fully established itself as a parliamentary republic. Finally, Calvinism produced men like John Knox, who left the Huguenot movement of France to go to Scotland and establish the Presbyterian Church. Presbyterians like Edmond Burke, a member of the British Parliament during the American Revolution, supported the independence movement going on in the colonies. Burke also took a fierce stand against the French Revolution.

Thus, Calvin's Biblical worldview[2] was brought to America by his many "sons:" the Puritans and Separatists of England, the Presbyterians of Scotland, and the Huguenots and Reformers of the

---

2. The Calvinist worldview was that Christians should exercise dominion in all of society. Many scholars hold that Calvin and Calvinism were powerful agents in the rise of modern republican government. Their emphasis on representative bodies - boards of elders – would spread throughout Northern Europe. Calvinists became change agents to overthrow the divine right of kings. Not that this was their original intention. But often one's influence goes beyond the original design. Generations of people were on the move to create a new society in Northern Europe, a society that culminated in the United States Constitution, with its deep distrust of human nature, its division of powers, and its provision for the rightful and orderly succession of rulers.

Rhine River and France. It is estimated that of the three million Americans at the time of the War for Independence, 900,000 were Scotch-Irish Presbyterians, 600,000 were Puritan/Congregationalist English, 400,000 were German or Dutch Reformed, and many were French Huguenots. Perhaps two-thirds of the American colonial world had been trained in the school of Calvin.[3] Calvinism could not help but have a large impact on the American Revolution.

But after 1760, King George the Third "kick-started" an American rebellion by usurping the self-governing rights long enjoyed in the colonies. Parliament was divided between those who supported this, calling themselves Tories, and those who did not, calling themselves Whigs. The two political parties also were divided between those who were for an absolute Church of England under the king (the Tories), and those who were more inclined toward freedom of religion (the Whigs). By this time the Protestant use of the designation "Puritan" was much less prevalent, but the Calvinist worldview was still very much alive in New England and was called Congregationalism. Church self-government and colonial self-government went hand in hand. In addition, another Protestant group, led by John Wesley, also was breaking away from the Church of England. This group, called Methodists, also was immigrating to the colonies. In England, Methodists were active in the Tory party, trying to soften its position on slavery and its opposition to freedom of religion.

It is important for the reader to understand the above background from which the American Revolution sprang. It was motivated and led by men whose desire was to found a nation on Biblical principles. Rather than a society structured from the top down, the Reformationists restructured society around individual accountability to God, to family, and to country. They believed in the "priesthood of the believer," and therefore opened freedom for the individual to approach God in direct prayer. Thus, confession did not make them subordinate to priests but directly accountable to God. This freedom helped produce a self-governing people without as much need for the police power of the state. They believed in the total depravity of human nature and therefore became inventive in finding ways to divide the power of government so as to limit the authority of those in it. They believed in Covenant theology and therefore in constitutional government. They believed in family enterprises for their economic security, rather than in security through feudal class obligations. Thus, they helped to build the rising middle class and helped abolish serfdom or peasantry. They believed in freedom of speech, which to them meant freedom to preach without censorship by the state. They believed in freedom of the press, which to them meant freedom to publish Bibles and tracts for evangelistic purposes. They believed in freedom of assembly, which to them meant freedom of worship without interference from a state church. They believed in freedom to petition the government for redress of grievances through lower magistrates, like members of parliament or colonial assemblies. The American Founders drew from that history when they wrote the First Amendment to the U.S. Constitution. To them, the only king was King Jesus. The Bible was sovereign, not bishops or rulers. Their idea of freedom was to surrender their lives to the lordship of Christ.[4] "Where the Spirit of the Lord is there is liberty."[5] American colonists believed in self-government in which the indwelling Holy Spirit helped create the manners of the people, as opposed to the government directing the manners

---

3. John Eidsmoe, *Christianity and the Constitution* (Grand Rapids, MI: Baker Books, 2005), 19.

4. Galatians 5: 1.

5. Second Corinthians 3: 17.

of the people, to paraphrase Noah Webster, one of our founding fathers.

The Enlightenment

The Enlightenment actually came to full fruition as a result of what was called the Thirty Years War in central Europe. This war began, like those before it, as a religious war. This time, small Calvinist states along the Rhine River were under attack by Catholic states in one last attempt by Spain to save some of what was left of Roman Christendom. However, France, under King Louis the Thirteenth, intervened, not on the side of the Catholics, but on the basis of maintaining a national balance of power between nation-states in Europe. While issues of religious freedom dominated the British and their colonies helping to create limited monarchy and actual republics, on the continent of Europe, absolute monarchy that was loyal first to national interests and not to religion was becoming entrenched.[6]

On the continent, Western Civilization began to put more emphasis on national interest and self-interest above religious interest. The state became absolute and the church was even considered the enemy. Enlightenment advisers to the king proposed reforms that called for equality and the elimination of privileged classes, but they still believed in the absolutism of the state. As the supreme example of absolutism, Louis the Fourteenth said, "I am the state". The Philosophe leaders tried to groom kings to be "enlightened despots." By the time of Louis the Sixteenth, the Philosophe leaders became very impatient and led a popular overthrow of the monarchy. This French Revolution called for the absolutism of the people without monarchy or church.

The Enlightenment was first of all a rebellion against Christianity. Fundamentally, the followers of this movement were distinguished from the Reformation followers by the following contrasting tenets. 1) To the Philosophes, "Man was the measure of all things;" to Christians, God was the measure of all things. 2) To the Philosophes, borrowing from Greek mythology, Eve was the hero of antiquity and God was a tyrant; to Christians, Eve represented the fall of man, and God's promised seed from Eve, the hope of redemption. 3) To the Philosophes, the general will was the measure of morality; to Christians, the Law of God was the measure of morality. 4) The Enlightenment was a humanist movement that rejected theology for ideology. Rather than make God king secularists made human consensus sovereign. 5) To these Philosophes, the nature of the common man was good, and society needed to return to what they called the "nobility of the primitive man." Of course, the Reformationists believed in the evil nature of man, absent a "new birth." 6) The Philosophe writers of the Enlightenment justified the absolute authority of the state as the source of the rights of the people. They believed in progress through human engineering of society. The Reformationists believed in limited government under the Law of God as the only source of popular liberty. They believed in progress that comes by the providence of God when his people are obedient to God's Law and submissive to the Holy Spirit's regeneration of the human soul.

On the other hand, like the Reformationists, the Philosophes found their inspiration in ancient classical times. That is, they were excited about rediscovering the wisdom of ancient Greek and Roman republics and desired to build ideologies based on that tradition. The Reformationists, however, were excited to go back to the original Greek and Hebrew languages to find freedom in the pages of the

---

6. For the first time, states were consciously introducing the balance of power in their foreign policy to keep the peace. Western Civilization from this time forward would try to maintain world peace by forming alliances of nations. They may, or may not, have understood that this concept of maintaining a balance of power between nations was in effect an act of God going back to his ordination of nations.

first complete Bibles canonized in classical times. Since both the Enlightenment and the Reformation influenced the 18th century, we sometimes say the West is both a Greco-Roman culture and a Judeo-Christian culture. But on some basic points these two traditions clash. I submit that although both have a common goal of republican states, there are two paths toward that goal. The one path was laid out in the American Revolution and the other in the French Revolution.

Since both the American Revolution and the French Revolution were republican revolutions, both affirmed freedom of speech, freedom of the press, freedom of assembly, and elected representative government. However, both those who followed the Enlightenment and those who held to the Reformation sometimes had difficulty fully extending freedom to all. But whereas flaws in the American experience can be cited and may have left us with deep wounds to heal, we should keep in mind that the American Revolution produced the most stable and free society in all of history. In contrast, the French Revolution immediately produced a reign of terror and a succession of failed reattempts to get it right. The French Revolution so disturbed the stability of all continental Europe that it only recently is claiming a seeming recovery.

Because French kings did not act radically enough or fast enough to reform society, the French Revolution became an attack on the absolutism of the monarchy, the church bishops, and the aristocratic second estate. It was led by intellectuals in the middle class (mostly atheists), and was joined by the small labor class in the cities. To purge society, they conducted a reign of terror and held mock trials resulting in the beheading of the king and many of those of aristocratic birth. Finally, the anarchy that resulted caused the army, under Napoleon Bonaparte, to take over the government. Fittingly, he became the supreme example of what were called "enlightened despots." As a popular total tyrant, he forced Enlightenment reforms on France and other nations that his army conquered. Elections were allowed, but only to endorse the tyrant. The reforms made him popular and helped restore order, but the totalitarian nature of this police state marked the French Revolution as a failure.

The French Republic gave the vote to the middle class and even eventually extended the vote to all males over 21. America did the same, but had no tradition from colonial times of an aristocracy of birth with titles and privileges.[7] Therefore America did not have the pent-up anger that existed in European society after centuries of class discrimination. America accepted a kind of natural aristocracy of society that was based on talent and hard work. In America, everyone knew that the promise of equal opportunity drew immigrants to the new world. We stressed equality under the law but not equality of condition, whereas France would move toward a more socialist equality within its republican experience. The French commitment to the absolutism of the state could only be maintained if the collectivist model of socialism was emphasized, rather than the Protestant Christian model of individualism and free enterprise.

The English tradition of limited monarchy that finally evolved into a republic owes its moderate approach to the Protestant Reformation. It has been said that John Wesley saved England from the class revolution that took place in France. Wesley's Methodism helped raise the hopeless peasant and labor classes out of a lifestyle that kept them in poverty. There was not only spiritual salvation but also social salvation in the Gospel of Christ. The Enlightenment expected that once the societal chains that held the common man in poverty were broken, then by way of their own good nature men would create a noble society of

---

7. The exception in the American experience was a Southern aristocracy built on slavery. I fully address this subject in Part Four.

equals. Instead, the tyranny of the aristocracy of birth was replaced by the tyranny of the majority. Actually, without the "new birth" of a new man in Christ, freedom becomes license without responsibility and it is "every man for himself." The reign of terror in the French Revolution soon demonstrated this.

It was Edmund Burke, friend of the American Revolution and enemy of the French Revolution, who said,

> Ours [meaning the English and American nations] is a moral order, and our laws are derived from immortal and moral laws; the higher happiness is moral happiness, and the cause of suffering is moral evil. Pride, ambition, revenge, sedition, lust, and ungoverned zeal — these are the vices that are the actual cause of the storms that trouble life. Religion and privileges of class are the pretext for agitators who think institutions are the cause of injustice. But the human heart in reality is the fountain of evil. You would not cure the evil by resolving there shall be no more monarchy, nor [the evil of bishop-led councils, by resolving there be] no more church.[8]

The First Republic of France lasted about 10 horrible years, and was replaced by the absolutism of Napoleon Bonaparte. Patterned after the tradition of Roman emperors, Napoleon called himself First Consul, and then later crowned himself emperor. He ruled from 1799 until England defeated him in 1815. He was responsible for spreading the ideas of Enlightenment all the way to Russia during his conquest of the continent. But Napoleon was defeated, and that led to the restoration of the monarchy for 33 years in France. Finally, in 1848, France had another revolution and set up the Second Republic, but Louis Napoleon overthrew that republic in short order. He became the second Napoleonic Emperor of France. It wasn't until 1875 that France finally achieved a lasting republic with freedom of religion. Even then France could not quite get it right and went through several Constitutions subsequent to its third one. Now France has freedom of religion, but under a secular state that is more and more dependent on police power to maintain any domestic tranquility. Actually this type of secular state cannot maintain national unity, since this freedom of religion means acceptance of such a pluralistic society that even religious adversaries without any love or common bond for one another are welcome. Freedom is being used for demonstrations in the streets that promote hatred for another, and thus liberty is still at risk in France today.

Over time, the American republic's two-party system has divided over which path to follow. Two men, both Virginians of our founding era, often are portrayed as representing these two diverging paths. One man, a Federalist, saw our form of government under the Constitution of 1787 as a growth of providential common-law principles reaching back to the Middle Ages, if not all the way back to Moses of ancient Biblical history. His name was John Marshall, and Federalist President John Adams appointed him Chief Justice of the U.S. Supreme Court. John Marshall helped establish the sovereignty of the national government over the American internal State governments, and the supremacy of the Constitution as interpreted by the U.S. Supreme Court. The other man was the founder of the Democratic-Republican Party, and he saw our form of government established in 1787 somewhat through the lens of the French Enlightenment. His name was Thomas Jefferson and he became president of the United States by defeating Adams. Jefferson always felt most governing should be left to the state governments of the union, or to the people themselves. He even led an effort called the Virginia-Kentucky Resolutions, which claimed the right of the States individually to nullify any na-

---

8. Russell Kirk, *The Conservative Mind*, (Washington DC: Regnery Publishing, Inc., 1995), 36.

tional law passed contrary to their interests, unless that law-making power was clearly delegated to the national government.

Both men have had an enduring influence that has shaped American history. But the popular opinion of our founding generations believed in and promoted the politics of the Judeo-Christian common-law connections of our republic. I will detail this point of view throughout the rest of this book. The early American judges on both federal and state courts also tended to share this view. It was not until the Progressive movement of the 20th century that judges appointed to the courts began increasingly to take the view that our constitution is a "living document" and not bound by Judeo-Christian roots. This idea of a "living document" is really a perversion of Marshall's court-guarded constitutionalism. Compared to today's prominent school of law view of constitutionalism, both Jefferson and Marshall were strict constructionists. Neither man would have agreed with the modern concept that the U.S. Supreme Court is meant to be a kind of continuous constitutional convention. Ironically, the Jeffersonian politics of state leadership in the union and strict construction of the constitution have become the strategy of conservative and Biblically based constituencies; while Marshall's position of constitutional law protected by the Supreme Court has become the strategy of liberal "enlightened" constituencies.

In our own time, we seem to be turning to the principles of the Enlightenment and rejecting the foundation laid by our founders. Just as the French Revolution helped produce totalitarian and centralist tyrannies, it is my opinion that any republic will fail if it experiences a continuous movement away from its Biblical foundation. Even the post French-Revolution secular republics of Europe had an original Judeo-Christian foundation. The transformation today of European nations (including Britain) into socialist secular societies puts them in danger of eventual collapse. American's economic dominance and its moral position as leader of the free world today is still based on its Judeo-Christian foundation. If America totally changes course and follows the European path, it does so at its own peril.

Part Two
Discovering Republicanism in Bible Law

The source of law for (any) nation
is (actually) the god of that nation.
All law is enacted morality.
Morality presupposes a religion as its foundation.
Law rests on morality, and morality on religion.
Weaken a nation's religion and you weaken its
morality, by undermining the foundations of its law.
The progressive collapse of law and order, and
the breakdown of society, follows.
Theology is therefore foundational to law,
order, and liberty.

—*Martin G. Selbrede*

From a Chalcedon Position Paper
Quoted in *"Faith for all of Life"*
Mar/Apr 2010

Chapter 4

The Author of Liberty

For a political scientist, the foundational principles upon which a free society depends are discoverable in the first books of the Bible, which were written by Moses. Particularly, and fundamentally, one finds the principle of limited government. That principle implies that national government should not hold all sovereignty, but must share sovereignty with other centers of authority. Further, it was never intended, in God's plan, that liberty be singularly a responsibility of the state. God ordained a separation of several civil authorities, and each checking the authority of the other helps maintain a free society. In Genesis, the social emphasis is about the role the family plays. The family should have significant and independent governing duties and rights within any nation. Godly families may even become, in God's providence, the seed that brings future blessing on a nation. In Exodus, the social emphasis is on the national rule of law. The story centers on freeing God's chosen nation from slavery which was under the typical totalitarian worldly state at that time. The new legal system would emphasize freedom under the law. The Book of Leviticus places its emphasis on separating one tribe for scholarly pursuits in the law and for the priesthood. The principle being the importance of a separation of "church and state," but also the influence the priesthood should have upon all spheres of authority in a nation. A moral center of national unity found in the law and grounded in religion is necessary for the stability of any state. The Book of Numbers places its emphasis on lists of princes of tribes and the role of a council of elders and an assembly of Israel. The principle involved is the importance of representative government. Then, Deuteronomy places its emphasis on the role of local city governments and a limited national government. Liberty depends on dividing and limiting the powers of government. The Hebrews created a system of separation of powers for government within local, tribal, and national levels of authority. Specifically, the above constitutional system was not laid out in one written document for the Hebrews, but it was God's design for the ancient Hebrew republic. Generally, an application should be made of all the above principles, for governing any republic.

God has ordained three institutions to be responsible for governing the lives of individuals. The three institutions ordained by God are the family, the nation-state, and the priesthood/church. The inference of Scripture is that the family has the responsibility for basic education and economic prosperity.[1] When parents, directly or indirectly, control the schools, education will prosper more so than when the state controls the schools. Home schooling, or at least locally elected school boards, should carry all the responsibility for education. The family-owned business always serves the interests of economic security for all much better than very large cor-

---
1. Deuteronomy 6: 6-9; 28: 3-6 and, First Thessalonians 4:11-12.

porate structures that so often are in control of business in this modern world. To the state, falls the exclusive responsibility to punish lawlessness and provide protection against foreign enemies.[2] The Biblical concept of good nation-state government is always one that is limited and not totalitarian in its authority. It is the priesthood/church that should control the responsibility of higher education, training in righteousness, and worship of the Supreme Sovereign of all.[3] The Biblical concept of proper religious authority is always one of independence from and not subjugation to the power of the state. But a fourth foundation of liberty is also taught in Scripture that is not an institution. That foundation is a godly and self-governing individual. A wise man put it this way, "How can a man rule a town if he cannot rule his own family, and how can he rule his family if he cannot rule his own heart, and how can he rule his own heart unless he is obedient unto God."[4] God's law is over all society, and human authority is divided within society. Only in the above contexts can liberty thrive.

It is the proper function of science to discover the primary laws by which all secondary or particular facts depend. In social science we call these primary laws fundamental political, economic and social principles, which support a society's organization. No national system can be understood apart from the knowledge of these foundational principles. If the Hebrew commonwealth is the birthplace of the first republic of human society, we must explore the principles underlying its system and compare and evaluate them with the underlying principles of other republics. This I will do. I also contend that without the truth revealed in the Bible natural man would never be able to establish a government in which human liberty can be sustained.

In both Part Two and Part Three, the heart of this work, my main inspiration has come from E. C. Wines and his book, *Commentaries On the Laws of the Ancient Hebrews: with an Introductory Essay On Civil Society and Government*. Wines wrote this classic work in 1853 and it is thus uncorrupted by the modern scholars of our time. The contents of his book are divided into two sections. Book 1 covers the uncertainty of pagan history and the credibility of Moses as an historian. In Book 2, Wines goes into detail regarding the organic law of the ancient Hebrew state. Chapter 1 of Book 2 covers 18 fundamental principles of political science that under girded the Old Testament Hebrew commonwealth.[5] All these principles also were foundational to the development of the American republic. I do not directly quote from each of these 18 principles, but in some form they are all worked into the thesis of my work. Any republic will have difficulty maintaining stability and freedom when it lacks or compromises these principles, which are older than the American Revolution or even ancient Greece.

Alexander Tyler, a Scotsman who lived at the time of the establishment of the American republic, said it was his observation that democratic-republics generally last at their height no more than 200 years. They are indeed fragile political systems. Their period of decline seems to begin early, and in some cases can be quite long. Based only on the time it took for elections to be introduced and eventually ended, the following are examples of the most outstanding early republics of history. The Hebrew republic lasted 516 years (1446 - 930 BC), the republic of Athens lasted 256 years, and the Roman Republic lasted 460 years. Obviously, not taking into account the long decline of the above republics, they seem to be exceptional in their longevity, according to Alexander Tyler's

---

2. Deuteronomy 16: 18-20 and Judges 2: 18.

3. Deuteronomy.10: 8-9 and 14: 27-29 and 17: 8-13 and 16: 16.

4. Anonymous.

5. See Appendix 3.

standard.[6] Our own American republic, having its beginnings in a long colonial history, is now over 400 years old. But if one counts our republicanism as beginning with the Constitutional Convention of 1787, it is only 224 years old (this being 2011). The British republic, if you count its beginning in 1689 with the Glorious Revolution, is now 321 years old. The above examples of republics are not the only ones, but will serve as the best to compare and contrast for purposes of this book.

Many today are confused about the reason as to why Anglo-American governments have produced the freest of all nations in history. The present-day republics of the United States of America and Great Britain are indeed exceptional nations in history. Modern scholars will say we drew greatness from the pluralism of cultures that Anglo-America uniquely allowed to immigrate into their nations. However, the diversity of people drawn to Britain and America is an effect of the greatness of modern Western Civilization, not the cause of its greatness. It was the valuable ideas upon which we were founded as a people of the Bible that has made us the freest people on earth. An unprecedented flow of immigrants into a nation from all over the world is evidence of something great about a nation. But they were not coming to bring their own old-world values; they were fleeing the oppression of those old-world values. Yes, we have benefited from a diversity of aesthetic contributions that come with all cultures, but we should not confuse this with what makes us the freest nations on earth. China's later dynasties were very cosmopolitan, but China was never known as a land of freedom. Whereas, Britain and America have become known as havens of freedom. Let me quote John Adams. He said, "I always consider the settlement of America with reverence and wonder, as the opening of a grand scene and design of Providence, for the illumination of the ignorant and the emancipation of the slavish part of mankind all over the earth." As I will demonstrate, the root of the great principle of liberty was not of our own making either. It came from the Hebrew Covenant of Law given to Moses.

According to E.C. Wines, the first principle of importance and significance in the Hebrew republic was that of the unity of God and his connection with true liberty. Rather than many gods, each of who was assigned to a different nation, the God of the Bible is one God over all nations. God is united in purpose and he alone is totally sovereign. Everywhere man is the source of tyranny, and everywhere God is the only source of liberty. This was a gift to the Jew first, but is available to the Gentile also. Interestingly, this freedom is also implied within the first commandment of the Mosaic Decalogue, which we call the Ten Commandments.[7] *"I am the Lord your God, who brought you out of Egypt, out of the land of slavery. You shall have no other gods before me."* The first commandment makes God alone absolute in the Hebrew commonwealth. One God and his law are the foundation of any hope of maintaining God's blessing of freedom.

Those who object to the teaching of America's Judeo-Christian founding, and who want us to believe we were founded on a secular philosophic foundation, find the first commandment of the Mosaic Decalogue especially offensive. This is because they want to make themselves sovereign and not God. The truth is, freedom and justice, like all good things, have their origin in God alone, because man, on his own, is not good. The creature cannot say to the Creator, " I am sovereign and have no need of thee." Only the one truly sovereign can grant liberty to others to enjoy freedom of choice.

---

6. Tyler added the word democratic to republics he was referencing. Later I will distinguish between republics that are democratic and those that are not.

7. Deuteronomy 5:6-10.

In the very next chapter of Deuteronomy (Chapter 6) Israel is reminded, "Hear O Israel, the Lord thy God is Lord only, and thou shall love the Lord our God with all thy heart, and with all thy soul, and with all thy might." Likewise, in our American republic we have a pledge of allegiance, in which we remind our selves that we are one nation, under God. Today the critics demand that this phrase be removed from our pledge. If it is removed, especially from our minds and hearts, our republic will not survive any better than did Israel's commonwealth, which fell as they sought after other gods of the nations surrounding them. If man is the source of freedom, then man can take away our freedom at will. But if we are bonded together by a belief that "we are endowed, by our Creator, with certain unalienable rights," those rights are secure. This is the importance of this inquiry that calls us to remembrance of our great founding. When we forget that our union of liberty and prosperity only exist under God, we may say to ourselves, as Israel of old:

> *My power and the strength of my hands have produced this wealth for me. But remember the Lord your God, for it is he who gives you the ability to produce wealth, and so confirms his Covenant, which he swore to your forefathers, as it is today. If you ever forget the Lord your God and follow other gods and worship and bow down to them, I testify against you today that you will surely be destroyed. Like the nations the Lord destroyed before you so you will be destroyed for not obeying the Lord your God.*[8]

In political science there is a maxim: You cannot have a government until you have a nation and you cannot have a nation without a common bond of fraternity. Note two things about the First Commandment of God's law. First, the Hebrew common bond was God, who had delivered them from bondage. Second, their freedom was dependent on obedience to him alone. But note also that this obedience was to be motivated by love, which is always a voluntary bond. Since the nature of mankind is selfish, such a brotherhood must have a means to be renewed; therefore the continual reminder, by God, of the consequences of disobedience and his offer of extended grace when the people would repent.

Some have always questioned why freedom can't develop independently of God. In fact, this was the issue subtly raised by the Serpent, Satan, in the Garden of Eden. The Devil was suggesting to Adam and Eve that God was a tyrant who was holding out on them. So too the ancient idolaters viewed Eve as the hero of that story and God the tyrant. They twisted the truth of God's Word passed on by the Hebrews. This is the way ancient cultures claimed they could have freedom without God. But that kind of freedom always turns into licentiousness. Beginning in Babylon and moving to Tyre, Memphis, Pergamum, and finally Athens, they worshiped goddesses (incarnations of Eve) and made sexual rituals religious festivals as a sort of celebration of their "freedom." I refer you, again, to the book *The Parthenon Code* by Robert Bowie Johnson, Jr. that ties the worship in the Temple on the acropolis of Athens to a twisted tale going back to the Garden of Eden, and especially Noah and the Flood. By doing so, the Greeks were really helping validate that these ancients knew of the truth of stories in today's Bible: from Creation, to the Fall, to the Flood, and to the Tower of Babel. From ancient times man has tried to make God a liar, sin freedom, and mankind pawns of the gods and in a struggle to become gods themselves. But note that the Hebrew God does not force himself on man or for that matter on nations. He asked Adam and Eve to choose life, he asked Israel to choose life, and today he asks you and me to choose Christ that we may be free indeed.[9]

---

8. Deuteronomy 8:17-20.

9. Deuteronomy 30:19-20 and John 8:31-36a.

The nations all around Israel had turned into terrible tyrannies and had become slaves to sin. Also, as we have already demonstrated in recent history, the path of France under the Enlightenment did not lead to true liberty but just the opposite. The pseudo one-party republics that arose in the 20th century (usually called communist peoples republics) that tried to wipe out Judeo-Christianity did not give the people freedom but a godless tyranny. There is no true liberty except under God.

The great destroyer of freedom in the time of the early Hebrew commonwealth was idolatry. The enemy of freedom today is a new idolatry of "self," based on a belief in the human evolution of our soul. In today's "Babylon," the choice is between those choosing the Christian path and those choosing the path of atheism. The basic lifestyle of those who chose not to believe God and those who do has not changed with time. Both the idolatry of ancient history and the atheism of modern history do not admit man is a sinner and in fact see the gods as tyrants and man the final hope of salvation from all ills of society. But have any human societies, other than those who submit to principles of government passed on by Judeo-Christian teaching, ever really created a people of true liberty?

E.C. Wines goes to great lengths to show how idolatry (polytheism) affected national societies of ancient history. All societies from Egypt to Babylon were based on the commonly held sentiment that the supreme god, after he had created the world, retreated unto himself and committed national governments to subordinate deities. Each subordinate deity was given special jurisdiction over different nations or over independent city-states. The temporal blessings for humankind like health, long life, fruitful seasons, safety, and victory over enemies were to be obtained by appeasing these gods.

Polytheistic religions did not stress the practice of virtue but demanded child sacrifice or orgies and unspeakable rites of worship. Therefore, at the time of the establishment of the Hebrew commonwealth, all nations were devoid of anything we would call a virtuous lifestyle. All women in Babylonia were expected once a year to repair to the Temple of Venus to prostitute themselves to strangers. Temples in all nations were the worst wicked sinkholes of moral pollution ever known from the time of Moses right up to the time of Christ. In the time of Christ, a single Temple in Corinth maintained 1,000 religious prostitutes, both male and female. In fact the Hebrews, having come out of Egypt, were exposed to similar temptations again and again.[10] An objective way to discover how immoral ancient times were can be gained by reading the laws laid down through Moses against sins of neighboring states such as bestiality, human sacrifice, prostituting one's own daughter, and many other examples.[11] It is not surprising that at times God told Israel to totally destroy some of these cultures. God also made stoning the punishment for these acts within Israel itself.

In our own new "Babylon" today, modern man again is less and less virtuous by Judeo-Christian standards. He continues to demand the "freedom," more appropriately called license, to live as he pleases without regard to the law of God.

Idolatry was the alternative to the purity and unity of monotheism, and all ancient immorality the result of polytheism. True freedom requires a virtuous people. "One God only shalt thou serve," was the great principle of Hebrew polity. The one true God became the true head of the Hebrew state. The Hebrews had no king but Jehovah. He gave them his law. They had come out of the slavery of a polytheistic state and God asked them to

---

10. See the story in Numbers 25, as an example.

11. Read the list of sins in Leviticus 18.

choose freedom through obedience to him alone. This is the significance of the principle of the unity of God. A nation requires something that brings it unity, or it forces unity through tyranny. It was treason for those in Israel to try to include the idolatry around them as part of their devotion to Jehovah. The Hebrew republic was the first whose nationalism was bound up in monotheism, and the first to be concerned with freedom and the virtuous life.

These ancient polytheistic states gave individuals the right to satisfy their own lusts at the expense of those who loved them. This was not freedom but license. True freedom requires discipline. It requires a sense of responsibility to others. It requires a willingness to submit to God. Though the Ten Commandments all were written in the negative, they were actually the first real bill of rights. They begin with, "I am Jehovah, which brought you out of bondage." The word "you" in this declaration is plural and includes every individual. But each individual's freedom extends only so far as it does not infringe on the freedom of his neighbor. "Thou shall love the Lord they God only; and thy neighbor as thyself".[12] The idea of rights coming with responsibility becomes obvious as you read on through the full Decalogue. Thus the law "thou shall not kill" is the right to life for all. The law "thou shall not commit adultery" protects the freedom and security of all families. The laws: "thou shall not steal and thou shall not covet," protect the freedom of private property for all. The law "thou shall not bear false witness" protects a limited freedom of speech and the press, as well as the preservation of the truth in court. So long as Israel obeyed the law of God, they were the freest people in history.

Returning for a moment to our own time in history, did you know, as you walk up the steps of the Supreme Court building in Washington DC, that your eyes view on the gable overhead a bas-relief sculpture of the world's great lawgivers? Each one is facing one lawgiver in the middle who is facing forward. That middle lawgiver is Moses, and he is holding the Ten Commandments. Did you know, as you enter the Supreme Court building and proceed to the doors outside of the great courtroom, that these massive oak doors have the Ten Commandments engraved on the lower portion of each door? Did you know, as you sit inside the courtroom and observe the wall above the judges' seats, that you can view another display of the Ten Commandments? My point is that you can hide books and history from the people regarding the founding of this nation, but it is harder to hide the symbols that are represented in its architecture and stone edifices.

The American republic took the wisdom of Moses and the adoration of Jehovah, through his Son, Jesus Christ, and founded the most successful republic in modern times. Like Israel, it is ours as long as we continue to remember that our liberty comes from God and our submission to his law. Despite what is taught today by historical revisionists, the great majority of our founders were believers in our union established under God. Once again, let me quote from Ben Franklin, who said while writing to a friend thinking of coming to America, "Atheism is unknown there; Infidelity rare and secret; so that persons may live to a great age in that country without having their piety shocked by meeting with either an Atheist or an Infidel. And the Divine Being seems . . . pleased to favor the whole country."[13] But, sadly, we have changed since the time of Ben Franklin. Atheism is openly proclaimed in our land and infidelity is widely accepted. How long can we remain a free people, I wonder.

---

12. Leviticus 19: 18b. and Luke 10:27.

13. Ben Franklin on atheism (1754), www.earstohear.net/heritage/BenFranklin.html. Franklin is also known for many quotes that reveal he himself was not a believer in Christianity. His observation above may not be evidence of his own beliefs, but only an honest opinion regarding his country.

In conclusion, God's Word teaches us that even family can turn into anarchy or tyranny when its members know nothing of submission. The deterioration of the modern family, and the attempt to redefine it, is a major cause of crime and lawlessness. I refer you to the commandment to "honor our father and mother." We must first submit to our Heavenly Father with all of our heart, so that we can learn to submit to one another. However, true submission cannot be forced on us, it must be an act of the free will. States, as well as families, become tyrannies when citizens have no concept of responsibility or duty and only submit out of fear.

Our Father God, the author of liberty, knew that the free will of man would cost him the life of his dear Son; but because he first loved us, we may even be willing to lay down our life for a friend, for family, or for country. Freedom is never free. Love must be voluntary or it becomes tyranny. God is love. Our God is no tyrant. When the people demand the right to do what is right in their own eyes, as the pluralistic modern republics require, it can only lead to anarchy. Pluralistic cultural license is not evidence of liberty. Only Judeo-Christian culture can produce true national liberty.

Chapter 5

The Twin Principles of Liberty and Equality

In this section of our study of the Hebrew republic, we will explore E.C. Wines' principles of national unity, political equality, and agrarianism as if they were one principle. This single principle I will call national unity. That is, I will speak of national unity as a kind of practical classlessness. This will not mean literal classlessness, which is never achievable. It will recognize a kind of natural aristocracy based on talent, education, and other attributes that always separate individuals in any society. It will, however, stand opposed to artificial divisions designed to separate classes in order to give political dominance to one group and forbid political influence to another group.

In Leviticus 26:13, God, speaking through Moses, declared,

> *I am the Lord your God which delivered you out of a state of slavery in Egypt [and have constituted you a nation of freemen].[1]*

In Deuteronomy 1: 16-17, Moses calls on those in authority to be careful not to be a respecter of persons based on one's position whether it be great or small or even a stranger in the land.

> *For the Lord your God is god of gods and Lord of Lords, the great God, mighty and awesome, who shows no partiality and accepts no bribes. He defends the cause of the fatherless and the widow, and loves the alien, giving him food and clothing. And you are to love those who are aliens, for you yourselves were aliens in Egypt. Fear the Lord your God and serve Him. Hold fast to him and take your oaths in his name.[2]*

Egypt, Babylonia, and the small states in Canaan (where the Hebrew state would arise) were all built upon a caste system. These systems were always disposed to subjugate a lower part of humanity without giving them hope of raising their station by hard work or by any achievement. Since they saw the heavenly realm divided into a hierarchy of gods, it would only naturally follow that within those societies of mankind there would likewise be a caste system. So under the laws of such states, there was a very harsh division of higher and lower classes. The higher classes were entitled to exclusive privileges and rights. Punishments for the same crime also would be more or less harsh depending on one's class.[3]

Even in the republics that developed later in Greek city-states and in Roman Italy, there were still harsh divisions of people by class. Most of the time, rights in these early republics applied only to

---

1. This quote comes from the *1599 Geneva Bible* and its footnote. (All other quotes are taken from the NIV Bible).

2. Deuteronomy 10: 17-20. Aliens if they were obedient to the law could actually become adopted citizens. This statement does not imply they could live by pagan religious standards within Israel.

3. See Appendix 4, Exhibit A. There you will find an excerpt of Hammurabi's Babylonian Code.

the upper class. But in the Hebrew republic there was national unity under the law.

> All of you are standing today in the presence of the Lord your God . . . your leaders and chief men, your elders and officials, and all the other men of Israel, together with your children and your wives, and the aliens living in your camps who chop your wood and carry your water. You are standing here in order to enter into a Covenant with the Lord your God, a Covenant the Lord is making with you this day and sealing with an oath, not only with you who are standing here with us today but also with those who are not here today" [posterity].[4]

Truly the Hebrew republic was a nation promoting equality under the law from its beginning and into its decline later under a monarchy. Below note how Moses makes an actual prophetic announcement proving it was God's intent that the Hebrew republic would be a foundation upon which other nations would learn to be free:

> *See I have taught you decrees and laws. Observe them carefully for this will show your wisdom and understanding to the nations, who will hear about all these decrees and say, surely this great nation is a wise and understanding people. What other nation is so great as to have their God near them the way the Lord our God is near us whenever we pray to Him? And what other nation is so great as to have such righteous decrees and laws, as this body of laws I am setting before you today?*[5]

Even though the above constitution of Moses had already been corrupted by most of Israel's kings, Josiah rediscovered and reapplied these righteous decrees and laws at the end of his life. Then, significantly, in the year 594 BC, less than 15 years after the Jewish King Josiah died, the *Draconian*[6] Code that separated Greek city-state classes was suddenly revised to be more like that of Moses. I think, it is logical to assume Athens was aware of this reform by Josiah and found a way to apply this Hebrew wisdom in their moment of crisis. The leader of Athens was Solon, one of history's great lawgivers, who became the father of Athenian republican government. Athens was on the verge of civil war between the rich and the poor. Solon gave all classes representation on an equal footing in his Council of 400. Each class assembly voted for 100 representatives apiece to sit on this Council, and thus they each exercised checks and balances over one another. This Solon reform saved Athens from a terrible civil war between the classes. But, despite this constitution, it only took a few years for several tyrants in succession to take over by stirring up class jealousy. The Solon constitution of 594 BC would survive only 86 years.

The Greeks had no Jehovah who held them accountable through an independent Levitical class devoted to a universal, absolute, and higher law. To them, the law only had a contemporary foundation, and it had no source beyond those who had made it for their time and in their own interests. In contrast, Hebrew law was *constitutional* in form and had to be applied equally to all and it was a fixed standard for present and future generations.

It was in 508 BC that the Athenian republic was again reformed. The tyrant Clisthenes gave the Athenians democracy by giving all males over the age of 20, regardless of the class of their birth, the equality of a one-man-one-vote single assembly.[7] This did not, however, lead to true liberty for

---

4. Deuteronomy 29:10-15.

5. Deuteronomy 4:5-8.

6. Literally, Athens was under what was called the Code of Draco before Solon. This code of law was more like the harsh laws of the Middle Eastern nations of that era, other than Israel. Ever since that time, Western Civilization has called harsh legal codes of law, "Draconian".

7. A just democracy can be an allusive goal. There are

all. Regardless of the population of each class under the rule of the Council of 400 all men were equally free to prevent or allow law to be made in Solon's republic. But since most of the males in the new single assembly were from the poorest class, it was the poorest that controlled the majority vote needed to make the law under Clisthenes' democracy. They began to banish one rich man and then another in order to take their property. This democratic-republic was really a tyranny of the majority, ruled by popular tyrants. The Athenian direct democracy lasted 170 years (508 to 338 BC) and was finally overthrown and became an absolute monarchy under Alexander the Great. According to Plato, one of the critics of this democracy was Socrates who was arrested and tried and convicted of treason because he criticized the state. Today he is thus often referred to as the first martyr for free speech, which ironically occurred in a democracy. Do you remember my reference to Alexander Tyler in Chapter Four? Now that we have taken a closer look at the Greek republic of Athens, it would appear Alexander Tyler was right when he said democratic-republics generally last no more than 200 years.

As far as the Roman Republic goes, which supposedly lasted from 509 to 49 BC, it too was fraught with civil wars between the upper class (called Patricians) and the lower class (called Plebeians). Its founders took power from the kings that had ruled Rome, and established the election of two Consuls as equal heads of state and allowed both to serve only one-year terms. Consecutive Consul terms were prohibited. The Consuls could only come from the Senate, which was made up of the patriarchs of the Patrician class.[8] However, the Plebeian class formed its own assembly, and began to elect two Tribunes to watch over the Senate. Tribunes had immunity from arrest while they served. If the Senate was about to do something harmful to the lower class, the Tribunes, sitting as observers, could call out "veto" (which means "I forbid") and, if they felt it was necessary, hold a plebiscite, or vote of the plebeians to intimidate the Patricians with a general strike. In 367 BC, the Licinian-Sextian Reform allowed the election of a Patrician and Plebeian Consul, giving the elected Plebeian Consul noble-status in the Senate. It wasn't until 287 BC that the assembly of the Plebeians was given full law making power with the Senate. This two-house democratic-republic lasted until 107 BC (only 180 years). During Rome's democratic-republic Consuls led its armies in many foreign wars, each time extending their terms of office while serving as generals. Marius managed to be elected Consul seven consecutive times. In 107 BC, civil wars broke out continuously between the classes until 82 BC when Sulla made himself dictator for life.

The Senate, with great difficulty, was able later to slowly regain sovereignty over generals.[9] But the Senate's powers were ultimately marginalized once again, between 64 BC and 44 BC. Those were the political years of the famous Julius Caesar. Caesar was the first general that broke the law by bringing his army with him to Rome, rather than leaving it in Gaul, a colonial territory of the empire. Like Sulla, Caesar made himself dictator for life. Not even the assassination of Caesar could save the republic. By the time of Christ's birth, an absolute emperor ruled Rome. Again, it appears that Alexander Tyler was right about the life span of democratic-republics.

---

many ways to form majorities and some turn into tyranny over the minority.

8. The Roman Senate was a little like the Council of Elders in the Hebrew republic in that both had hereditary clan chiefs serving as representatives of the people.

9. Starting with the Punic Wars against Carthage, between 264 and 146 BC, Rome turned more and more to generals but senators kept them under control by making them keep their armies in the colonies of the growing empire. However, as Rome's Empire grew and grew Roman citizens became more and more loyal to the generals they served under, rather than to the assembly or senate.

The survival of any republic is usually threatened once it becomes a democracy. A democratic republic is eventually weakened when the majority realizes they can vote for candidates on the premise that once elected they will make the largess of the treasury of the state available to the masses without the necessity of earning it by their labor. Then the state becomes a tyranny of the majority, and is bankrupted and or violently over-thrown, ending up under a dictator. May we not forget the foundation upon which our freedom and prosperity rests.

So much for the glory of Greco-Roman culture, from which the Enlightenment drew its inspiration in the 18th and 19th centuries AD, when republics were coming into vogue once again.

How can a nation claim to be a free people if it has no national unity extending that freedom equally to all? The republican ideals of the Greek and Roman republics probably originated with the Hebrews, but without a means to encourage national unity, their application turned destructive. If their great ideas were to work, they needed to rely on the supposed good nature of man to overcome his bad tendencies. But in reality the nature of man is far to self-centered without the schoolmaster of God's law to bring one under self-control. The French made the same wrong assumptions about human nature in the birth of their republic. If one would find the right foundation from which to build a working republic, one needs to return to the Hebrew republic between 1446 and 1050 BC. Not that the fallen nature of man did not also trouble that republic, but as we have begun to discover, and will continue to explore, the Hebrew republic provided a national means for recovery when the sinful nature of man threatened it.

According to E.C. Wines, "the members of the body politic, called into being by the Law of Moses, stood upon a more exact equal level and enjoyed a more perfect community of political rights, dignities, and influence than any other people known in history, whether of ancient or modern times." The key to their success was in their attention to national unity.

The key to political equality is in the ownership of land. If the king, as in ancient Egypt, owns all the land, he will be absolute. If the privileged nobility, as in ancient Rome, are the few that own the land, then all others will be their serfs. But if the land is divided among all those who compose society the true power and authority of government will reside in a true and lasting republic. General private property rights are just as fundamentally important to the maintenance of a republic as is the right to vote.

God's plan for the free commonwealth of the Hebrews was that, as they entered the land and took possession tribe by tribe, each tribe's clans were to be assigned lands based on a lottery.[10] The larger the clan the greater the land inheritance granted. The smaller the clan the smaller the land inheritance distributed. This was not the tradition in Europe, before the founding of the American republic. In Europe, at its moment of transition into modern times, a class system had long ago established in two estates all ownership of land. These two estates were the nobility and clergy. The masses were not free or equal. They were known as serfs, and their estates were considered property of the higher estates. If they even tried to leave the land they were born on, their lord had a right to hunt them down and bring them back. The idea of the equality of man, in Western Civilization, had been lost for 2755 years (970 BC to 1785 AD).

The beginning of the loss of national social equality for Israel became evident most dramatically during the reign of King Solomon. 970 BC was the start of Solomon's rule, which ended up a tyranny and an absolute monarchy. Solomon, unconstitutionally, assumed the right to take cities from tribes of the Galilee region as collateral for

---

10. Numbers 33: 53-54.

debts he had with King Hiram of Tyre; and he conscripted labor, unconstitutionally, from his people on a very harsh basis, and from some aliens in Israel who previously had enjoyed equal rights with the Hebrews. He now made them lifetime slaves for his projects. These projects were sometimes for the king's own aggrandizement or for fortifications that housed stables of horses in his standing army. All these were violations of the Covenant of Moses and were considered tyranny by the tribes.[11] Chapter 8 will provide the detail regarding the unconstitutional nature of these acts.

Like Joshua, the founders of the American national republic, 2755 years later, established a powerful national unity by making land ownership freely available to everyone. America was a vast open land with room for wide and open ownership. It was easy for our founders to copy the example laid down by the ancient Hebrews, of which they were astute students. The US Constitution forbids titles of nobility and, though we never held a lottery for the distribution of lands, we did allow the taking of land simply by squatter's rights and thereafter the right to obtain title. Some of our founders did insist on buying the land from the indigenous natives, but not everyone. One complication was the tradition of the Indians that had no place for private property in their culture. To them, no one could own the land any more than they could own the sky. Upon winning our independence as the United States of America, our early Continental Congress passed the Northwest Ordinance of 1785, which allowed for the sale of land in the west at about a dollar an acre. But this price need not necessarily be paid until after its settlement and development. A very attractive draw of immigrants to America would be the ease by which one could obtain land. Those of the lower classes of Europe flocked to America, for this would mean opportunity of advancement that they would never be given in their homelands. Even the pauper who might be imprisoned for debts could be brought to America and sold into indentured servitude, after which he would be rewarded with 50 acres of land. This idea too came from Moses.[12]

In the interest of complete honesty regarding the claims I have made, I cannot continue with my analysis without first explaining that Israel was not totally free of lifetime slavery during her republican years.

> *"Your male and female slaves are to come from the nations around you; from them you may buy slaves. You may also buy some of the temporary residents living among you and members of their clans born in your country, and they will become your property. You can will them to your children as inherited property and can make them slaves for life, but you must not rule over your fellow Israelites ruthlessly."*[13]

God permitted lifetime slavery in Israel, if the one enslaved was not an adopted or naturally born Israelite citizen.[14]

This is not acceptable to us today under Christianity. Why was it allowed then? Perhaps you will accept the following explanation, but it is only my opinion. I have no Biblical reference to back it up. God seems to be dealing with humankind in a progressive manner. For his own reasons, he did not send the Messiah immediately after Adam and Eve sinned. Nor has God made any Christian perfect after they accepted him as Lord of their life. He does, however, promise that one day we will have a redeemed world free of the curse of sin and resurrected bodies free of the sin nature. Therefore, I suggest that Israel and its promised land is an imperfect picture of what God has in store for his people. Israel at that time was to

---

11. First Kings 5: 13-16 and 9: 11 and 15, plus 12: 1-18.

12. Deuteronomy 15: 12-15.

13. Leviticus 25: 44-46.

14. Leviticus 25: 39-42 and Deuteronomy 24: 7.

be an example of the difference between a free people's economy and government for those who choose life under the Law of God, and the kind of economy and government that exists for those who choose to be their own masters. As Jesus taught the disciples in the parable of the wheat and the tares about the need for good and evil to live together while awaiting the "harvest season," perhaps the same principle for purposes of visual illustration applied to Old Testament times as the free and the enslaved lived side by side.

On this side of the cross, it took a very long time before the Christian conscience was raised to the point of leading the struggle against the institution of slavery totally.[15] Eventually, it was the British and American churches that led the way. Despite the fact that many churches remained on the side of slavery, note how in the "Kingdom of God" the side of righteousness always wins out in the end. It was the Reformation Christians, like the Quakers and the Methodists, who stood out first as the crusaders for ending slavery in the British Empire, but then slowly, as the crusade ignited the passion of the northern States of America, it became an interdenominational Christian cause. For a continued examination of this subject, I refer you to chapter 11 of this book.

The issue of slavery is first an economic matter and only secondarily a political matter. How would one describe the economy of that ancient Hebrew commonwealth? First, there was no birthright aristocracy class in the Hebrew republic. Every head of a family was given private property rights and equal opportunity to create new wealth. Some would create businesses, and some would end up as free labor dependent on others for a living. As free labor, they would at least own their home. The Hebrew economy was likely the first capitalist economy. Some became very wealthy but all were assured of equal opportunity to make the most of their life. This was not the norm for ancient times, or most of human history. The Hebrew republic encouraged the virtues of industry and frugality as well as a good work ethic. The national unity of the Hebrew people was based in their equal-opportunity system that prevented the otherwise inevitable development of a burdensome upper class supported by a massive enslaved lower class. But, despite the freedom of citizens, the Hebrew economy also allowed some slavery of non-citizens. Small family business was the backbone of the Hebrew economy. Its dominate-class was the middle class.

The most unique aspect of the Hebrew republic's economy was how it was administered under its covenantal Sabbath Year cycle, occurring every 7 years. The Sabbath Day of Exodus 20 was for worship of the Creator and was to be observed once a week. However, the Hebrews also had what was called the Sabbath Year, and it laid at the heart of their economy. The Sabbath Year was for the purpose of literally "resting" in the promise of redemption for citizens and the land. All debts were canceled between citizens, and the manumission of all citizen-indentured servants took place every Sabbath Year. The land was not to be worked for the entire Sabbath Year. God's people were to trust in what the land on its own would yield in harvest or what surplus they had accumulated from harvests in the years preceding the Sabbath Year. Letting the land rest was a reminder that God alone owns all we think we possess. We are his stewards of the earth. This is also a picture of how Christ, who came as our redeemer, cancels our debt of sin and frees us from a life of slavery to sin. However, those who were not citizens of heaven, so to speak, represented by the Hebrew lifetime slaves, did not enjoy this year of liberty from slavery. Indentured servants were always contracted labor, for free, to pay off a debt, and they of course are the

---

15. Though Paul recognizes the legal existence of slavery in New Testament times, he seems to imply that we Christians should not separate ourselves as bond and free, and in the Letter to Philemon urges him to accept a runaway slave as a brother in Christ. (Philemon 1:16.)

ones manumitted every seven years. The Sabbath Year was only for the true citizen of the "promised land," whether natural born, or adopted.[16]

Then after seven Sabbath Years (49 years), Israel observed a Year of Jubilee. For two years in a row they let the land rest. The 50th year, or once a generation, Israel celebrated the return of every citizen to his family property, and each to his own tribal clan. This inheritance had its origin back when Joshua assigned each tribe its lot. Over the 50 years, property may have changed hands as economic deals were made to pay off debts or obligations. During such capitalistic trading, one's title of ownership was sort of held in escrow, and one always had the right to exercise an option to buy back the property or have a kinsman redeem it. Also, during the passing of years, people would move for many reasons, but in the year of Jubilee, they had the right to return and freely be restored to the inheritance that had belonged to their family going back to the founding of Israel.[17] An alien even had the right to marry into a Hebrew family and become a citizen by adoption. The Book of Ruth, in the time of the Hebrew republic and its judges is partially devoted to this adoption and a kinsman's redemption of property rights.

The principles involved in the economy established by the Law of Moses are several. First, God is making it clear that Israel did not own anything but were only his stewards of the land. Also, the assigned possession is an unalienable property right, always returning to the heir. This economic system promotes accountability, and the resulting rewards and penalties depend on whether one's stewardship is good or poor. Also it is a system that promises the next generation its own fresh start on its own merits. I suggest it is also from this Jubilee concept that the modern world gets its idea of bankruptcy laws.[18] Significantly, the Year of Jubilee opened with a somber emphasis on the Day of Atonement. A whole year of making things right with God and one another starts out with national repentance and forgiveness. This Day of Atonement must have had deeper meaning in terms of national revival than all the annual Days of Atonement preceding the Year of Jubilee.

What a picture of God's grace this is, as lost inheritances are returned even after possibly unfaithful stewardship. Is it a picture of how, despite our small contribution in good works in this life, compared to others, we all will inherit eternal life in the next world? The real gift of Easter will one day be our Christian Jubilee. The final Day of Atonement was Good Friday. Our future day of resurrection will set us free, finally, once for all. It is fitting therefore, in America's founding, that the Liberty Bell in Philadelphia had engraved on it, "Proclaim liberty throughout the land to all its inhabitants," with the scriptural reference of Leviticus 25: 10. I am sure you can see that this economy under the Covenant of Moses made Israel an exceptional nation, prohibiting the division of the people into patricians and plebeians. These ideals found in the Mosaic commonwealth could not be perfectly applied to the American republic, but our founders did apply the underlying principle of equal opportunity to our own historical development. Ancient Israel was dominantly a middle class society; the dominance of a middle class in any society can only be found in the exceptional nature of Judeo-Christian societies called Western Civilization today.

In the Hebrew republic there existed a massive middle class unheard of in any nation until the rise of the American republic about 2,800 years later. Both John Adams and Thomas Jeffer-

---

16. This Sabbath Year may be a type of how the Kingdom of God (Church Age) is made up of both Bond Slaves (Gentiles) and free men (Jews), both natural born and adopted. Romans 11: 11-24 But, within the "Kingdom" are also both weeds (life time slaves) and wheat (the Saved). (Matt. 13:25-30.)

17. Leviticus 25:1-28 and 39-43 and 47-55.

18. The first society to borrow this legal notion of bankruptcy was Athens, under Solon.

son agreed that America was a yeoman's nation of small farmers and businesses. It remained so until the 20th century. John Adams said,

> The happy agrarian life is divided into the hands of the common people in every State, in such a way, that nineteen twentieths of all property would be in the hands of the middle class; let them appoint whomever they will for chief magistrate and senators, the sovereignty will reside in the whole body of the people.[19]

But, another founder, Alexander Hamilton, viewed the future of America in giant commercial enterprise, banking, and trade; it has been Hamilton's vision of America that has more recently won out over that of Jefferson's vision. Jefferson often debated him on the importance of an agrarian economy of small farmers, and small businesses, under family ownership, for the continued vitality of the republic. I wonder if Jefferson might have understood, like so many of his contemporaries, that his view was also that of the ancient Hebrew republic?

The modern growth of giant corporations, made up of nameless and faceless stockholders without a common family-type bond of responsibility to hold them together, has sometimes resulted in tyranny as destructive as any state tyranny. It may not be impossible to maintain our dominant middle class within the modern centralization of corporate power in America; but, if we do maintain this required component of our national unity, it will surely require an overriding Christian ethic at work in the exalted board rooms of corporate America. Republics are most easily maintained in an economy of small business and masses of small farms, all family owned.

The Hebrew commonwealth was a nation of hard-working small farmers for the most part, and must have seemed a strange sight to all other nations surrounding them. All societies around this Hebrew nation of hard-working small farmers and businessmen despised the tilling of the ground and turned it over to slaves. America's Southern plantations did the same until the Civil War abolished slavery. Therefore the South did develop an aristocracy. However, the middle class is the backbone of a true republic. A republic that is an agrarian society of small farmers, and family businesses does instill love of country and ownership like none other. It is hard to keep a sense of national unity when a global economy rules, and wealth is held by great concentrations of transnational companies. Is America now also engaged in the politics of pitting class against class? How secure is our national unity today under its corporate impersonal business class?

Given the fallen nature of man, and the curse on creation itself, nothing is secure without the sustaining hand of God. The Judeo-Christian God is a God of grace and this thus separates such believers from all other worldviews. Our redemption and the redemption of creation rests in the providence of the sustaining Word of God. Thus history, in the Judeo-Christian worldview, requires divine guidance and sustaining providence for those who trust in the truth and light given by revelation of God. But history for unbelievers is at the mercy of God's judgment, and their only hope is in repentance and acceptance of the grace of God. In addition, God has ordained all governments of nations to also sustain some order in which lawlessness is restrained. There can be no freedom without order; but just as true, there can be no freedom without brotherhood (equality). Finally, there can be no equality unless all, including the ruler(s), operate as servants under God's law.

By the above generalizations regarding the agrarian nature of America's economy in its founding, I do not intend to deny the early trend of the industrial revolution of the 19th century.

---

19. Rev. E. C. Wines, *The Roots of the American Republic*. (Marlborough, N. H.: The Plymouth Rock Foundation, 1997), 12.

That industrial revolution both contributed to corrupting and promoting fairness and equal opportunity in America. Because most Americans remained small farmers all through the 19th century, the industrial revolution helped them prosper as never before. Our nation did not reach the point of even half the people living in cities until about 1920. The larger impact of industrialization didn't come until well into the 20th century. Today, in the 21st century, only about 5 percent of us work on farms, and even farms have become big business. But then too, the machine age actually helped to weaken the tyranny of slavery as a viable system going on into the future.[20]

The rise of factories in cities had a mixed effect on America's middle class. In some cases it helped produce sweatshops known for their tyranny over labor. In some cases it expanded a healthy and continued prosperity for the middle class. An example of the later case occurred in my own hometown of Kalamazoo, Michigan. Going back to the beginning of the 20th century, Kalamazoo was blessed with a growing prosperity mainly fueled by a new family-owned pharmaceutical company. The employees of the Upjohn pharmaceutical company worked for bosses who were known for their loyalty. They paid a living wage and offered many services to their workers, such as free transportation to and from work and health insurance, all without the coercion of a labor union. While the company later became a successful public-traded stock company, it still remained mostly owned by the Upjohn extended family, which remained a generous benefactor of local community interests. This was true right up the end of the 20th century.

But, the Upjohn Company eventually was bought out and consolidated into ownership that was not local and had no family like attachment to Kalamazoo. In the 21st century, the extended family of the Upjohn lineage sold their extensive stock holdings and, in the spirit of the heritage of that family company, they reinvested their wealth in starting another small business locally. In addition, many scientists lost jobs locally as first Pharmacia and now the Pfizer Company downsized. Following the consolidations, some of these scientists borrowed money to start new drug exploration companies of their own locally. So, it remains true that centralized economic control does continue to grow in the American economy, fostering a threatening economic tyranny. But, it remains true, as well, that small, locally owned, family-type business is not dead and remains the model for promoting equal opportunity and middle class expansion in our future economy.

In conclusion, I hope you now appreciate the Biblical source and foundation of the great republican principles of liberty and equality and fraternity. But remember, it is not the state that holds the promise of these ideals, because centralization of power always leads to tyranny. It is obviously not the giant transnational corporations that save a nation from economic tyranny, either. It is small, family-oriented, local business that is the key to the preservation of these ideals. The ideals of liberty and equality are twins and both have their source in God's revelation to Moses. Human attempts to duplicate the fruits of liberty and equality have always failed, unless modeled within a Judeo-Christian framework. That framework is one of independent and free enterprise that is family owned and managed. As someone once said, " the best welfare system is a dependable job, and there is no better security for old age than owning your own business."

Look around the world today. You will see that most nation-states still are organized around a few very rich and powerful members of an upper class, a very small middle class, and a massive lower class living in utter poverty. Only in nation-states with a history of a Judeo-Christian past development will you find the dominant class to be

---

20. I explain the fall of slavery in chapter eleven. Slavery was an evil that could not wait for a natural death and our nation did not wait for its natural demise.

of the middle class. In such exceptional societies you will also find freedom and extended equal opportunity. Even the poorest in the United States of America today live in luxury compared to the masses of peasants in most nation-states. May we not forget the foundation upon which our prosperity rests.

Part Three
The Hebrew Constitution

Righteous are you, O Lord, and your laws are right.
The statutes you have laid down are righteous,
they are fully trustworthy.
My zeal wears me out, for my enemies ignore your words.
Your promises have been thoroughly tested,
and your servant loves them.
Though [the nation has] forgotten and has been taught
to despise [your truth], I will not forget your precepts.
Your righteousness is everlasting and your law is true.

Psalms 119: 137–142

Chapter 6

A Federal System of Republics

The term constitution, as defined in a dictionary, is "a body of fundamental principles or established precedents according to which a state or other organization is acknowledged to be governed." It may come in the form of written documents adopted over time, or it may be established in a single founding document. It always defines a set of established institutional centers of authority. In the case of the Hebrew republic, I choose to separate the Law of the Covenant from the Hebrew constitution. The Law of the Covenant sets forth God's commandments regarding human behavior and relationships, for example, the Ten Commandments. The Hebrew constitution sets forth God's established system of governance, for example, the offices and assemblies of authority set up by Moses. I refer to the Hebrew constitution with a lower-case "c" because it is not contained in a single document, but is a development one discovers in Israel's written history. I refer only to written Constitutions with a capital "C". A written Constitution requires a single complete document created at a national convention of citizens that defines the limited powers of a national government, and which can only be amended by a vote of popularly elected delegates or representatives. It was we Americans who introduced the idea of a written Constitution. The main body of the American Constitution deals almost totally with institutions of national authority, but many of its amendments deal with rights of the people designed to limit the powers of those governmental institutions. The American Constitution is about the limitations of power as much or more than the required authority of the government. Interestingly, we borrowed our constitutional principles from the histories of the Hebrew republic and British common law, and then made them into a single written document we call the Constitution of the United States.

This part of the book will be about Mosaic principles that define institutional centers of divided authority. The Hebrew constitution was the first introduction of the general principle of "limited government." In this chapter, I will explain how the Hebrew commonwealth limited human authority under a "federalist" system.[1] As noted previously, a republic is a state in which there is government by consent of the governed, and individual civil liberties to guide justice and check tyranny. This is best achieved in a nation that checks and balances the powers of national government by giving great powers to fully equipped regional governments, and also allows the retention of a free private sector. One way to check the power of central government is to form a confederation, which gives the national authority no sovereignty and thus makes it totally dependent on regional states. An alternative system is a federal system that divides sovereignty between a national gov-

---

1. Federalist (federalism) is exclusively an American term. The Hebrews had no concept of this term, but in reality they were given a system that, in today's terminology, fits the requirements of a federal system.

ernment and local governments. Federalism is an interdependent system of regional governments and a central government. Our founders experimented with a confederation but quickly realized it wouldn't work and called the new system they invented, at the Constitutional Convention of 1787, a federal system. Its advocates were called Federalists. When one compares our federal system to the ancient Hebrew commonwealth, one discovers they both have an established division of interdependent local and central constitutional governing authorities.

Since you and I live in the 21st century, when republics have become quite complicated, it is important that we not draw the conclusion that the Hebrew republic had all the "bells and whistles" of modern republics. All republics, whether modern or ancient, are not equal. However, all republics have simple basic characteristics. Foremost, a republic is always representative government. Representative government requires some method by which the governed have the power to choose and hold accountable those who govern them. Some republics only give the power to govern to the few called the nobility. Some republics make everyone of a responsible age equal in the power to choose leaders. Not all republics are democracies. Some republics divide government between various representative bodies, and some centralize authority in a national parliament. In addition, all republics are subject to a national common law rather than the rule by the whim of man. They always provide a system of justice under "due process of law."[2]

This topic is too large to cover in one chapter. It will take all of Part Three to describe the constitution of the Hebrew republic. I will divide the topic in the following manner. First, I will deal with how the Hebrew republic was government by consent of the governed. Second, I will examine the Hebrew tribal republics within a "federal" structure. Third, I will examine how the decrees of Moses established amazingly modern civil liberties and due process of law within its justice system. Fourth, I will examine the national legislative power of the commonwealth's states-general. Finally, I will examine the national executive power of the Hebrew commonwealth. All these lessons will incorporate E.C. Wines' principles of the Mosaic constitution numbers 5, 6, 7, 8, 9, and 16.[3] For the big picture of the constitution of Moses, see the diagram titled: *The Hebrew Commonwealth under the Mosaic Constitution* in Appendix 5 (page 157).

Government Under God and Under the Consent of the Governed

If a government is under God, does it have to be a theocracy? Can a government be both under God and under the consent of the governed? As regards the case of the Hebrew commonwealth, I will show you that the answer to both questions was yes. Yes, the Hebrews and all aliens living with them were required to practice only one religion, and it therefore was a theocracy. But, totally different from all other theocracies of that time in history, it was a theocratic republic rather than a totalitarian state. The American republic, on the other hand, has never been a theocracy, but was founded under Judeo-Christian Biblical principles. We have essentially been a Christian nation, although that Christian dominion recently has weakened considerably. We prefer the term "under God" to theocracy. We constitutionally forbid the establishment of a single Christian denominational national church. Also, we have usually allowed other non-Christian religions to function within our nation. In Part Four of this book, I will further explore the American republic as it has evolved. Of course, my concern in Part Three will mainly be with an analysis of the Hebrew republic.

---

2. Chapter 7 will introduce the concept of "due process of law."

3. See Appendix 3.

Theocracy usually is defined as rule by a high priest, or rule by divine right of a king as head of a state church, or a union of kingdoms ruled under one "holy father." Theocracies that allow local kings or secular rulers, such as the medieval Roman Catholic papacy, or the present-day Islamic Ayatollah, always assume the right to overrule secular authorities arbitrarily. As such, theocracy usually implies absolute rule from the top down into society. The Hebrew theocracy was different, reflecting that the nature of its God was not about despotism but about freedom. The Hebrew constitution laid out by the lawgiver Moses (as God's spokesperson) was one of direct rule by God, as represented by his Law. But this was a Covenantal Law system that required the consent of the governed. All Hebrew human institutions for making decisions were responsible for the administration of the Law of God and could make other laws only if they did not contradict that higher law.

To administer the Covenantal Law, Moses was instructed to establish human authority under a separation of powers between a birthright high priestly office and a "federated" states-general of secular leaders. The secular tribal princes were elected by the clan chiefs and installed in office by a God appointed national judge. All balloting was by means of an assembly voice vote. The national judge was raised up by God and not by birthright. The judges in the Hebrew commonwealth's history were from many different tribes.[4] We will learn that the commonwealth leaders were urged to try to avoid a king, who, they were warned, would end up taking away the freedoms God had installed in his law. One can only conclude that this unusual government was a theocratic republic. Importantly, however, one should not conclude it was a democracy, which makes majority rule absolute. Nevertheless, it was government by consent of the governed through popular representatives. In its pure republican form, the Hebrew commonwealth only had tribal elections of princes and local city elections of jurors (or local judges) who held court at the city gates. There were no national elections until their constitution was amended to allow for a king.

The states-general, in the Hebrew republic, was a gathering of leaders serving elected office at the tribal and city levels. The original Hebrew government was certainly not anything approaching a monarchy, or even rule by a high priest. From time to time, the national judge would fill a temporary role as a national military leader, or as one who could preside over the states-general meetings when called. The national judge also could act as a one-man supreme court, but sometimes these judges preferred to submit cases to the commonwealth's states-general. We will see that most governing was left to elected city officials, as well as to elected tribal-princes and their birthright clan chiefs within each tribe. The most common national gathering of the people was during the nation's yearly religious festivals at Shiloh under the high priest and the Levitical priesthood. Secular national government assemblies were called for only in emergencies. This system of checks and balances was indeed unique. All the above provisions made up the Mosaic constitution.

Though God alone was absolute in the Hebrew republic, note in the Book of Exodus how he required that the people ratify his law at Sinai (or Horeb as it is called in The Book of Deuteronomy).[5] At Sinai, God spoke directly to the people so that all could hear the great Decalogue of Law. Then the people were given the opportunity to ratify the fundamental Law given by Jehovah (God). Note, the leaders of the tribes (elders) were addressed by Moses and were voting on behalf of the people to sub-

---

4. See Appendix 6.

5. Exodus 19: 7-9 and 20: 18-21. There could be no Covenant if the people did not voluntarily join, and no Covenant without God's sovereignty. Ratify is really the proper term—the concept of Covenant requires that two parties enter an agreement.

mit to this great Covenant. For Moses to address more than a million people and all of them to hear his voice would have been a miracle, but there is nothing here to suggest this was a miracle. However, the people were very aware of the miraculous and dramatic thundering voice of God. They all could hear the Ten Commandments from the mouth of God, but only their representatives were addressed by Moses and asked to vote. It is obvious that this was all oral and that the tablets of stone containing the Ten Commandments had not been made yet. In Chapter 20 of Exodus, it is written, "And God spoke all these words" of the Ten Commandments. But the people trembled with fear and told Moses, "Speak to us yourself and we will listen. But do not have God speak to us, or we will die!" So, after this first introduction, God speaks only to Moses and then Moses speaks to the people through their representatives. In context, God wanted all the people to hear for themselves his Law as well as to have their leaders ratify it. In verse 7 of Exodus 19, again note the words of the author, "So Moses went back and summoned the elders of the people and set before them all the words the Lord had spoken." The people (obviously through their representatives) responded together, "We will do everything the Lord has said." So Moses brought their answer back to the Lord. God then gives much more detail only to Moses in the chapters that follow. By implication, Moses then passed it on to the representatives of the people, who passed it on to the masses.

Then, in Chapter 24 of Exodus, Moses was asked by God to ascend up the mountain again and to bring with him Aaron, Aaron's two oldest sons, and the Council of 70 Elders of the commonwealth.[6] The elders were princes of the tribes and leaders of clans within each tribe. They, like Moses, were given permission to see something of the presence of the Almighty (God). Next, they were made aware that Moses would go up the mountain alone, God would put in writing on stone tablets the Decalogue of Law, and Moses would receive other instructions from God. A Covenantal constitutional system was being put in place by consent of the governed. Moses was gone 40 days (I assume the elders had returned to the people), and during that time Aaron was "forced" by the people to build the golden-calf idol. The representatives of the people (the Council of 70) apparently did not try to stop this rebellion. Moses returned and, upon witnessing the idolatry of the people, smashed the stone tablets on the ground in anger. But later in compassion, Moses interceded for the people and was given permission by God to return to the mountain to receive new stone tablets of the Law, which Israel would keep in a sacred box to be called the Ark of the Covenant.[7]

Significantly, it became a requirement that all the law (perhaps more than the Ten Commandments) be read to the people on a regular basis for their recommitment and dedication. In his Book of Deuteronomy, Moses wrote down more constitutional detail of the law and gave it to the priests, the sons of Levi, and to all the elders of Israel. Then Moses commanded them:

> *At the end of every seven years, in the year of canceling debts, during the Feast of Tabernacles, when all Israel comes to appear before the Lord your God at the place he will choose, you shall read this law before them in their hearing. Assemble the people, ... men and women and children, and the aliens living in your towns ... so they can listen and learn to fear the Lord your God and follow carefully all the words of this law.*[8]

Thus, in a regularly scheduled manner, these leaders had to read the law to everyone. Of course, this took place in many scattered groups of appropri-

---

6. Exodus 24:1-3 and 9-18.

7. The Ark was kept in the tabernacle (temple) in its most holy chamber throughout most of Israel's history as a republic.

8. Deuteronomy 31:10-12

ate size so that all could hear the reading. Every seven years, as all the people listened to the reading of the law, they consented either aloud or quietly in their hearts to be obedient to it.

In this same vein, again requiring formal popular ratification of the law, a one-time special ceremony of dedication had to be held by Joshua and all the elders of the tribes once they had obtained their inheritance of lands. It occurred in a valley where a great stone monument was erected, and the blessings and curses (recorded in the Book of Deuteronomy for the purpose of alerting the people of the results of their obedience or disobedience) were read by the Levites, with representatives of the tribes standing on either side of the valley facing one another to hear and consent to the reading.[9]

Truly, the Hebrew nation was ruled by a written common law, which included their historical founding of offices for decision-making and their Covenant with God. Their constitution was ratified over and over again by representatives who gave affirmation in the presence of all the people. It was the first republic or government by consent of the governed under the law.

Hebrew Tribal Republics

The Hebrew nation evolved in a manner similar to all nations in ancient times. Every nation arose from a patriarchal beginning. When the extended family grew large enough, it would divide into tribes, and finally tribes would surrender to a central national government. Usually the central government would be under a king. What set the Hebrew nation apart was that God was to be king. From beginning to end this nation developed in cycles of rebellion and surrender to God.

The credibility of Biblical history, as compared to most ancient histories, lies in its admitted and recorded imperfections regarding its heroes and rulers. All other ancient national histories lack the honesty one finds in Biblical history. For example, the ancient histories of other nations made their rulers gods who functioned as king and priest to the people. The history of the great patriarchs, Abraham, Isaac, and Jacob also is more complete than the histories left by most other national patriarchs. Uniquely, these Hebrew patriarchs learned to listen to the oracle voice of God and submit to his guidance and to hope in his promise to make them the first free and holy nation.

The tribal history of the Hebrews is much less complete than their patriarchal history. They became tribes under the twelve sons of Jacob and their descendants while in Egypt for 400 years.[10] Little is said about those 400 years except for the beginning under Joseph and the end under Moses. The Hebrews, while in Egypt, began to choose princes and other magistrates to provide leadership over their tribes named for the sons of Jacob. These princes and their related clan chiefs were often collectively called the Elders of Israel.[11] Israel was a new name given by God to Jacob in his last years, and later was adopted as the name of the nation, as formed under Moses. In Chapter 1 of the Old Testament Book of Numbers, it is recorded that each Hebrew tribe took a census of its people, and it named the respective princes, as heads over each tribe[12] This numbering was done while they were still at Mt. Sinai. The national government that was emerging was formed not entirely under one man, but also around the leaders of well organized tribes.

Moses did not record that the qualification requirements for these leaders should be based in birthright, but they were to be men of courage and integrity who feared God. Doesn't this imply that these leaders were to be men who had proven

---

9. Joshua 8: 30-35 (as Moses instructed in Deuteronomy 27 and 28).

10. Acts 7: 6.

11. Exodus 3:16.

12. Numbers 1: 1-16.

themselves worthy of the office? Did Moses appoint the princes and other magistrates himself, or would he have only sworn them into office after the tribes elected them? It seems the latter is the case. In Deuteronomy, Moses says,

> *How can I bear your problems and your burdens and your disputes all by myself? Choose some wise, understanding, and respected men from each of your tribes, and I will set them over you.*[13]

How else could this be accomplished if not by election? According to E.C. Wines, the heads over thousands, hundreds, fifties, and tens, within each tribe, were elected in each city to serve in judicial capacities and even military offices. I agree with E.C. Wines, except for the leaders of thousands, and will address that more thoroughly in my chapter on the national government.

It is often overlooked that God's interests cover the totality of human existence and not just religion. It was part of God's purpose to ordain and bless the religious place of Israel in history, but God also specially defined Israel's government in detail. As one would expect, the Scriptures are filled with indirect, and sometimes direct, references to political, economic, and social systems within God's chosen nation for display before all of humanity. We already have shown that the Mosaic constitution clearly promoted social and legal equality, and it only follows that it would be inclined to popular elections.

The above paragraphs imply an election system. Now let me point to another clue, provided in the Book of Numbers, regarding my inference that Hebrew princes were elected by their tribes. Four times the names of the princes of the tribes are given. First in Chapter 1, then in Chapter 2, again in Chapter 7, and again in Chapter 10, the exact same names of tribal leaders are given, always accompanied by the statement that each is the son of the same specifically named father. Obviously, the same princes of each tribe are continuing in office, and because their fathers are always named, this may be an inference of bloodline requirements for the office. However, suddenly in Chapter 13, new leaders, the sons of fathers not named before, are listed for each tribe. These new leaders are given the responsibility of spying out the land of Canaan and planning for its conquest. In context, this transition of leadership seems to be the result of new elections. Such leaders did not arise through birthright but were chosen by the tribes. In the Hebrew republic, terms of office were probably nearly lifetime terms. It is clear that these newly elected princes of the tribes mostly were a disappointment to Moses. However, they were not removed immediately by new elections, rather the nation had to wait for them, and most of their generation, to die before entering the 'promised land' forty years later under other newly elected leaders.[14]

After Joshua had finished the conquest of Canaan, we are given a chance to see the tribal republics in action. It will thus be the Book of Judges that will give us a look at the individual tribal republics. Some say in the last chapters of the Book of Judges, a theme develops around the expression, "In those days Israel had no king, and everyone did what was right in his own eyes." This *is* a time when the Hebrews had no king, as other nations around them. In any republic the people develop a duty to be self-governing. They have elected leaders who are accountable to them. Judges is about

---

13. Deuteronomy 1:9-15.

14. All but Joshua and Caleb came back from spying in the land of Canaan with reports that discouraged the people from beginning the conquest of the "Promised Land." But the sin did not alone rest with the frightened leaders. The sin rested with the whole nation that had again and again complained and lost faith in God. This was the final straw and all Israel was judged with 40 more years of wandering in the wilderness. Finally, Joshua and Caleb, along with newly elected princes of a new generation, would lead the nation into the "Promised Land."

how the Hebrew tribal republics did not govern themselves very well, or so it would seem. As you would expect in a republic, the sins are likely to be rooted in the attitude of the people and, of course, reflected by their leaders. Israel's elected princes and magistrats, fearing the people more than God, failed at times to lead as they should. The people, of course, did not blame themselves when things went wrong, but instead blamed their plight on not having a king, like other nations. Toward the end of the history recorded in the Book of Judges, the inference seems to be that Israel was experiencing a breakdown of national unity as some gave themselves over to foreign gods and cultures. Increasingly, some in Israel were looking for human leadership in the form a king and were disobedient to the Law of God.

I will now begin to give you what is probably a new perspective on the Book of Judges. I have noticed that in the Book of Judges the writer seldom deals directly with the nation as a whole, but rather writes about certain tribes in alliance dealing with problems under each national judge. Tribes are individually named and held accountable as self-governing units. In the appendix of my book you will find a map of the tribes. There I have listed the only tribe or tribes connected in the text with each national judge.[15] Of course, this does not mean that there are no national events taking place in the Book of Judges. Indeed, two chapters from now I will talk about one in connection with my examination of the national government. Note that when certain tribes are mentioned as being in alliance to deal with foreign attacks on their part of the nation, I am not implying that the issue had no impact on the entire nation. But I am trying to demonstrate that any given national judge did not necessarily hold all tribes accountable for a specific time of oppression, and therefore did not make them all responsible for providing men of arms in defense of the nation in every case.

Mostly, the Book of Judges is about the tribal governments and not about the entire nation. During the life of Joshua, all the tribes swore to one another to fight together under his leadership until all had their inheritance; once that had been accomplished, the alliance no longer existed. At the very start of the Book of Judges, upon the death of Joshua, God tested the faithfulness of the princes of the tribes to govern as they should with only Jehovah as their national head. In fact, after the completed conquest during the continuing lifetime of Joshua and that of his contemporary elders and princes of tribes, some of whom outlived him, the people of Israel served the Lord faithfully.[16] But some of the next generation of leaders allowed the people to prostitute themselves to foreign gods. Therefore the Lord was very angry with Israel and said,

> *"Because this nation has violated the Covenant that I laid out before them and has not listened to me, I will no longer drive out before them any of the nations Joshua left when he died. I will use them to test Israel and see whether they will keep the way of the Lord and walk in it as their forefathers did."*[17]

Israel would not again have another strong leader to rely on nationally, like Moses or Joshua, until Samuel. In between Joshua and Samuel, tribal government was much more active than national government.

The tribes that governed badly get all the attention. Those tribes not mentioned at given time periods probably are governing better than the others. Tribes were equal in respect to political dignity and rights. Even Simeon, which had fewer men of arms, had to be consulted by Judah, whose men of arms were much greater in number, before each would join in military action against their lo-

---

15. Study Appendix 6.

16. Joshua 24: 31.
17. Judges 2: 20-22.

cal Canaanite enemies.[18] When it says, "the children of Israel asked the Lord", it is referring to the practice of going to the high priest, who consulted with God for them. When it was determined Judah shall lead in battle in Chapter 1 of Judges, it does not mean all other tribes agreed to let the prince of Judah lead them all. Rather, it means Judah and Simeon made an alliance to fight together this one time. Chapter 1 of Judges then goes on to record how other tribes, each responsible for its own territorial lot, either did or did not drive out local Canaanite nations that still were occupying the land with them. Every story in the Book of Judges is about local struggles with indigenous nations in the area or with invaders of various specific areas of Israel. Seldom is all of Israel joining in a national army under a judge to take on enemies. The Hebrews often faced people with iron weapons and horses, neither of which was a technology or resource available to Israel.[19] Indeed, any victory over Israel's enemies was a miracle, and the author of Judges always records "the victory was the Lord's."

When the princes of tribes failed to drive out the indigenous nations in their lots then God would raise up a national judge to come to the rescue. In every instance, of course, when specific national judges were called to the rescue of one region or another of Israel, it is clear that they were acting in the interest of all of Israel. However, the absence of details regarding the rule of princes of tribes and other magistrates should not be used as evidence that tribes were not self-governing.

The emphasis in the Book of Judges is on the alternate necessity of a succession of national judges to maintain tribal integrity and self-government. Sometimes the judges acted independently of any tribe, individually attacking the enemy. Sometimes they were leading an undefined army that may have included all the tribes. For the most part however, they were leaders only of specific tribes in battle. Sometimes they seemed to have no enemy to defeat and were mentioned only with respect to their role of deciding cases appealed to them from lower courts regarding the law.[20] When a tribe (or even a single tribal city) refused to join in war when asked by a judge, it was punished.[21] Again, this is evidence that the Hebrew commonwealth was not a confederation in which individual tribes could shun national authority. Actually, every judge was recognized as a commander in chief when needed, but commanded no standing army as under the rule of a king. That is, princes had to raise their own tribal men of arms and submit to a central command by the national judge. As one reads the cases for each judge, it becomes clear that the army is often made up only of certain tribes, and that the judge dealt only with oppression of those tribes. All tribal governments continued to exercise their own limited sovereignty but under one universal Covenant.

After Joshua died, and before Othniel is judge, there seems to be no national judge. This was probably also the time of the civil war with the Tribe of Benjamin, which is mentioned in the last chapters of the Book of Judges. Later I will analyze that case study as the means by which national government was to function without a national king. National judges come on the scene not to act in a national executive fashion, but to fill a temporary role as commander of an alliance of tribal men of arms, and to fulfill a judicial role as a kind of one-man-supreme-court when needed. In this way no tribal prince could take on a national executive role over the other tribes. All tribes were equal in a "federal" union with a sovereign national government when needed.

---

18. Judges 1: 1-10.

19. Judges 1: 19 (this is the first hint of this reoccurring problem).

20. Judges 4: 4-5.

21. Judges 12: 1-7.

At a turning point in Israel's history as a republic, one tribe, Gad, makes Jephthah prince over its clans, and then takes him to Mizpah (often a place of meeting for the states-general) to be accepted as judge of all Israel.[22] The writer of Judges says, "The elders of Gilead said to him, we are turning to you, now come with us to fight the Ammonites, and you will be head [prince] over all who live in Gilead." It would appear that the people did not possess the vote, but their clan leaders held suffrage rights. Then the writer goes on to say, "And he repeated all his words before the Lord at Mizpah."[23] The Tribe of Gad clearly elected Jephthah their prince, and God blessed the decision through the high priest who anointed him into office. Of course, when Jephthah led an army made up of soldiers of more than one tribe, he was recognized as judge of all Israel at that point. His army was made up of soldiers of Manasseh and Gad to fight the king of Ammon. Interestingly, later in Chapter 12, the Tribe of Ephraim questions the authority of Jephthah, and Ephraim must be defeated in battle over the issue of whether he was qualified to be judge. His role as judge was short and only applied to the required military role. I think it is fair to say that he was an exception in the experience of national judges because he was a prince and at the same time national judge just for this crisis.

The judgeship of Jephthah represents a turning point for the republic. The Hebrew historical record does not record that Jephthah gave Israel a certain number of years of rest. All judges preceding Jephthah were recognized for restoring a long time of peace for the young nation. In contrast, Israel's republic will have zero years of rest following the judgeship of Jephthah. Clearly the history of Israel in the Book of Judges implies a national republic in federal union with tribal republics. Clearly the princes of tribes were elected, although probably by a vote of elders of clans within the tribe. Those elders probably held birthright positions themselves.[24]

It seems rather clear that national judges were not elected, thus only Jehovah would be head of all Israel. Jehovah alone appointed judges in various ways. Sometimes Scripture records that "the Spirit of the Lord came upon him" as a judge is introduced. Sometimes it is recorded that "the Lord gave them a deliverer." Sometimes one reads that a prophetess was used of God to destroy the enemies of Israel. Sometimes the Angel of God came directly and visibly to the judge-to-be and appointed him. When the son of Gideon, named Abimelech, tried to make himself king, God had him struck down and killed. The Angel of God announced to the mother of Samson that she would give birth to the next judge of Israel. It is as if these national judges were watchmen raised up by God to keep check on the tribal governments of Israel. Later, prophets will try to play a similar role with kings of Israel. Samuel, the last judge of Israel, is sometimes referred to as both a prophet and a national judge.

The hidden story in the Book of Judges is in its chronology. To better understand this, refer to my Timeline of the Hebrew Republic.[25] Note the 300-year period marked off at the start of the timeline. The King of Ammon (according to Judges 11:26), even before the time of Jephthah, had been subjugating the three trans-jordanian Hebrew tribes claiming possession rights going back 300 years. Jephthah, a good student of history, reminded the king of Ammon that the Battle of Heshbon

---

22. Judges 11: 1-11.

23. The tribal lot of Gad was called Gilead, and it stretched along most of the eastern border of the Jordan River. When a place is called Mizpah it means a fortress. There are several different places in this era of the judges that are referred to as Mizpah.

24. On whether the Clan Chiefs were elected or birthright positions, I disagree with E.C. Wines who says they were elected. I will go into this further in chapter eight.

25. See Appendix 7.

(in 1407 BC) was fought against the king of the Amorites in the last year of Moses' life, and that Moses had never made war on the Ammonites. Nevertheless, hundreds of years after Moses, Ammon had claimed dominion for twelve years over Gilead, the lot of the Tribe of Gad, and her neighboring tribes Manasseh and Reuben. So during the entire six years of the judgeship of Jephthah, he led Israel with just a few cooperating tribes against Ammon, and redeemed the independence of the tribes east of Jordan, thus ending 18 years of Ammonite dominion.

The first part of the Book of Judges records the history of the judges from Joshua to Jephthah. It is mostly a record of military campaigns against unconquered Canaanites and outside invading enemies of Israel. The impression is left in the reader's mind that for most of those years Israel was at war. A careful reading reveals otherwise. The time from Othniel to Jephthah covers 248 years. In that time frame, parts of Israel were under dominion of foreign powers for only 65 years.[26] For just a little more than a quarter of that 248 years, parts of Israel periodically had been under God's judgment, but otherwise the whole land had rest. There seems to be much more time for the republics to be functioning well in this era of Israel's history, as compared to the time in which they were in rebellion. As you read the first ten chapters of Judges, again and again it references short periods of time during which a judge is raised up to deliver the people from their enemies. All the early stories of Judges are about these periods of short duration, and the lives of the judges are tied to the detail of that deliverance. Although, the book references again and again that each judge helped establish a long period of rest or peace in the commonwealth, nothing is said about those years of peace.

On my Timeline Of The Hebrew Republic, I indicate the length of influence of each judge by the long period of rest associated with that judge.

However, within each judge's era of influence is included the short story of tribal oppression by Israel's enemies. For example, Othniel freed Israel of eight years of servitude to the king of Aram.[27] Everything we know about Othniel has to do with that eight years or its conclusion. However, Othniel played a role in Israel for 40 years. According to chronological experts like Dr. Floyd Nolan Jones, the correct method of measuring time in the Book of Judges is to place the period of oppression within the time of recorded rule by each judge, and not to add it to that time.[28] Otherwise, we would end up with scripture contradicting scripture in regard to time frames. The good story just under the surface of the Book of Judges is how the Mosaic Covenant and constitution must have been operating successfully in this period. How can we not believe the Hebrews lived by this wonderfully free rule of law at that time? The purpose of the Book of Judges is to warn Israel of the results of disobedience to the Mosaic Covenant, not to make us question whether it even worked. Actually, a separate study of the Book of Ruth gives us an example of how the commonwealth functioned in peace in the time of the judges. This peaceful coexistence of the tribes may have been the rule rather than the exception. Observe the note on the Time Line of the Hebrew Republic regarding its total years of existence compared to its total years of oppression.

Great republics in history all have followed the example of this first one. That is, one can expect a cyclical sequence of events in the rise and fall of free societies. The cycle of progressive phases in the Book of Judges was: 1) Israel prospers under freedom and obedience to the Lord; 2) a generation arises that compromises by flirting with un-

---

26. See Appendix 7.

27. This was the king of the people then called the Arameans, who were from Damascus, north of Israel (today's Syrians).

28. Dr. Floyd Nolen Jones, *The Chronology of the Old Testament* (Green Forest, AR.: Master Books, 1993), 73.

godly lifestyles in disobedience to God's Law and God allows an enemy to oppress them; 3) Israel cries out for deliverance and is given a special deliverer, whereupon Israel once again prospers under freedom and obedience to the Lord. However, the ultimate end is that phase two finally becomes very long and the republic cannot fully recover.

Most republics have been short lived unable to sustain a balance between freedom and responsibility. Eventually all republics seem to fall, either to foreign oppressors, or to their own home grown oppressors. Israel experienced both kinds of oppressors. It took the providential hand of God, rising up a deliverer to save the Hebrew republic each time it cycled down into a potential state of servitude. The final demise of Israel's free republic came from within at the hands of its home grown oppressors. Once the Hebrews were ruled by kings, their disobedience to the Covenant Law eventually resulted in their national demise, as foreign invaders successfully took total possession of their land.

It has been said that the American republic seems to have experienced the following pattern of development: from bondage to faith, from faith to liberty, from liberty to abundance, from abundance to complacency, from complacency to apathy, and from apathy to dependence, and finally may fall from dependence back to bondage. Will we too finally see our nation return to bondage and tyranny? Will it be home-grown-tyranny or foreign domination that destroys the greatest of truly free republics in history? Part Four of this book will explore the evolution of the American republic. For now I will continue to explore the Hebrew republic and its decline and fall.

Decline of the Hebrew Tribal Republics

Note on the timeline, located under Appendix 7, that during the 12 years of the judgeship of Jair all the way to the start of Samuel's judgeship, first eastern Israel was under the oppression of the Ammonites and then southern Israel was under the oppression of the Philistines. This is the period of the decline and fall of the Hebrew republic. The piecing together of these last 63 years of the Hebrew republic requires making a connection between the Book of Judges and the Book of First Samuel. The last part of Judges and the first part of First Samuel tell different stories, all of which are taking place in an overlapping fashion. Note on the timeline how the lives of Samson and Samuel overlap. Note also that the times of influence by the four judges before Samson are all relatively short. After Jephthah, the main story is a lengthy Philistine oppression. This Philistine oppression is referenced in different contexts in both the lifetime of Samson and the lifetime of Samuel.

The chronological placement of the last two stories in Judges interrupts the flow between the Book of Judges and the Book of First Samuel. First there is the story of a man named Micah. Micah hired a false priest and purchased foreign idols as household gods. But a group of Danites kidnapped his priest and idols intending to leave southern Israel and move far to the north to reestablish their tribe with its own false gods in that northern territory. Then, in the last chapters of Judges, there is the story about a civil war with Benjamin that most likely took place at the start of the Book of Judges. It is important that one treat these two stories at the end of the Book of Judges as a kind of parenthetical interruption, and go back to the story of Samson's judgeship to tie it in with the first chapters of the Book of First Samuel.

The key lies in establishing the lifetime of the High Priest Eli.[29] Eli lived to be 98 years old. He died when the Philistines stole the Ark of God right in the middle of their 40 years of oppression of southern Israel. Establishing the date when the Ark was stolen will help establish the overlap-

---
29. First Samuel 4:14-18.

ping lives of Samson and Samuel. The Philistines held the Ark captive only seven months. Samson fought the Philistines for 20 years without being able to break their dominion in southern Israel. After the death of Samson, it was Samuel who called the states-general together at Mizpah so he could militarily lead them to a victory over the Philistine dominion.[30] The Bible tells us that the Ark had been at the house of Abinadab for 20 years just preceding the judgeship of Samuel.[31] This means that the Ark was held at the house of Abinadab all 20 years of Samson's judgeship.[32] Therefore, Eli died 20 years and 7 months before Samuel would be made judge and very close to the time the Spirit came upon Samson as judge of Israel. Go back to the Timeline of the Hebrew Republic and note by easy calculation that Saul was made king in 1050 BC (counting back from the rule of Solomon, David, and Saul). One can calculate that there were 26 years between the start of Saul's reign and the start of Samson's judgeship. This makes the death of Eli to be 1050 + 26 or 1076 BC.[33] 1076 + 98 is 1174 BC, the birth of Eli. Eli was high priest his last 40 years, so the lives of both Samson and Samuel, from birth to adulthood, overlapped the last part of Eli's time as high priest of Israel. Samson died prematurely and Samuel lived on almost through the whole reign of Saul.

Having established the overlapping lives of Samson and Samuel, let me take you back to the overlapping events of their time. The major threat to Israel in this period came from the Philistines. Philistia had no single king over her entire territory. Their cities were independent and operated as city-states in confederation. They had five major city-states: Gaza, Ashkelon, Ashdod, Gath, and Ekron.[34] These cities, one of which still exists today, were all along the Great Sea coastline southwest of Israel. Great decisions of this confederation were made by a vote of the five lords. The Philistines were known for their superior weapons of iron. They held a monopoly over the making of iron in the era of the judges.

It is recorded:

> *Not a blacksmith could be found in the whole land of Israel . . . and all of Israel went down to the Philistines to have their plowshares, mattocks, axes and sickles sharpened . . . on the day of battle not a soldier had a sword or spear in his hand save the king.*[35]

By human standards, Israel should not have been able to stand up to Philistia. But the Hebrews didn't rely on human standards. Whenever they defeated an enemy, the battle was the Lord's. That is, all nations around them feared them because they knew of the miracles performed by God on their behalf, going back to the exodus from Egypt.

The Philistine dominion was 40 years and ended at the Battle of Mizpah at the start of Samuel's judgeship.[36] On the Timeline of the Hebrew Republic, note that Samuel was made judge when Samson died in 1056 BC. Therefore, the start of the Philistine dominion over southern Israel began in 1096 BC (40 years earlier). It was already a reality when the Angel of the Lord told Samson's mother she was to give birth to the deliverer.[37] 1096 BC takes one back in Israel's history to the last two years of the judgeship of Ibzon, whose judgeship was followed by the judges Elon and Abdon. These leaders did nothing to deliver Israel. Samson became judge when the story is told in First Samuel that the Philistines captured the

---

30. First Samuel 7:5-6.
31. First Samuel 7:1-6.
32. Judges 15:20.
33. This is also confirmed by adding the years of the judges: Jephthah (6), Ibzon (7), Elon (10, and Abdon (8), a total of 31 years. It has been established that Jephthah became judge in 1107. 1107 minus 31 equals 1076.
34. See map at Appendix 6.
35. First Samuel 13:19-22.
36. First Samuel 7:12.
37. Judges 13: 1-2.

Ark of the Lord. Though the Philistine dominion ended with Samuel's military victory at Mizpah, the Philistines continued to try and bring back that dominion during King Saul's reign. The total Philistine threat to Israel was 80 years—for 40 years they ruled over southern tribes, and for 40 years they fought against a united Israel without success. But, It was King David who finally ended Philistine warfare with Israel.

In the preceding two paragraphs we have an overview of the time frame in which the Hebrew republic started its decline. What follows are the main actors in this short history. The story in First Samuel, Chapters 1, 2, and 3, about the birth and boyhood of Samuel overlaps the time of the story in Chapter 13 of Judges about Samson's birth. Samuel grew up in the "temple" during the time of Jephthah's judgeship, and Samuel was called-by-God at that time to be a prophet of the Lord. But next in line as judge was Samson, whose birth was announced by the Angel of the Lord to his mother as the one who would "begin" the deliverance of Israel from the Philistine dominion of southern tribes. As a man, the Spirit of the lord moved within Samson, and he became a legend for his strength and a disappointment for his rebellious ways. The death of the High Priest Eli, with the Philistine seizure of the Ark of God, brought on the judgeship of Samson and ended the judgeship of Abdon. Samson never led an army, but like Greek stories of individual heroes fighting single-handed battles, he did all of his fighting alone, with super human strength. However, whereas Greek heroes were associated with the Greek pantheon of gods, Samson is pictured as an ordinary human being empowered only by the Almighty, and whose sins were abjured and lead to his downfall. Judges are seldom pictured without also revealing their own inclination to sin, and like the nation as a whole in need of surrender to the Lord of Lords. Samson helped hold back a complete nationwide oppression by the Philistines, but was not an example of godly leadership. When Samson died bringing down the Temple of Dagon, chief god of the Philistines, and killing himself and more than 3,000 Philistines, it did not end Philistine and Israeli warfare. The Philistines next planned an invasion that would become an extended war lasting all the way through the reign of King Saul.

The new judge of Israel was Samuel. But six years after the assembly of Mizpah recognized that God had made Samuel judge, the people demanded a king to rule over them. Though Samuel is mainly remembered for helping to establish the monarchy in Israel, he remained judge after the king was anointed. Israel's repentance under Samuel, at Mizpah, lasted such a short time that the nation continued under the discipline of Jehovah all through the reign of King Saul. Actually one could say that the rise of the monarchy under Saul was not complete. Rather, a kind of dual government existed through most of Saul's reign. Samuel remained a fully functioning judge, and Saul a fully functioning king, simultaneously. It is obvious that 1050 BC marked the end of the Hebrew republic as they had known it up to then. However, it did not end the constitutional nature of the government. Samuel continued to be called Israel's judge until he died.[38]

I should explain the reference, in First Samuel 8: 1-5, to Samuel making his sons judges in Israel. Since Samuel was still national judge until he died, I assume this refers to approving their election as lower court judges in Beersheba. The inference by the Council of 70 (all the elders of Israel) that his sons might be eligible for national judge after Samuel died, is evidence that Israel was leaning toward making the judgeship into a true hereditary monarchy. Remember, the national judgeship was never passed on by birthright. The elders all knew this, but they didn't want the popularity of Samuel with the people to cause a demand that one of his

---

38. First Samuel 7: 13b-17.

sons become king. Note, also, that Samuel reluctantly helped the nation find a candidate for king.

Almost immediately after he was made king, Saul was tested and failed the test. The Hebrew republic had an established separation of "church" and state. This separation began with the division of authority between Moses and Aaron. Thus Saul was not to perform the priestly duties of the Levites. He was to submit to God in this way. Saul was told to wait for Samuel to make sacrifice and to ask for God's blessing on a battle against the Philistines.[39] The result of Saul's disobedience was his loss of God's blessing as king. Later in Saul's reign, he did not kill all the Amalekites and their herds and flocks, as instructed by God through Samuel, which led to Samuel's search for a successor king.[40] What was emerging was what we today call a constitutional monarchy. God really was king and Saul was accountable to him and his Law.

Perhaps you already can see that three branches of government were coming together in the Hebrew republic at this moment in Israel's history. It is a moment in her history when it would be even more important to limit the authority of human government. They now had a king as head of state, a prophet as a supreme-court judge to keep the government under the Law of God, and a states-general of tribal princes and elders to act as a legislative branch when needed nationally. However, under the kings, a legislative branch almost never seemed to be called upon.

One more observation regarding the Hebrew commonwealth in transition needs to be made. In a free republic, the root of all ills of society lies with the people themselves more so than with their leaders. The people nationwide had rejected the lordship of Jehovah. This apostasy included the Tribe of Levi, Israel's priests. It lasted 66 years. It began with the Philistine capture of the Ark of God and only ended with the taking of the throne of Israel by David and his bringing of the Ark to Jerusalem.[41] Shiloh was no longer the national seat of the republic. Without the Ark residing in the tabernacle, the duties of the priesthood had fallen away along with the major national festivals of the people to be held three times a year at Shiloh. The Ark, while in Philistine hands, had produced God's judgment on the Philistines through a plague of tumors that was spread by rats in all five of their cities. In terror, the Philistines had placed the Ark on a cart to send it back to Israel. In superstition, they tried to appease the God of the Hebrews by also placing golden idols of rats and tumors on the cart. It arrived at Beth Shemesh, where God killed 70 Israelites when some tried to look inside the Ark. At that moment, Israel and Philistia both feared the Ark, but Israel didn't seem to see the importance of what the Ark was supposed to mean as a symbol of government under God. You might say Israel was close to making the Ark into an idol. In addition, Israel seemed to be without a high priest during this national apostasy. The Ark was kept for nearly 66 years in the house of Abinadab at Kiriath Jearim.

Seemingly, only Samuel was keeping the commonwealth together. But with the coronation of King David, the monarchy was again under God

---

39. First Samuel 13:5-14.

40. First Samuel 15: 17-19 plus 28-29, and 6: 1. This event will be significant in the future of Israel. In an earlier time, the Amalekites had attacked Israel under Moses' leadership as they came into the Promised Land. God had sworn to include them in the list of Canaanites slated for annihilation. (Deuteronomy 25: 17-19). Saul was supposed to carry out that sentence. When Saul didn't kill Agag the king, this remnant of Amalek became known as the Agagites. About 500 years later, the Benjaminite, Mordecai faced this enemy again in Susa, capital of Persia. Haman, the Agagite, had a plot to kill all the Jews in exile in Persia. The Book of Esther in the Bible is all about God's providential revenge and the salvation of Israel from this holocaust. Is this an example of God's sovereignty in history and yet how man is free to make history himself, and thus not all history is a reflection on God or his will in totality? Think about it.

41. The 66 years were determined by adding 20 years for Samson, and six years for Samuel, then 40 years for Saul.

and not absolute. The forms of the republic would remain shakily in place during all the reign of David and most of the reign of Solomon, but future kings took absolute power and Israel slipped slowly away into final oppression by other nations, as a judgment of God. The first amazing federal system of republics died, having been an example to all would-be free nations yet to come in history.

Chapter 7

Local Judicial Power and Due Process of Law

If the concept of republican government is government by consent of the governed, then all the governed must have equal protection under the law. In an earlier lesson titled "The Dual Principles of Liberty and Equality" (Chapter 5), I showed how the Hebrew commonwealth was the first nation to lay down this important foundation of equality under the law. It is time now to examine the Mosaic justice system in this regard. One of the main levelers of society in a free republic is what we call the civil liberty of due process of law. All republics should protect the rights of what may be called a fair trial. Here again, the Hebrew republic is the leader in history. Later, the Roman Republic helped refine judicial justice even more. However, the underlying philosophy that one is innocent until proven guilty in a neutral court did not originate with the Romans, as often claimed. The institutional process of justice required to put the above philosophy in practice requires adversarial hearings between the accuser and accused before a local jury. Moses did not call the local assembly that sat before the gates of every Hebrew city a jury, but such assemblies were the first juries. The final perfection of this concept of justice we owe to the English and Americans, taking their lead as much, or more, from Moses as from Rome.

The natural state of human government is one in which a central government is sovereign and absolute authority resides in its appointed judges. The police power of the state is given to these judges and any subject of the realm is assumed to be guilty when brought before them. Over time we have come to call this an inquisitional system, and it may resort to torture to get a confession. Again, the natural order of man-made government is always tyranny. True justice is dependent on government under the sovereignty of God's law. It is human nature to pervert even the best of justice systems, but all true justice has its roots in Judeo-Christianity.

This idea of the rule of law in free republics is not simply a matter of some great human lawgiver (such as Hammurabi)[1] making a Code of Law in stone for all to live under. It is more than that. It requires that the king or ruler himself swear allegiance to a universal law. It also requires that all classes be under the same Law without preferential treatment for a noble class. The administration and enforcement of civil liberties must not come from the ruler down, but from the people up. That is why the great powers of the criminal justice system have always been reserved to local American institutions rather than to the national government. As in the ancient Hebrew republic, almost all police powers, including prosecution, trials, and correctional institutions in the Ameri-

---

1. The concept of an *"eye for an eye, and a tooth for a tooth"* is found in both Hammurabi's Code of Law and the Mosaic Law; but Hammurabi had no concept of due process of law. It makes no sense to conclude, as some do, that Moses borrowed from Hammurabi. (See Appendix 4, Exhibit A).

can republic, are part of local governments. Such wisdom came from God through Moses.

Since police power of the state can so easily be turned into tyranny, under God's Biblical template for justice these powers are kept as close as possible to local, not central government. For this reason Moses warned Israel against ever adopting the constitutional office of a king. However, experience had made Moses very wary of man's inclination to be rebellious, and God advised him there could be a time when the people might insist on trusting in a human king rather than in God as their king. Moses advised Israel:

> *When he [any future king] takes the throne of the kingdom, he is to write for himself on a scroll a copy of this law, taken from that of the priests, who are Levites. It is to be with him, and he is to read it all the days of his life so that he may learn to revere the Lord his God and follow carefully all the words of this Law and these decrees and not consider himself better than his brothers and turn from the Law to the right or to the left. Then he and his descendants will reign a long time over his Kingdom in Israel.*[2]

The above quote not only allowed the people of Israel to amend their constitution, but also is a warning that such an amendment may very well destroy their republic in the end. As we continue this study of the history of the Hebrew commonwealth, we will see that in fact this will be the key cause of the fall of this first experiment with free government.

Let me continue to explain due process of law in Israel's republic prior to the time they would adopt monarchy. Moses required that the "brothers" be locally empowered to uphold the law.

> *Judges and officers shalt thou make thee in all thy gates, which the Lord thy God giveth thee throughout all the tribes; and they shall judge the people with just judgment . . . .*[3]

Again and again, the Law of Moses reassures the citizen of his right to equal justice without partiality to the small or great, and by prohibiting bribes. Judicial authority was mostly exercised locally at the gates of cities, but all cities of the commonwealth were under a national uniform rule of law. The last court of appeals was to be the national judge.[4] But in special cases a national supreme court of tribal elders also could sit with the final say.

Perhaps the greatest assurance of justice for which the Judeo-Christian culture is known comes from its constitutional system of adversarial hearings before a local jury. The English common law drew this system of justice right out of the Scriptures. Starting with Alfred the Great, and then more specifically with Henry the Second, the English system of justice was one of due process of law. The former king drew the concept of jury trial from Saxon Christian heritage, and the latter king from Norman Christian heritage. Neither king justified his system from some ancient understanding of Roman justice, but rather drew it right out of the Books of Numbers and Deuteronomy. Rome had no tradition of jury trials. Even ancient Greek jury trials were more or less forms of mob rule and not government under the law. You cannot find an older or even a truer source of due process of law than that of Moses' writings.[5]

The Tribe of Levi did not receive a tribal lot, but rather was assigned cities within the other tribal lots. In this way the Levites were readily available to all of Israel as her lawyers to oversee the administration of justice, as well as the duties of the priesthood. Also assigned to the Levites

---

2. Deuteronomy 17: 18-20.

3. Deuteronomy 16: 18-20.

4. Deuteronomy 1: 16-18.

5. See Appendix 9.

were six cities of refuge.[6] These cities were like jails where an accused person awaits trial, but, as places of refuge, they were not a place of confinement behind bars without freedom to go on about one's life. "They will be places of refuge from the avenger, so that a person accused of murder may not die before he stands trial before the assembly."[7] A local city assembly (or jury) would sit in judgment. This Hebrew "jury" had power to act as judge and jury. A case had to be tried at the gates of the city in which (or near which) the crime was committed.[8] The assembly, or jury, would be made up of judges selected by the people of that city. Ancient Sumerian and Canaanite cities also held court at city gates, but the city-state king, who both made the law and judged those in violation of it, appointed those who held court or did it directly himself. The Hebrew system was impartial, guided by one universal-law throughout all Israel, and not subject to any city-state king's whims.

According to Rabbi Yanki Tauber, the above Biblical "assembly" was the birth of grand juries.[9] The assembly at the gate of the city of refuge would have power to investigate if a crime had been committed.

If a malicious witness takes the stand to accuse a man of a crime, the two men involved in the dispute must stand in the presence of the Lord before the priests [Levites acting as lawyers] *and judges who are in office at the time. The judges must make a through investigation, and if the witness proves to be a liar ... then do to him as he intended to do to his brother.*[10]

These jury assemblies were also to act as trial courts in the jurisdiction of the city where the crime was committed.

If a man hates his neighbor and lies in wait for him, assaults and kills him, and then flees to one of these cities [of refuge], *the elders of his town shall send for him, bring him back from the city, and hand him over to the avenger of blood to die.*[11]

But this was not to occur without a trial:

One witness is not enough to convict a man accused of any crime or offense he may have committed. A matter must be established [before a trial jury] *by the testimony of two or three witnesses.*[12]

Rabbi Yanki Tauber says Jewish tradition developed this part of the law into what were called the "Minor Sanhedrins."[13] The Major Sanhedrin (the Council of 70) was a national supreme court; but every city had its own "Minor Sanhedrin" which held court at the city gates. Not just cities of refuge held court, but every city had these jury trials at the city gates.

If a man has a stubborn and rebellious son, which will not obey the voice of his father, or mother, and when they have chastened him,

---

6. See Appendix 6.

7. Numbers 35:12.

8. Deuteronomy 21:1-2.

9. Rabbi Yanki Tauber, Birth of the Grand Jury, *Crime and Punishment,* http://www.meaningfullife.com/torah/parsha/devarim/shoftim/Crime_and_Punishment.php.

10. Deuteronomy 19:16-21.

11. Deuteronomy 19:11.

12. Deuteronomy 19:15.

13. The term sanhedrin was adopted in the Hellenistic (Greek) era, and was kept as a system of local courts and a supreme court all during Judah's history as part of the Greek and later the Roman empires. But, all members of the Great Sanhedrin and minor sanhedrins were appointed and not elected. Because one of the functions of minor sanhedrins was to be a school there name was changed to synagogue. But, the synagogue was dominated by a local civil authority and the Pharisee scribes served both as Rabbis and as jurors (taking the place of the judges at the city gates back in republican days). The Great Sanhedrin was headed by the High Priest, a position offered to the highest bidder by Rome. Obviously the Jews had long lost their republic of Moses by the time of Christ.

he will not obey them: Then shall they lay hold on him and bring him unto the elders of his city, and unto the gate".[14]

These were the elders or other respected brothers of elders elected by those men of military age to be local judges.

The father did not have life and death power over his son, but had to bring him before a jury and prove the crime. In contrast, all other societies of that age, and long afterwards, gave fathers life and death power over members of the family. This made the Hebrew constitution of justice very unique. According to Jewish tradition, a majority of two or more was required to convict. This requirement for a jury acquittal or conviction is probably based on Moses' standard that: "One witness shall not rise up against a man for any iniquity, or for any sin, but at the mouth of two or even three witnesses shall the matter be established".[15] Since not even one eyewitness sufficed to convict, neither was one more than half of an assembly of judges sufficient to convict. Later in English-American jurisprudence this was source of the idea of a required unanimous guilty verdict.

The Mosaic system of justice also made a careful distinction between accidental and vengeful crimes.[16] It allowed the ancient code of vengeance only if an offense was committed willfully, with malice, and in the presence of witnesses, and it severely punished a false accuser. There was a requirement of careful investigation of charges and concern for false witnesses, and even the safe guard of cities of refuge. If one fled to a city of refuge, the assembly there must hold investigative hearings, and if the accused was suspected of guilt, he was sent back for trial in his hometown. How can we not agree that the Mosaic constitution was the origin of due process of law, and the birth of the philosophy of innocent until proven guilty?

When it came to punishment, it seems there were many options, such as stoning, hanging, or flogging, and for hard cases, confinement in a city of refuge. Such confinement, if never resolved by a trial, was to last until the death of the high priest serving at the time. In most cases, this confinement allowed a long period of cooling off for the accuser, and perhaps the discovery of the real person at fault. In the Middle Ages, Christendom copied this policy for those accused if they fled to the sanctuary of a monastery or cathedral. The option of restitution was also encouraged by the Mosaic law.[17] Though there is mention of prisons used during the reign of the kings, during the Hebrew republic they may have preferred indentured slavery as an alternative means of confinement for property crimes. Even when it came to the resolving of an unsolved murder, there was still a requirement of the shedding of the life of a sacrificial animal.[18] Regardless of the degree of seriousness of the crimes of the people God required the shedding of blood for the remission of sin. Sin sacrifices were really part of the justice system. In other nations, right up to the 19th century AD, most crimes were punished by the death penalty, upon conviction. It has been the American system of justice and its due process that brought back the spirit of the legal system intended and grounded in the ancient Law of Moses.

No ancient system was as fair and just as that of the Hebrew republic. Actually, this was the boast of Israel,

> *Behold I have taught you statutes and judgments even as the Lord my God commanded me, that ye should do so in the Land whither ye go to possess it. Keep therefore and do them for this is your wisdom and your understand-*

---

14. Deuteronomy 21:18-21.

15. Deuteronomy 19:15.

16. Deuteronomy 19:1-13.

17. Exodus 22.

18. Deuteronomy 21:1-9.

ing in the sight of the nations, which shall hear about all these statutes and say, surely this great nation is a wise and just people.[19]

This legal system must have caught the attention of the Greek city-states that then in some ways tried to copy the Hebrew concept of justice. Not that they applied due process to everyone equally, but they did practice assembly jury trials. Today it is America that is acclaimed throughout the world for its liberties and due process of law. How many are aware of how much we owe to the ancient Hebrew commonwealth of Moses for our rights today?[20]

The first people to govern through assemblies were the Hebrews. Moses said to pick men of integrity who feared God to govern over 1,000s over 100s, over 50s and over 10s, and as specific tribal officials. At that time there was no distinction made between members of an assembly as far as giving some the power to make the law, some the power to interpret the law, and some to administer the law. All assemblies before the gates of each city could serve in all three ways. But the Hebrews were the first to give assembly members the title of judge to settle disputes between "brothers" without partiality. As I stated earlier, the Hebrews enacted the first adversarial system of justice in which all who were accused had equal rights to make their case before the local assembly. There is no indication of whether the persons who were witnesses could also be members of the assembly on either side of the case. These kinds of refinements came later, starting with the Romans.

The Greeks probably borrowed their idea of rule by assembly from the Hebrews. They too assigned the role of juror and lawmaker to city-state assemblies. But they had a harsh distinction between classes and did show partiality to higher classes over lower classes. Finally, at a point of near civil war, they turned to democracy. This allowed the lowest class, with the most numbers, to determine the law by majority vote. The Greeks soon turned the tyranny of the upper class into a tyranny of the majority, revealing the weakness of the rule of man without the Law of God.[21]

The Romans were the ones to refine the justice system into separate roles for separate individuals. They separated the powers to make the law and judge the law. They moved from juries to single appointed judges. A person accused of crime by another citizen, or even a lower level of government, now was to stand trial before one of the judges appointed (sometimes elected) in Rome. The accusers were to come before this Roman court, wherever it set up jurisdiction in the empire. These accusers were to come with their evidence and witnesses, thus for the first time separating the role of prosecution from the role of judges.[22] Keeping the Hebrew concept of innocent until proven guilty, the Roman system trained its judges to be fair and neutral under Roman law passed down through history by lawmaking assemblies. But, again like the Greeks, Roman law was not universally applied to all classes of people without partiality. Roman judges also introduced the practice of written opinions that became a body of legal precedence for future judges to apply.

Later, the Christians of the Middle Ages, by combining the influence of Hebrew, Greek, and Roman republics, introduced the idea of citizen juries picked by lot to decide justice before a mediator judge. The first English king of signifi-

---

19. Deuteronomy 4:5-6.

20. See Appendix 9.

21. In modern secular republics, their tendency to become socialist has a similar effect.

22. In the 1st century of Christianity, St. Paul, as a Roman citizen, stood trial before a local governor of Rome and exercised his right to appeal to Rome; but when he arrived in Rome under guard, his accusers did not follow and therefore he was held under temporary house arrest and never did stand trial because Rome required that prosecutors be present to make their charges before a neutral judge.

cance to do this was Henry the Second of Norman heritage.

Such great principles of governing must be taught to each generation so that they become religious acts of the heart. So Moses admonished Israel,

> *Hear O Israel: The Lord our God is one Lord; and thou shalt love the Lord thy God with all thine heart, and with all thy soul, and with all thy might. And these words, which I have commanded this day, shall be in thine heart. And thou shalt teach them diligently unto thy children and shalt talk of them when thou sittest in thine house, and when thou walkest by the way, and when thou liest down, and when thou risest up.*[23]

At the end of chapter five of Deuteronomy and the summary of the Ten Commandments in verse 29, God says:

> *O that there were such an heart in them that they would fear me, and keep all my commandments always, that it might be well with them and with their children forever.*

The governing constitution of the Hebrew republic mainly depended on well-run local cities within each of the tribes. At the same time, protecting the nation from disintegrating under so much local authority, there was also a national legal bureaucracy and priesthood of Levites. This rule of due process of law, if not corrupted by evil and unrepentant men, effectively checked tyranny and lawlessness. Centuries later, even the French observer of the new American republic, Alexis de Tocqueville, wrote, "They did not receive their powers from the central authority, but on the contrary, they gave up a portion of their local independence to the state."[24] He may not have understood that this concept of limited national government came from the ancient Biblical text of the Moses constitution, but he understood it was a corner stone of the American republic and its resulting free society. As I always taught my students, one of the greatest powers reserved to the States and local governments in our union is that of criminal justice. We greatly limit police power in our national government, and therefore almost all police are local government officers. Almost all criminal law cases also are local or State affairs, not a matter of national juridiction.

---

23. Deuteronomy 6:4-7.

24. Alexis de Tocqueville, *Democracy in America*, (New York, NY, Washington Square Press, 1964), 38.

Chapter 8

The National Government

Ideally a national commander in chief, when called upon to defend a free people from their enemies, will willingly accept the responsibility as a limited assignment and not make it an opportunity to become king. In reality, seldom do ideals rule in governments. However, like Gideon of Bible fame, America's deliverer in her founding was a humble and God-fearing public servant.[1] George Washington was a man whose victories were miracles, and who also had no ambition to be king. Like the Roman Senator Cincinnatus, Washington was a general who returned to his plantation and family and tried to fade away after the war. America's founders, after the War for Independence, drew lessons directly from the above histories of the ancient Hebrew republic, and Roman Republic regarding establishing a limited national government.

Like the national Hebrew republic established by Moses, America's first national government had no national chief executive but only a national states-general. This national states-general was called the Continental Congress. It authorized the drawing up of the Declaration of Independence and a national constitution called the Articles of Confederation. Like the tribal states-general of the ancient Hebrew republic, the Continental Congress was the heart and soul of all national governing authority. But, unlike the Hebrew states-general, the Continental Congress could not act as a national supreme court. America had no national supreme court until one was adopted at the Constitutional Convention of 1787. Also, just as the Hebrew republic had no national standing army but relied on the tribes to provide men of arms, the American confederation had to rely on the States[2] of the union to provide militiamen to fight to protect our national union. Similar comparisons will occur often in this study, and from such correlations I believe one has good reason to suspect that our founders relied on a Hebrew template as much or more so than on a Greco-Roman template for building the framework of the early American national republic.

However, as with most confederations of history, the American confederation failed because it did not protect any real national sovereignty. Soon the several American States were quarreling and even forbidding free travel and trade among themselves. It began to look like they would lose their independence without a national government strong enough to defend their continued freedom from great European powers. But, as I noted in earlier chapters, the States agreed in 1787 to form a new national convention to revise the

---

1. Judges 8: 22-23. Gideon did not desire to be king, and, as all judges were supposed to do, he went about returning to private life after serving as general. However, Gideon was less honorable than Washington in his retirement, which led to one of his sons trying to make himself king.

2. It is proper to capitalize the "S" when using the word state to refer to the States of the American union, but not if the word state is used to refer to the general organization of any national government.

87

Articles of Confederation. The result was what they called a federal union. This federal union delegated independent powers to the central government, but reserved all other powers to the States or to the people. If America had failed to amend its national government system, the War of 1812 would not have been our second war for independence, as it became known. America would have lost its independence.

Many have noted the above similarities between the Hebrew commonwealth and the early American republic and mistakenly have concluded that both were weak confederations without an effective national government. However, I have already made the case in Chapter Six for how the Hebrew commonwealth was not a confederation. These critics of the Hebrew commonwealth base their conclusion on an incorrect analysis of the Book of Judges. This analysis, which I have already refuted, is centered on the following key verse in the Book of Judges. "In those days there was no king in Israel, but every man did that which was good in his own eyes." However, this so-called key verse does not appear until the end of Judges, after more than 300 years of a mostly stable Hebrew commonwealth. The condition of near anarchy reflected in the above quote is meant to point to the then-declining condition of the republic in its last 57 years. The Hebrews had successfully maintained a free republic until Israel's extended conflict with the Philistines. Actually, since God did not give the Hebrews a king in the first place, and as most confederations have proven to be too feeble and divided to survive, you would expect God's plan of government with twelve equal tribes to have some built-in national sovereignty to protect the integrity of the nation. So, what were the strong provisions in the Mosaic constitution for national sovereignty in the face of possible intertribal anarchy?

The following statement is a summary of several provisions protecting the national authority of the Hebrew republic. The national interest was generally upheld by every tribe because: 1) the constitution revealed in the Book of Deuteronomy was centered in one God as the oracle king, 2) a states-general assembly had national authority to force rebellious tribes to act in the national interest if necessary, 3) there was one tabernacle of worship and all tribes were required to attend important religious festivals three times a year under one high priest, 4) there was one national judge who could function as "prime minister" of the oracle king, 5) there was one scholarly class of lawyers of the Levite Tribe that possessed cities in every tribal territory, and most importantly 6) there was one codified law over all tribes. This was the Hebrew "federal" union and it functioned well enough in the face of foreign enemies and inter-tribal conflict to last 396 years.[3] The above list of checks and balances built into the Hebrew commonwealth provided a solid foundation for this first national republic of history. Excessive central government would have weakened the republic and its freedoms. In fact, this happened later under their kings. Just as true, too little central governmental power would have led to weakness and loss of republican freedoms by foreign conquest. So how did Israel maintain some national legislative, judicial, and executive authority?

The Legislative Function of Israel's National States-General

Now I will begin to reveal the presence of an actual national legislative body in the Hebrew commonwealth. If one searches the Old Testament for the words elders and assembly, one will find many references in which these words are used in the context of a governing body. We have already observed the use of the word assembly for a local jury in deliberation. Whenever a judge calls for a meeting of the elders or assembly of leaders,

---

3. See Appendix 7.

it involves a representative body coming together to be part of a decision-making process.

In the Book of Deuteronomy, Moses makes a series of speeches in which he addresses various topics on Israel's constitutional rule of law. More often than not, Moses is addressing how the "chosen nation" is to be governed. The Hebrew word Deuteronomy has a meaning that implies it is a practical review of the law.

> *Hear now, O Israel, the decrees and laws I am about to teach you ... Do not add to what I command you and do nor subtract from it, but keep the commands of the Lord your God that I give you.*[4]

We might call this short statement in Deuteronomy the *supreme law of the land clause* of the Mosaic constitution. Some think this means there was no need or provision for a national legislature, and therefore the council of princes and leaders of thousands was to act only as a supreme court. But E. C. Wines argues that although the Law of God could not be added to or subtracted from, other laws consistent with God's Law still would be needed.

Under a constitutional rule of law, governments always need two levels of law. A written fundamental Law is the supreme law of the land, but statutory laws are also always needed to administer to details and specific problems. Note the following example of the Hebrew states-general making a law. One clan of the Tribe of Manasseh came before Moses, the High Priest Eleazar, and "the leaders and whole assembly,"[5] and asked for a legal act regarding policy affecting a clan's inheritance. Despite the fact that Moses consulted the oracle king (Jehovah), note that this also required the presence of the princes and all the assembly. Again, as with the Ten Commandments, God required the ratification of his statutes by the people's representatives. In this case, the whole assembly of the states-general put questions before Moses, and Moses and Eleazar put the same questions before the Lord. A short time after this first meeting of the whole assembly, which made a law concerning the right of a women to assume leadership of a clan, all the clan leaders of Manasseh again came before "Moses and the leaders as heads of the tribes of Israel"[6] to further amend the law. The point is, one must carefully look at the context to determine who made up the assembly of the people in a given text. In this case, the assembly was obviously a representative body of the tribes in the process of making a national law.

According to E. C. Wines, the national states-general was bicameral with an upper and a lower house.[7] The upper house was referred to as a meeting of the elders, or leaders and heads of thousands. When the lower house was added to the meeting of the upper house, the body was referred to as the whole assembly of Israel. It is recorded, "Make two trumpets of hammered silver, and use them for calling the community together and for having the camps set out." When both trumpets were sounded, all leaders followed by their electors were to assemble around the Tent of Meeting. If only one was sounded, just the leaders (heads of the clans of Israel) were to assemble before Moses.[8] There were leaders of 10s, 50s, 100s, and 1,000s within the nation. Each would move out in an orderly fashion to lead their tribes in a certain order as they prepared to march with their belongings to the next campsite. Later, according to E C Wines, it was also a way of calling both the lower house and the upper house to do governmental business by the blowing of two trumpets, and for calling the upper house to do business by the blowing of just one trumpet.

---

4. Deuteronomy 4: 1-2.
5. Numbers 27: 1-11.
6. Numbers 36: 1-13.
7. Numbers 27: 1-2 and Psalms 107: 32.
8. Numbers 10: 1-4.

After the Hebrews settled in the Promised Land, God established that three times a year all males should meet together for worship as one nation in one place he would choose. This place became Shiloh, in the tribal lot of Ephraim, according to Joshua 18:1. When needed, national magistrates were instructed by the Lord to meet at Shiloh, other than for worship. Sometimes a national assembly was for judicial purposes, and sometimes for legislative purposes. The national judge could also hold court there, assisted by a lawyerly council of Levites. The authority of this national assembly was final and not to be ignored, under penalty of death.[9] Mostly the people were to be governed locally in their tribes within each city, but one always had the right to appeal to the national authority. If a states-general meeting was needed, it could meet at Shiloh, as it might have to call upon the advice of the Levites or even consult with God through the high priest.

Actually, the national states-general was a part-time national government. Representatives of the people would gather when called to act on some matter, and their staff advisers were always the Levites. The use of trumpets to call a meeting might have been the practice, but of course a herald would have to ride to the appropriate cites and it would have taken days to call the states-general together.

When one comes across the term, "the whole assembly" gathered together for this or that, one needs to carefully examine the context to determine if it is possible that this could mean the entire nation or if it meant some specific assembly of Israel. It might be called a "holy assembly" and be made up of those conducting some form of worship. It might be called for governmental decision-making. As an example, Joshua in his last days "summoned all Israel," which meant "their elders, leaders, judges and officials."[10] In this assembly of the whole states-general, Joshua delivers a farewell address. Apparently this governmental meeting took place at Shechem, the place where Israel renewed its commitment to the Sinai Covenant at the start of Joshua's judgeship, and the place at the end of his life where "Joshua [and the people's representatives] drew up for them decrees and laws."[11] Under later judges, the place of meeting for the states-general was a place convenient for the national judge at the time. The place of meeting by Israel's states-general seemed to vary in the nation's history. They had no national secular capital city.

In the Book of Numbers, the people are organized as citizen-soldiers under tribal princes and leaders of thousands. In the Book of Joshua, the leaders of the states-general are addressed as though the mantle is now laid on them collectively to faithfully lead the people true to the Law. After Moses, and after the five or so years of war in which Joshua led in the conquest of Canaan, national judges seemed to be leaving governing more to the tribes. Every tribe (like a regional state) had rulers over thousands, over hundreds, over fifties, and over tens, and other officers.[12] The inference at first seems to be that these were military officers when needed, but once the fighting was over and tribes had their lands assigned to them, these leaders also assumed governmental roles.

Twice in the book of Numbers, in Chapter 1, and in Chapter 26, a national census was taken for military purposes. In Chapter 1, only the princes of each of the twelve tribes were named. No clan leaders of 1,000s were named. For some reason, the newly elected princes are not named in the census taken years later as found in Chapter 26. That census only names the clan leaders of 1,000s in each tribe. Thus, we are able to put together a model of the Council of 70, often called the elders of Israel,

---

9. Deuteronomy 17: 8-13.
10. Joshua 23:1-2.
11. Joshua 24:1 & 25.
12. Deuteronomy 1:15.

or, as I refer to it, the upper house, or senate, of the states-general.[13] This senate was made up of the 12 princes of the tribes plus 58 tribal clan chiefs.

If you carefully number the clans named for each tribe of Israel you will find that there are only 57 recorded in Chapter 26 of Numbers. Interestingly, this fits with the fact that the Tribe of Manasseh apparently lost a seat in the senate when the chief of one of its clans produced no sons.[14] For this reason the Zelophehad clan is not named as a clan in Chapter 26. But if you study Chapter 27 you will see that the members of this clan were concerned they therefore would not have assigned lands when the tribes took possession of territories. Though the clans of the Hebrews were usually patriarchal, it appears the states-general legislated an exception if there was no male heir. When you add the clan of Zelophehad to Manasseh (as legislated in Chapter 27) you have 58 clans in the Council of 70. The 12 princes, again, are not named in this listing, only the clan chiefs. Review again the model of the upper house of the states-general in the Appendix 8.

Just before the death of Moses (Israel's first judge), we read of a new arrangement calling for a kind of joint leadership between the high priest and the judge as regards states-general meetings. Moses was to bring Joshua and "have him stand before Eleazar the Priest and the entire assembly" for a commissioning ceremony.[15] From this time on, Joshua was to stand before Eleazar whenever he acted as judge of Israel, and the high priest would confirm decisions by inquiring of the "urim" before the Lord.[16] This practice of calling on the judgment of the "urim" is not totally understood. Experts think it was akin to casting lots in order to make a determination to take or not to take some course of action. It was an added role of the high priest and seemed to be part of the system of government mainly during the judges-era. Perhaps business in the states-general consisted of the judge presiding over issues that were considered by the assembly, the development of oral consensus, and, to test the common sense of the assembly, having the high priest prayerfully cast the lots of the "urim." God's judgment (reflected in "inquiring of the urim") regarding any assembly consensus was thus affirmation, or acted as a veto.

Much later in Israel's history, after the fall of its republic and after the rise of monarchy, and after years of exile under foreign empires, the Council of 70 was revived and was called the Sanhedrin. According to Jewish historians, when the Persian emperor allowed Israel under Ezra's leadership to return to its homeland, the Jews tried to revive their ancient republic. But Israel failed to renew many of the liberties of the Mosaic constitution. Even when the Hebrews gained independence from the Greeks, their government was more "Hellenistic" than truly republican.[17]

In the Christian era of the West, we also do something that, to nonbelievers, might seem rather mysterious. We seek God's will in prayer through a legislative chaplain before each day's legislative decisions are made. As long as our leaders are Christians, they expect the Holy Spirit to give them an affirming sense of comfort or discomfort about decisions pending before them. Of course one thing that has not changed at all in history is that we always have had God's law to guide us when we question what God's will is. God's will never contradicts his law. It appears Joshua and

---

13. See Appendix 8.

14. I spoke of this problem several paragraphs earlier regarding a legislative act of the national states-general. Again review Numbers 27: 1-11 and all of chapter 36.

15. Numbers 27: 19.

16. Numbers 27: 18-23.

---

17. The "Hellenistic" era of Greek history is her empire period, which was rule by kings and aristocratic councils. It was a time after her republican era, between 338 and 146 BC. (Israel fought for and won independence from the Greeks in 167 BC, and maintained it until taken over by the Romans in 63 BC).

future judges would have to consult God through the high priest before confirming any major action of the states-general. Only Moses, as the first judge, had the dispensation to inquire directly of the Lord.

The states-general of the Hebrew republic consisted of the leaders of tribes, of clans, and of cities. The upper house was made up of princes of tribes and clan leaders of 1,000s. Cities had elected judges and magistrates over 100s 50s and 10s. These men could be both military officers and governing authorities. If the "whole assembly" was summoned, it included these city officials who could collectively be called the lower house of the states-general. All men of arms numbered in the census taking process were not members of the states-general. When we studied the tribal governments, we established that princes, as leaders of tribes, were elected. However, no mention was made of leaders of 1,000s, as clan leaders, being elected. Obviously membership in a tribe was directly tied to a genealogical record kept for members of clans, and the elders of clans held birthright positions. That is the clear context of the Numbers Chapter 26 record.

Clan membership established one's right to assigned lands and even one's rights as a citizen under the Law. One could even redeem his right to lost property through the genealogy record in the year of Jubilee. To protect tribes from loss of territory, an only child, if female, was required to marry within her own tribe. Thus, the states-general required that the daughters of Zelophehad marry their cousins. Otherwise the Tribe of Manasseh, from which Zelophehad came, would have lost that clan's lands to another tribe into which his daughters married. The national unity of Israel was tied to perpetual ownership of all lands assigned by lot at the founding of the nation. Apparently the oldest daughter of Zelophehad even gained the right to sit at her father's clan's birthright seat in the Council of 70.

Normally the system was male-dominated, but women at times did assume roles that usually only men occupied. One of the judges raised up by God over Israel was Deborah. In the context of the story of Deborah, it seems that she was the right person for the job because no man was man enough for the job at the time.[18]

Again, when references are made in the Old Testament to the congregation of Israel, all the assembly, or all the children of Israel, it can mean either a representative assembly of all Israel or literally be a way of referring to the whole nation. One must read it in context to make the distinction. Under Moses, when the spies returned and 10 gave a bad report and spread fear throughout the camp about giants and great walled cities too powerful to conquer, the whole community (or nation) became as cowards. "Then Moses and Aaron fell face down in front of the whole assembly *gathered* there."[19] Since it is not a reference to just the elders, this assembly must have been larger than the Council of 70. This was a meeting of the upper and lower house, or whole states-general. When Moses tells the assembly about God's judgment on them for their lack of faith, he could not possibly be directly addressing the whole nation of more than a million persons.

When only the upper house is called, the terminology used is a "meeting of the elders," or a "meeting of the leaders of the assembly." Unlike the upper house, the lower house probably never met by itself. That fits with two trumpets calling a meeting together of both houses, and one trumpet calling only a meeting of the upper house. For an example of the lower house in action, consider the recorded story of the Gibeonite deception in the time of Joshua. The Gibeonites, fearing Israel after hearing of its victories at Jericho and Ai, pre-

---

18. I sort of make a joke here; but examine this bit of Israel's history in Judges 4 and 5 and decide for yourself if Barak did or didn't have a role to play but wasn't man enough.

19. Numbers 14:5.

tended to be from a distant country and to have come to honor and make an alliance with Israel. It is recorded, "Joshua made a treaty of peace with them . . . and the leaders of the assembly ratified it by oath." After discovering the deception, it is recorded, "The whole assembly grumbled against the leaders," finally imposing an amendment to the treaty.[20] This kind of action cannot be anything but an act of a representative system. The upper house ratifies a treaty made by Joshua, and the lower house, adding its input, forces an amendment to it.

How does this compare with other ancient republics? It is unlike Greek city-states where the assembly included all who were required to bear arms in defense of the people. Also, the Hebrew republic was not a democracy in the sense of Greek city-states later in history. There is no evidence the Hebrews cast ballot votes in the assembly; the Hebrew republic was strictly a representative system. According to Numbers 26: 51, there were over 600,000 men of arms nationally. This means that the total population of the Hebrew nation was probably at least five times larger (taking into account wives and large families of children). Could Moses address an assembly of 3 million?[21] The answer is obviously no. Imagine trying to be heard by even 100,000 at the University of Michigan stadium without amplification. Greek city-states were usually smaller than or no greater than 20,000 in total population, and therefore one could effectively address those men of arms who probably numbered something like only 1,000. In the Hebrew republic elections were probably held less frequently than they would have been in Athens. Hebrew terms of office seem to have been lifetime terms.

The case for elections is made entirely by inference, but I think convincing inference. It is clear that representatives of the people existed, even though some held birthright positions and some had to be chosen by those with birthright positions. It is clear that these representatives were given the right and the duty to ratify both decisions of who would be prince over each tribe and what laws would govern them. It is also clear that the Hebrew commonwealth was free of aristocratic class rule because most all families were middle class. However, later, under the monarchy, middle class status would decline and slavery would increase. What would one call the government established by Moses, if not a republic?

Interestingly, there is a surprising parallel between the Hebrew constitutional republic and the English constitutional monarchy of modern times. Note in my diagram of the national states-general that I place the judge over the Council of 70 (a kind of House of Lords) and not separate from it. The real king was God, who was separate and above the states-general. Moses was more like a "prime minister" for God, who was the head of state. A prime minister represents the king's agenda before the representatives of the people. In the English government, back at the time of the American Revolution, there was a king who picked a prime minister from parliament, and a parliament divided into two houses. The upper house, called the House of Lords, was seated by birthright, and had both judicial and legislative power. The lower house was elected from districts and had the final say in making the law. In British history, the lower house of parliament arose out of middle class citizens of the nations cities. In the Hebrew government, the upper house was mostly a birthright office and it had both judicial and legislative power. In the lower house of the Hebrew assembly, all positions were elected from cities and it was only a legislative body. Very highly qualified legal historians of British history (like Sir William Blackstone) confirm that England's national common law evolved primarily from trying

---

20. Joshua 9: 15-21.

21. Could Moses have even addressed over 600,000 men of arms?

to copy the Hebrew Old Testament constitution. The British republic has outlasted the usual 200-year or shorter lifespan of most republics, and now holds the record for longevity, as national republics go in history.[22]

Of course, in the Hebrew republic, the tribes and cities were to govern themselves for the most part, and a national states-general would form only as needed. Every year the whole nation (men able to bear arms) had to go to Shiloh on three separate occasions.[23] This requirement, of necessity, helped maintain national unity. The whole nation was to meet at the start of the year (in our month of April) for celebration of the Passover, the national day of salvation. Fifty days later (at the end of our month of May), the nation gathered for the celebration of the Feast of Weeks to honor the giving of the Law at Sinai. Then finally, in the fall (in our month of October) the Hebrews came together nationally for the Feast of Tabernacles, which was preceded by the Day of Atonement in which the high priest entered the Holy of Holies to sprinkle blood on the Ark of the Covenant for national confession and forgiveness of sins. At this last festival time of the year, the attendees lived in tents or temporary shelters in remembrance of their 40 years of wandering in the wilderness and their anticipation of a future "Day of the Lord," when God will indeed rule in men's hearts and all will dwell together in the "Promised Land." The national capital was not a site of permanent secular rule where the states-general would be continuously seated. The national capital was Shiloh, the seat of the Tabernacle of the Lord and high priest.

The House of God was the focal point of the nation. In essence this should keep the Lord God sovereign in Israel. Keeping the Sabbath weekly within their local communities also kept the nation united under God.

The National Judicial Function of Israel's States-General

The Hebrew republic had no national chief executive, but did have a national judge who acted as commander in chief when needed. This commander in chief relied on the national states-general to provide men of arms, and sometimes this military role doubled as police power over tribal relations. Likewise, the states-general was required to fill the role of judicial arbitrator over conflicts between tribes.

A case study of this federal union at work is found in the Book of Judges Chapters 19 through 21. In this text, the Tribe of Benjamin came into conflict with national interests, and as a result we are able to observe the executive and judicial national authority of the states-general. Despite the fact that this case is described in the Book of Judges after the history of Samson, we can be fairly certain it occurred earlier between the Joshua and Othniel judgeships. A reference is made to the High Priest Phinehas, son of Eleazar (the son of Aaron) as presiding over this case. Clearly this had to be before the time of the High Priest Eli and the final years of the republic.

A gross violation of the Law regarding homosexual acts associated with Canaanite idolatry had occurred. This corruption was infecting the cities in Benjamin's lot. But the source of the evil was located in the lot of Judah in the city of Jebus, independently ruled by the Jebusites. This Canaanite tribe of Jebusites had not yet been conquered by Israel, but later under King David their city would be taken and renamed Jerusalem. The Jebusites were "sodomites" and their lifestyle had pervaded the Israeli city of Gibeah in Benjamin's lot.

---

22. However, in more recent times the British parliamentary republic has evolved into a democracy where the lower house is totally sovereign and the House of Lords and monarchy are insignificant. I will take up the issues of democratic-republics verses representative-republics thoroughly in Part Four.

23. Deuteronomy 16:16.

The National Government

All of Israel was sworn to uphold the Law of Moses throughout the nation. The problem in Gibeah had not yet been addressed. It finally came to national attention when a certain Levite was traveling through Benjamin's lot. Under Israel's "federal" union, free and protected travel by fellow Hebrews throughout all tribal areas was required. Especially protected were the traveling rights of Levites who had no territory as their lot, but were a class of lawyers and priests whose responsibility was to uphold the Law nationally.[24]

In this case study, this Levite from the tribe of Ephraim, north of Benjamin, had to travel through Benjamin into Judah to try and bring back his runaway concubine.[25] He was returning home and, fearing the Jebusties in Jebus, bypassed that city to stay overnight in the town of Gibeah. He was not given his hospitality rights (or traveling rights) and was going to sleep in the streets, but an old man returning from the fields to his house saw him and invited him into his home. In the evening some wicked men beset the house and sought to sexually violate the Levite. The end result was that both the homeowner and the Levite released their female family members into the streets to save themselves. (You and I could find much fault with this decision by the men in this story, but that discussion will have to occur at another time because it would divert me from my intended object here.) The gang rape that took place killed the Levite's concubine. So, as a call for national retribution, the Levite cut his dead concubine into twelve parts and had each part delivered to the leaders of the twelve tribes. (I know, ugh!) We may shrink back from the brutality of this story, but it reflects the reality of that time in history. The Hebrew justice system, however, does not reflect the reality of those times. Stick with me as I take you through the constitutional due process Israel used to solve this issue.

Since in those days Israel had no king, how did it deal with issues like this nationally? It is recorded, "Then all Israel from Dan to Beersheba and from the land of Gilead came out as one man before the Lord at Mizpah. The leaders of all the people of the tribes of Israel took their places in the assembly of the people of Israel."[26] This was not the ordinary occurrence in Judges where only a few tribes participate. It was every tribe east and west of the Jordan, as well as all tribes between Israel's northernmost city and its southernmost city. They all showed up with their men of arms, some 400,000 strong. Obviously, no one tribe had a right to openly violate the Law of God. But the federal authority had to be very carefully weighed against the tribal authority of Benjamin.

A national court of the states-general was required to investigate the charges of the Levite. The Levite did not bring charges against the whole tribe of Benjamin, but only the specific inhabitants of Gibeah. But the tribe of Benjamin was responsible for bringing the defendants before the states-general assembly. When Benjamin refused, and decided to protect the accused, the case became larger and all of Benjamin now came under the charge of treason to the federal union.[27] So strong was the rebellion that the army of Benjamin twice defeated the national army. Finally, in a third assault, the national army wiped out every member of the tribe, except for 600 men. To save the tribe from losing its lot in the federal union, the states-general

---

24. Deuteronomy 18:1-13.

25. According to Genesis 25, the Hebrews (starting with Abraham himself) took secondary wives (often referred to as concubines); but under the Law of Moses, all people, whether concubines or not, were supposed to have rights and protections.

26. Judges 20: 1-2 (also see map in Appendix 6). The whole assembly of Israel came together as one for executive and judicial action.

27. Judges 20:12-14 & 26-28 & 35.

had to find a way to provide wives for the survivors. Benjamin was restored to the union once she repented of her sin. Note also that when the city of Jabesh-Gilead did not participate in this national action, as part of the Tribe of Gad, it was punished.[28] The states-general of Israel had to have a presiding officer, but there was no national judge in Israel at this time.[29] According to Judges 20: 27-48, the elders of Israel inquired of their High Priest, Phinehas what the Lord God would have them do. I assume he inquired of the "urim" and the answer came back, "Go . . . and they put all the towns to the sword." Even as they did so, the whole nation wept bitterly for their brothers.

Similar to our own Civil War between the American States in the 19th century AD, this ancient civil war in Israel's history strengthened the national authority of the nation. For at least three generations, Israel (like America) continued to function with great loyalty to the local authority of each tribe (State), but also recognized a strong national authority. However, a trend toward demanding more and more national authority had been stimulated. This finally led to the kingship of Saul. In American history, following the Civil War the national government assumed more and more authority slowly diluting powers of the States. Likewise, later under the kings, Israel's several tribal authorities would be under constant danger of extinction. Even federal unions are difficult to sustain. Note also that Israel's and America's republics were federal unions that allowed no right of secession by tribes/States in the union. This, again, is evidence that Israel's commonwealth was not a confederation, but more like our federal union.

The Formation of National Executive Power under Israel's Kings

Moses did make allowance for Israel to one day have a king, perhaps anticipating that her people, in their sinful nature, would lack the self discipline required for republican government. But let's look at how Moses actually warned Israel about monarchy at the same time.[30] Moses required that the king be a leader ordained by Jehovah and a natural born citizen, and that he accept the conditions of his rule from a prepared scroll approved by qualified Levites. The conditions of such a king's rule included: 1) he was not to acquire great numbers of horses; 2) he was not to take many wives; 3) he was not to accumulate large amounts of silver or gold; 4) he was to read the Law of God, copied by his own hand, every day of his reign; and 5) he was not to consider himself better than his fellow Hebrews. The inference here is that kings would be inclined to put themselves in the place of God and act like worldly kings from the nations surrounding Israel. Given these restrictions, one should not conclude that Moses was making an endorsement of a king as absolute head of state.

It is clear that God preferred that Israel learn to rule itself without a human king. We have seen how God alone was to be their king. No provision existed for a single head of state. The executive heads of the tribes were elected, and there were other locally elected magistrates, but that was all. When military leadership was needed to defend Israel from foreign enemies, God would raise up such leaders from among men who were not part of the tribal governments. These were the national judges and shouldn't be confused with other local judges. Israel also had no national capital city, and the states-general met only as needed in various cites and various tribal lots. God was Israel's king, and his high priest had the only national gathering site, Shiloh, where the Tabernacle was kept. If

---

28. Judges 21: 2-23.
29. See Appendix 7.

30. Deuteronomy 17:14-20.

Israel had had a king and a capital city from which he ruled, it would not have been long before it was the king who was sovereign in the eyes of the people, and not God.

Of course, the time did come when the people demanded a king. Samuel's role in this regard helps explain a lot about the free republic of this Hebrew state. It is recorded, "so all the elders of Israel gathered together and came to Samuel."[31] The Council of 70 demanded that Samuel give them a king. Knowing the law of Moses, Samuel warned the elders of all the tribes regarding the danger of their request. I might add, Samuel was not opposed to giving the nation a king for the reason that he would lose power as Israel's national judge. He had no powers of state except to be a national military leader when needed. Further, the republic had no national head of state, only a national senate of princes and elders. Samuel knew that what the elders requested was unconstitutional, but they would not listen to his objection — only in that sense were they rejecting Samuel. However, God told Samuel that they were actually rejecting him as their king by rejecting Samuel's advice. Because theirs was a theocratic republic, God nonetheless allowed them the right to have a king, but only under limited constitutional authority.

God pointed out to Samuel the man he was to pick as king. Later, Samuel addressed the states-general of the nation regarding how they were also to have a voice in picking their king. Again, God is not a dictator, and he already had provided a means whereby the nation could amend the constitution to allow for a king. At Mizpah, a fortified place often used for states-general meetings, God then used Samuel to go tribe-by-tribe and clan-by-clan to finally pick out Saul of the Tribe of Benjamin. The representatives of the people shouted,

"Long live the king," and Samuel explained to the people's representatives the regulations of the kingship. He wrote them down on a scroll, which he presented to the high priest of the Lord.[32]

As I will continue to demonstrate, here the precedent was set to require that the states-general elect the king. As with the Law itself, and now with the selection of a king over Israel, this republic was both under God and by consent of the governed.[33] Only now did the republic have a chief executive, but kings soon would make the office totalitarian.

Saul displayed a bit of cowardice in this overwhelming experience of being picked as king, and it did not go unnoticed. But after a time of adjustment, the Spirit of the Lord came upon Saul and he led Israel bravely in battle against invading Ammonites. A king not in full submission and dependence on God is weak, but filled with the Spirit he is mighty. Apparently, Nahash, king of the Ammonites, was again threatening Gilead and that may have prompted the people's demand that they have a king to lead them against this old enemy. (The Philistines had recently been defeated by Samuel and had not yet returned to attack Israel again.) Some tribes were not sure that they wanted to trust Saul, but with this victory they united behind him, and Samuel called another states-general meeting at Gilgal to reaffirm Saul's right to rule.[34] It is recorded that Samuel charged the representatives of the people at Gilgal,

---

31. First Samuel 8:4.

32. First Samuel 10: 24b-25.

33. When God told Samuel to listen to the people and grant their request, he was affirming that Israel indeed was ruled by consent of the governed and now must correctly go about amending their Covenant with Him.

34. First Samuel 11:14-15. The repeated meetings by the states-general to select Israel's first kings will occur again and again, only adding emphasis to the importance of the election of her kings.

If both you and the king who reigns over you follow the Lord your God, good! But if you do not obey the Lord and if you rebel against his commands, his hand will be against you as it was against your fathers.[35]

Of course, as we discussed in the last chapter, Saul lost the endorsement of God when he twice disobeyed the instructions of the Lord given through his prophet-judge Samuel. Led by the Lord, Samuel sought out David, and though David was still a lad, anointed him to be the next king. The Philistines would be involved in a war with Saul all through his reign, and though Saul took his own life as he faced defeat in his last battle, Israel would eventually win the war under their next king, David.

Following Saul's death, Abner, Saul's military commander, brought Ish-Bosheth, Saul's last living heir, across the Jordan River to Mahanaim as a kind of temporary national capital in Gilead. There Abner, in an attempted coup, made Ish-Bosheth king with the support of Gad, Asher, Issachar, and leaders of Ephraim and Benjamin. Judah did not participate in the coup, and made David king in Hebron. Since not all the tribes are listed as joining Abner, several probably abstained, neither voting for or against the coup. For two years Israel had two kings.

The issue of succession to the crown obviously became the next test for the republic. Judah, following the constitutional requirement of allowing God to help Israel pick the king, made David king when Saul died.[36] Abner, in the name of all Israel, whose total support he did not have, made Ish-Boshseth king as the birthright son of Saul. But if a kingdom is won by birthright will not the citizens become subjects of the whims of a man and no longer free?

David, as the Lord's anointed, had been loyal to Saul all this time. David was not vindictive toward Ish-Bosheth and knew about the requirement of an election. However, Joab, David's military commander, was forced into a civil war with Abner. In the full context of this war, it became clear that Abner, after consulting with the various princes of the states-general, discovered that they were withdrawing their support for Ish-Bosheth.[37] It is recorded that, finally,

Abner . . . came to David . . . and said, Let me go at once and assemble all Israel [meaning the states-general] for my Lord the king, so that they may make a compact with you, and that you may rule over all that your heart desires. So David sent Abner away, and he went in peace.[38]

Abner made peace with the council of tribal elders and they all supported making David king. But, as required by Moses, and as carried out in the case of Saul, it was now required of David that he make a contract with the states-general and that they affirm his right to be king. He was then elected by the Council of 70 meeting in Hebron, and was anointed by the high priest[39] It was so important that this process be completed in all its required parts, with a contract, and affirmation of the states-general, and God's anointing, that it was done despite the fact that this was the third time David had been anointed king.[40]

But just as Samuel had warned Israel, the commonwealth was corrupted under the rule of kings. He had warned,

This is what the king who will reign over you will do: He will take your sons and make them

---

35. First Samuel 12:13-15.

36. Remember Samuel, led of God, had already rejected Saul and picked his successor David.

37. Second Samuel 3:17.

38. Second Samuel 3:21.

39. Second Samuel 5:1-3.

40. It was David that captured Jerusalem from the Jebusites and made it the national capital. See Second Samuel 5:6-16.

serve with his chariots and horses . . . Some he will assign to be commanders of a standing army, others to make weapons of war . . . he will take your daughters to be perfumers and cooks and bakers. He will take the best of your fields and vineyards and olive groves . . . he will take a tenth of your grain and of your vintage and give it his officials . . . he will take a tenth of your flocks and you yourselves will become his slaves. When this day comes you will cry out for relief and the Lord will not answer you in that day."[41]

David, though not perfect, was always a repentant king when he sinned, but his successors were far worse, helping to destroy the constitution of Moses and the republic.

David's sons devoured one another over the issue of who would take the throne next. First Absolom and then Adonijah and Solomon fought over the throne. Samuel had provided checks and balances in the selection of each king of Israel, but when the time of succession came there was always a power struggle. To keep the constitutional nature of the republic, there was to be a two-step process in selecting a king. First, God would make known his choice. Second, the states-general had to ratify that choice. But when David was old and the time approached to pick a successor, two of David's wives[42] and two of his most trusted military commanders competed for the right to decide who would be king next. The story is told in Chapter One of the Book of First Kings. The first alliance was formed between: Haggith (the mother of Adonijah---David's oldest son), Joab, and a pretender high priest, Abiathar. Abiathar was a descendent of Eli whose family had lost the blessing of God (as recorded in First Samuel, Chapter Two). Joab might have had the support of the army but no longer had the support of David. The opposition was formed between: Bathsheba (mother of Solomon), the rightful high priest, Zadok, and with Benaiah, David's chief bodyguard. One added member of the opposition was the prophet of God, Nathan. Since at this time there was no clear single holder of the office of high priest, the prophet Nathan gave Solomon the clear endorsement he needed from God as the right successor.

King David quickly anointed Solomon before Adonijah could win the people's support. He proclaimed Solomon king, but the selection process had to be repeated because a vote of the people's representatives was required, and the high priest had to anoint the monarch. David had no right to decide the matter himself. Finally, now that the coup had been put down, David called a meeting of the assembly of Israel (the states-general) and a proper coronation was held.

Then [the states-general] *acknowledged Solomon son of David as king, a 'second' time, anointing him before the Lord to be ruler and Zadok to be priest. So Solomon sat on the 'throne of the Lord' as king in the place of his father David. He prospered and all Israel obeyed him.*[43]

Soon Solomon took unto himself hundreds of wives, accumulated great sums of silver and gold for himself, established great stables of horses, and conscripted an army of his fellow citizens and of mercenaries. All of the above actions of Solomon violated the Mosaic constitution. The accumulation of all these violations, and the effect each had on the Hebrew republic's loss of freedom, led to a crisis when it was time for a successor king to take over. Some of Israel's princes of tribes demanded the option to check the power of the successor king. Rehoboam, son of Solomon, met

---

41. First Samuel 8:10-18.

42. For the king to have several wives was also a violation of the constitution. See Deuteronomy 17: 17.

43. First Chronicles 29: 2-23. Note the reference that this is the second time. Note also whose throne the scripture says Solomon sat upon, not David's but the Lord's.

with the states-general of Israel and was asked to lighten the "heavy yoke" of taxation and forced labor his father had imposed on Israel. Rehoboam dared to reject the request and threaten to impose even higher taxes and harsher conscription of labor. The response of the princes was the cry, "To your tents, O Israel! Look after your own house, O David!" Most of the tribes refused to submit to his authority and they elected another king. The Kingdom consequently was permanently divided into two states that would be in conflict with one another from time to time. The very essence of a republic's right to government by consent of the governed was at stake. The states-general rejected the king proving that their right to ratify his reign was more than just a formality.[44] The point was made but the cause was lost. The Hebrew republic had not survived the imposition of monarchy upon it.

God's nation must freely accept him and his Law, and must also freely vote to ratify its own leaders. God is no tyrant and neither should his model government for nations be a tyranny. The same principle applies to we Christians who must be called by the Holy Spirit and also must confess our place before men as a member of the "kingdom of God."[45] What a God we serve; the same yesterday and today, and who seeks a universal community (the church), not of robots, but of free men and women whose freedom is dependent on loving obedience to the Law of God.

God, through Moses, warned that kings would make themselves military dictators. Thus God established the "national guard" system of tribal military units for the Hebrew commonwealth. In all republics of history, the greatest fear is that of giving a national magistrate the power to command a standing army. Absolute monarchies or military dictatorships are born this way. Thus the Roman Republic, whenever it was at war, called on a patrician to be elected by the senate as dictator for one year only. Also, only the Roman Senate could declare war. After serving as dictator this patrician would return to his plantation to cultivate the soil and otherwise serve as a senator equal among other senators. Later, as Rome was constantly at war with Carthage, generals were appointed for longer periods of time but were never allowed to bring their armies back to Rome. The armies were kept in colonial areas of the empire to keep the peace. Of course, in the end, Caesar did bring his army out of Gaul to Rome and that was the end of the Roman Republic.

Thus, in the earliest of all republics (the Hebrew commonwealth) you would expect a prohibition against a standing army. In the Book of Numbers there are accounts of tribal numbering of all men old enough to bear arms when needed. The precedent for Rome's military reserves coming from clans to submit to temporary central command was laid way back in the time of Moses. However, if Hebrew cities within a tribal territory refused to answer the call for men of arms they were punished.[46] The "judge" or temporary general raised up by the Lord was always from outside of tribal government. Further, the use of a cavalry, the main weapon of ancient warfare, was prohibited by the constitution of Moses.[47] On one occasion when a large number of enemy horses were captured, Joshua was directed to *hough* (hamstring) them. This was accomplished by cutting the sinews of the horse's legs. The practice either killed the animal or rendered it useless.[48] Note that David also in like manner destroyed the horses captured from Damascus.[49]

---

44. Second Chronicles 10: 16-19.

45. Romans 10: 8-10.

46. Judges 5: 23 & 8: 4-9.

47. Deuteronomy 17: 16.

48. Joshua 11: 16.

49. Second Samuel 8: 4 (note David also sinned by keeping 100).

It was Solomon who totally broke this constitutional limitation on making war. He was known for his many stables of horses and his standing army. The prohibition regarding the accumulation of horses was also a means whereby the republic prevented the development of a nobility class that naturally evolved around an equestrian class in ancient civilizations. Symbolic of this principle, recall that the King of Kings rode into Jerusalem on a donkey on Palm Sunday. His "kingdom," to be established by the church, was to be won peaceably by souls freely surrendering to the Holy Spirit, not won by war as the worldly kingdoms are won.

Constitutionally, the Hebrew commonwealth was to be a nation at peace with other nations, but one ready to defend itself against any aggressive hegemony of enemies. Thus it did not have a king and standing armies like other nations. Note the following scriptures regarding these matters. One will find in Deuteronomy Chapters 2 and 3, a prohibition against forceful passage through the nations of Edom, Moab, and Ammon, thus avoiding war. However, if these nations made war on Israel after granting peaceful passage through their lands, Moses had the right to defend his nation. God would himself provoke those nations he wanted Israel to wipe out so as to give their lands to Israel. This was the way they ended up taking over Gilead, east of the Jordan River. They were told to completely wipe out nations west of the Jordan under Joshua's leadership, because the cup of iniquity for these nations was full in God's scheme of history. But at times, even when Joshua was leading, Israel was instructed to give a city the chance to surrender without the necessity of war.[50]

In an age when battles were the business and delight of nations, and empires rose and fell, the Hebrew commonwealth was not to follow that example. Its greatness would not consist in standing armies, but in the calm virtues of industry and equality, and in the freedom of God-given laws. How much like that has the American republic of modern history also been? For the most part, ours has not been a nation seeking empire, but peace and the freedom of self-determination for all nations. The American federal republic did not allow the formation of a standing army until the 20th century; has always had the constitutional provision that Congress shall declare war; and has tried to avoid militarism through civilian control of our military. The issues of war and peace in God's scheme seem to require a duty to defend justice, but also to avoid the temptation to build empires of tyranny.

The national government of the Hebrew republic had no king or president. The American republic also had no elected head of the national state under the Articles of Confederation. The Hebrew republic finally turned to a king of limited authority, but that did not prevent the republic from slowly losing its rule of law and its freedoms. The American republic also revised its Constitution to allow for an elected head of state to be called the President of the United States of America. Trying to avoid the evolution of dictatorship in the American republic, our first president set the precedent of serving no more than two four-year terms. However, the power of the executive branch of the American national government has slowly grown larger and larger. Our hope is that our national congress and U.S. supreme court will be able to prevent the rise of an absolute presidency. The Hebrew republic also had a body that served as a national council, which could sit as either a legislative body or a supreme court. But the states-general of the divided kingdoms was seldom mentioned in the Books of First and Second Kings and was seldom called on because kings were more often than not absolute in their exercise of power; kings also were no longer elected.

---

50. Deuteronomy 20: 10-18.

For 120 years, Israel had a constitutional monarchy with the requirement that the king make a contract with the states-general. There was never a national people's ballot to elect kings, but the Council of 70, as a kind of "electoral college," was required to ratify the one who God had ordained to be king. The states-general was supposed to determine succession by election and not by birth right. Prophets would be raised up by God to challenge Israel's kings when they strayed from this constitutional system, which was introduced by the judge/prophet, Samuel. As long as kings feared the prophets and knew the people's representatives would back this rule of law, Israel maintained a constitutional monarchy. Psalm 119 is full of admonitions written to keep rulers and citizens respectful and obedient to the Law of God. But following the splitting of the kingdom into two kingdoms, kings became the downfall of the Hebrew republic, and with only a few exceptions they were not obedient to the Law of God.[51]

Separation of "Church" and State in the Mosaic Constitution

As one last point regarding the limited national government under the Mosaic constitution, I will address the separation of authority between God's anointed priests and the secular government. God separated the duties of Moses and of Aaron, and of every national judge and succeeding high priest. Once Israel adopted the rule of a king, it was doubly important that he be forbidden from assuming the role of high priest. In neighboring nations, kings always had both the role of high priest and chief of state. The first governmental system with a separation of "church" and state was the Hebrew commonwealth. It was not a separation that granted the secular government power to regulate the church and restrict its role in society, as officials have applied this principle in American society today. Rather, it was a separation that kept the secular government from inserting itself into religious matters. In the reign of King Uzziah of Judah there is a scriptural reference to how this king disobeyed this separation of church and state, and the consequences. It is recorded that King Uzziah was a good king who submitted to the law of God, until in the last part of his reign when he became proud and entered the Temple of Solomon to burn incense in worship of Jehovah. The priests tried to prevent it, but he became angry with them and thus God struck him with leprosy and took his throne from him.[52]

Obviously some aspects of the Hebrew republic lasted for a long time even under the rule of kings. One of the last kings of Judah even tried to reunite the tribes of Israel (the Northern Kingdom) with Judah (the Southern Kingdom) and return to the forms of the republic as established by Moses.[53] His name was Hezekiah. He is sometimes called the reformation king. But his reforms generally were rejected by the Northern Kingdom. God's final judgment came on the Northern Kingdom with the invasion of the Assyrians during Hezekiah's reign. Finally, Judah was over-thrown by the Babylonians 100 years after the conclusion of Hezekiah's reign.[54] Once Israel was split into two kingdoms, the role of the priests was so corrupted that revival of the constitution would be impossible. Likewise when most of the churches of America become willfully apostate, we too will see our freedoms crumble beyond repair.

We have now reviewed all the Biblical support for the fact that the ancient Hebrew com-

---

51. See First Kings 21. In this record we read of King Ahab taking over Naboth's vineyard and Elijah the prophet condemning it, saying, "Have you not murdered a man and seized his property?"

52. Second Chronicles 26: 16-23.

53. See page seven through thirteen in Chapter One (I review the reformation efforts of Hezekiah and Josiah).

54. Second Chronicles 30-31.

monwealth was indeed a republic. It was the first republic of human history. If first, and an interconnection can be established with succeeding Gentile republics, why should we doubt that the first was the seed of all that followed? We have discovered that indeed Moses left a template from which the most successful republics of history have found the secrets of establishing free republics. Moses himself declared to Israel,

> *See I have taught you decrees and laws as the Lord my God commanded me, so that you may follow them . . . Observe them carefully for this will show your wisdom and understanding to the nations, who will hear about all these decrees and say, Surely this great nation is a wise and understanding people.*[55]

---

55. Deuteronomy 4:5-6.

Part Four
The American Republic

The following is a quote from a military sermon preached by the Reverend Jacob Duche' in Philadelphia, before the War of Independence began. A sermon that was dedicated to General George Washington and his army.

> I have made choice of a passage of scripture [Galations 5: 1], which will give me an opportunity of addressing myself to you as FREEMEN, both in the spiritual and temporal sense of the word; and of suggesting to you such a mode of conduct, as will most likely, under the blessing of Heaven, ensure to you the enjoyment of these two kinds of Liberty. STAND FAST, THEREFORE, IN THE LIBERTY, WHEREWITH CHRIST HATH MADE US FREE . . . .
>
> If spiritual Liberty calls upon its pious votaries to extend their view far forward to a glorious Hearafter, CIVIL LIBERTY must at least be allowed to secure, in a considerable degree, our well-being here. And I believe it will be no difficult matter to prove, that the latter is as much a gift of GOD in CHRIST JESUS as the former, and consequently, that we are bound to stand fast in our CIVIL, as well as our SPIRITUAL FREEDOM . . . let us nevertheless, STAND FAST as Guardians of LIBERTY.[1]

---

1. Peter Lillback, *George Washington's Sacred Fire* (Bryn Mawr, PA: Providence Forum Press, 2006), 430.

Chapter 9

The Future Depends on Understanding the Past

We present-day Americans have almost no memory of our beginnings as a nation that drew its values and principles of government from the Bible. When a generation that knows not its own origin and history arises within a nation, that nation is doomed to a gradual crumbling of its very soul and strength. Like Israel of old, we need to heed the words found in Deuteronomy 8: 11-18,

> *Be careful that you do not forget the Lord your God . . . who brought you out of Egypt, out of the land of slavery, otherwise when you prosper in freedom you may say to yourself, my power and my strength have produced this wealth for me . . . .*

Also, we would do well to remember the Song of Moses in Deuteronomy 32, which says in part,

> *Remember the days of old, consider the generations long past. Ask your fathers and they will explain to you when the Most High gave the nations their inheritance.*

In this chapter we will hear from the words spoken and recorded by our forefathers. They will be profound words not heard in a classroom for many generations.

Today our children are being taught in school that our founding as a nation was of our own invention, and that all the founders were secularists who had, by then, rejected their Reformation heritage. They also are being taught that by our might and our strength alone we will maintain our freedoms and prosperity. Their teachers do not consult the words of our founding fathers, and least of all do they understand the miracles of providence that earlier generations were taught.

Rousas John Rushdoony a prolific writer and scholar on America's providential history helped me regain an appreciation for our Puritan founders. Rushdoony suggests that the most profound spokesperson of the Puritan forefathers was the Reverend John Cotton. Much of the Calvinist Protestant thinking regarding establishing America's Biblical republic came from the sermons of John Cotton (1585-1652). Cotton gave life to a dynasty of powerful Christian clergymen in New England: Increase Mather (a son-in-law) and Cotton Mather (a grandson). Their lives span a century and a half of colonial history. All three men played prominent roles in the history of New England. John Cotton was so respected back in England that he was invited to attend the Westminster Assembly of Divines in London during the time of Oliver Cromwell. The following is R. J. Rushdoony addressing modern government in America, quoting John Cotton's thoughts on Biblical civil government:

> "Man is a creature under God the Creator; but also under the curse of The Fall. Therefore the godly order means limited powers and limited liberty. Sinful men and sinful institutions seek to destroy these limits.

Both true power and true liberty can only be grounded on Scripture. Power, moreover, is ministerial, not legislative. In church and state, it is the man of sin, antichrist, who seeks to be legislative—i.e. the creative source of the law. According to this perspective, man's goal cannot be the good society but can *strive* to be a godly society, with a restrained and restraining government, since man is a sinner. Godliness and not paradise must be the objective of civil government and the church."

Rushdoony interjects:

> Thus civil government for John Cotton meant among other things, three things certainly. First, it meant limited power; second, limited liberty; and third, no universality of authority. That is, there should be no intervention of civil government into [what God intended to be] separate and independent spheres of law. By way of contrast, the modern messianic state aims at a self-contradiction. First, it grasps at unlimited power. Second, it promises unlimited liberty. Then it claims, increasingly, universality of jurisdiction. John Cotton further said, "Church and state are of the same genus, or order, with the same author, God, the same subject, man, and the same end, God's glory. On the level of species, however, the two diverge. Here the end of the church is salvation of souls, while the state's end is the preservation of society in justice. The subject of the church is the inward man and is limited to those who are in a state of grace; while the government, in order to preserve all society must see to it that the outward man, ungodly as well as godly, attend to the Sabbath. Moving along parallel lines, church and state should avoid dissolving into one another by not delivering spiritual power into the hands of the civil magistrate . . . and conversely, by not holding a man responsible in church for his political opinions."[1]

There were 80 years between the death of John Cotton and the birth of George Washington. In part, it was the time of the Salem witch trials in New England and the slow death of the once popular title of Puritan. Although those who once identified themselves as Puritans dropped the name, Americans did not drop their Calvinist doctrines. In England Cromwell's Puritan commonwealth had become very unpopular. Also, for the English it was the time of the restoration of the monarchy and the glorious revolution that made the monarch a figurehead and gave rise to true parliamentary government. Some have suggested that thus England and America then rejected all things Puritan. After all, it was also the time of the rise of the philosophes in Western Europe. The truth is English parliamentary government had deep Biblical roots that reveal a lingering Puritan influence from the Cromwell era. In similar estimation, just because the rival philosophies of the Enlightenment in Europe were invading the American scene, we should not conclude John Cotton's ideas of a Christian civil government had died in America. The excesses of Cromwell in the United Kingdom and of Salem, Massachusetts in the time of Cotton Mather were temporary though serious aberrations. They did not interfere with or alter the republican Christian revolution taking place in both nations.

The concept of a Biblical civil government, most importantly, did not vanish from the politics of the American Revolution during the development of new State governments, nor even from influencing the national Constitutional Convention of 1787. In fact, the practice during much of our colonial history, and especially during and after the American War for Indepen-

---

1. Rousas J. Rushdoony, *This Independent Republic*, (Fairfax, VA.: Thoburn Press, 1964), 154-5.

dence, was for respected members of the Christian clergy to give what were called "election sermons" to newly elected State and national officials. When one reads the text of these sermons, the consistent theme throughout them is a belief that political liberty and religious Biblical truth are vitally intertwined. Governors and legislators are again and again reminded of the debt we owe to the ancient Hebrew republic and the modern European Christian Reformation for our constitutional liberties.

For example, the following is the Biblical text of an election sermon on the commencement of the adoption of the new State Constitution of Massachusetts, in 1780. The Biblical text addressed by the Rev. Samuel Cooper was, Jeremiah 30: 20-21: *Their congregation shall be established before me (God), and their Nobles shall be of themselves, and their Governor shall proceed from the midst of them.* This quotation taken from the Geneva Bible refers to the prophecy that, upon the Jewish return from captivity, the Jews not only would be restored to their homeland, but would be returned to the freedom of their God-given republican government without a monarchy. The preacher was telling Governor Hancock and the newly elected Massachusetts legislature that Israel's Mosaic constitution was that of a free republic, consisting of a chief magistrate, a Council of 70, and general assemblies of the people.[2] Having lost their republic to absolute monarchy and having suffered captivity in Babylonia, the Jews were to be given a second chance according to this prophecy. The promise was achieved in the reformation led by Ezra and Nehemiah under the protection of Artaxerxes I, Persian Emperor from 465-424 BC. Actual independence of the Jews had to wait until 167 BC, achieved through the Maccabean Revolution against the Greeks.[3] The problem was the Jews could not maintain this Mosaic reformation which slowly turned into an oligarchy which propped-up an absolute High Priest theocracy. The Jews even lost this right of limited self-government and independence later, when Rome took over and appointed the Herod dynasty to keep them in line. The Rev. Cooper could not have anticipated that the Jews would re-establish a more perfect independent republic in 1948 AD, but his message was that this was of God and that the model for the Constitution of Massachusetts was based, in part, on the ancient Mosaic template. In effect, this sermon raises the challenge that America, like Israel, will enjoy great liberty only so long as it is faithful to the one who is the source of liberty.

Each generation of a nation depends on the one before it to pass on the grand heritage of their nation's history. When nations neglect this responsibility, they risk the demise of their heritage. On the other hand, when those who are given the responsibility to lead a nation draw upon the heritage of the leaders who preceded them, that nation moves with destiny and purpose. Such a nation learns to sense that it is part of something greater, something providential. Our founders knew they had experienced the hand of God rescuing them step by step through the War for Independence, and they identified with ancient Israel's rescue from Egypt under Moses.

We are all part of a chain of events larger than ourselves. Yet, we have a choice. Will we allow ourselves to be a link in God's providential movement of history; or will we choose to be linked with all those who think they are going their own way, but are really marching straight into slavery and tyranny? The latter was the effect of the French Revolution that fed into the European socialist and communist revolutions a century later. As I have documented in this book, the founding fathers of the American republic carefully held at bay the politics of the French Revolution so as not

---

2. Ellis Sandoz, *Political Sermons of the American Founding Era, Vol 1* (Indianapolis, IN: Liberty Fund, 1998), 634.

3. See Appendix 4, Exhibit B.

to undo our founding on the Christian principles of the Reformation.

In the generation following that of George Washington, America remained a Christian nation. It was Alexis de Tocqueville, writing about America as a visitor from France, who said the following: "In the United States of America, the sovereign authority is religion." He cited evidence of this, including the American refusal to accept the testimony of an atheist in court.[4] Our first Chief Justice of the U.S. supreme court, John Jay is attributed to have said, "Providence has given our people the choice of their rulers and it is the duty as well as a privilege and interest of our Christian nation to select and prefer Christians for their rulers."[5] As recent as 1892, our U.S. supreme court openly declared this to be a Christian nation.[6]

The purpose of this chapter is to try and redirect our nation's attention to the chartered Biblical course laid out by our founders. Sir William Blackstone (1723-1780), the English expert on common law and the greatest influence on American legal education up until the 20th century, said that, "much of Western constitutionalism originated in the Hebrew polity found in the Bible." Our greatest early chief justice of the U.S. supreme court, John Marshall, was one of Blackstone's disciples. English common law came from the Bible, and the American Constitution came from English common law. In the Mosaic constitution: the Council of 70, the Congregation, the chief magistrate (whether judge or king), the Levitical legal offices, and the prophetical office constituted many checks and balances restraining the exercise of tyranny. Tyranny in that time and in our own is the natural order of things. The Mosaic constitution thus became an example to build upon by the Greeks, Romans, English, and Americans for free and just governmental systems never before made possible. The roots of both insignificant republics and the more significant, such as named above, all come from God, through his prophet Moses. America's founding was the beneficiary of a providential chain of events in history.

"Righteousness exalts a nation, but sin is a disgrace to any people."[7] If America would strive to be a righteous nation, it must imitate God's constitution as laid out in the Bible for his chosen nation. Flagrant attempts to amend that Mosaic template will eventually turn a national people over to the tyranny of sinful rulers. In an election sermon given by the Rev. Samuel Langdon, who was President of Harvard University, he goes to great lengths to demonstrate how we owe our model for government not to the Greeks or Romans, but to ancient Israel. The sermon is titled, "The Republic of the Israelites / An Example to the American States." The sermon was given in 1788 before the New Hampshire State convention regarding the ratification of the U.S. Constitution. New Hampshire would be the State that finally made ratification a national reality, being the ninth one to support ratification (an agreement of at least nine States was required). At one point Langdon observed,

> they [the Greeks and Romans] were far from being worthy to be compared with the laws of Israel, as to the security of life, liberty, property, and public morals . . . .[8]

The Christian God treats individuals and nations the same. Both the repentant person and the repentant nation-state, if they would become Christian, must voluntarily, out of love and faith in God, obey his laws. To obey is to know God's blessing; to willfully disobey will result in negative consequences. If you want to know why a na-

---

4. Alexis de Tocqueville, *Democracy in America* (vol. 1 and 2, unabridged)

5. William Jay, *The Life of John Jay*, (New York: J & J Harper, 1833), Vol. II 376.

6. *The Church of Holy Trinity v. U.S.* (1892), 143, U.S. 457, 458.

7. Proverbs 14: 34.

8. Ellis Sandoz, 950.

tion is suffering from crime or even governmental tyranny, look at how disobedient it has become toward God's laws. The seeming paradox of the text I write is: God is sovereign, but his model of government is government by consent of the governed. The Judeo-Christian God is no tyrant. Man is created a free moral agent, but subject to universal unchanging natural laws put in place by the Creator.

In the Reformation of the church, Christians learned the meaning of individual self-government. From that came the virtuous citizenry required of modern republics. First there must be popular consent to God's laws, which must be enforced by elected leaders consistent with the national allegiance to the Law of God. However, a nation may elect leaders who are not Christians and still remain a Christian nation. It is still entitled to be called a Christian nation so long as its system of government is under the freedom of God's principles of governing, and enough of its citizens exercise the right to vote as guardians of those Christian principles. If those principles are amended the blessing of God given freedom, will begin to erode. If Christians are not elected the nation may remain Christian so long as its system of government is not drastically changed. Our nation was not founded as a Christian theocracy, *but* its founding was undergirded by Judeo-Christian culture. Of course, to a certain extent, America has always had its atheists, and its immigrants who are adherents of Eastern religions. Such immigrants had to tolerate the keeping of the "Sabbath" and Judeo-Christian morality however, and, of course, quickly took advantage of freedoms they were not afforded in their own homelands.

The problem is, over time, America has experienced a general rebellion against God and has amended its ways and its laws. Thus, our land may be in danger of slowly but surely losing its Christian rule of law and falling under the tyranny of men.

The future depends on understanding the lessons of the past. Education today has de-emphasized history. In its place, teachers uphold the latest doctrine of an evolving, humanistic, progressive future. Under classroom instruction today, we follow each fad that comes along. In contrast, Biblical Christianity is a faith placed in proven principles and built upon lessons learned by our forefathers. May God help us rediscover the proven Biblical principles of government and our place in his providential time-line of history.

My challenge for our nation is as follows: since God judged his chosen nation when it rejected him and turned to false gods, why should we, who are founded on Christian principles inherited from God's chosen people, be more secure in our own disobedience? Will we too lose our inheritance because of the sin throughout our country as we reject holy laws of righteousness? God's warning is clearly sounded through the Prophet Jeremiah:

> *Cursed is the one who trusts in man, who depends on flesh for his own strength and whose heart turns away from the Lord . . . but blessed is the man who trusts in the Lord, whose confidence is in him. He will be like a tree planted by the water that sends out its roots by the stream. It does not fear when heat comes, its leaves are always green . . .* [But] *The heart of man is deceitful above all things . . . who is there that really understands this?* [9]

For this reason our nation's founders greatly limited the authority of national government and reserved most of its powers to the States and to the people. May our nation's memory be stirred to again demand that our national government limit its powers so that our freedom might be secure.

---

9. Jeremiah 17: 5-9.

Chapter 10

Maintaining National Liberty

Today, it is often assumed that the ultimate perfection of free government is a democracy. However, the Hebrew republic was not a democracy, and neither was the early American republic. Actually, absolute democracy can become a human corruption of truly free government. If total sovereignty lies in majority rule, the society may turn into a tyranny of the majority. This was the downfall of the ancient Athenian republic, as well as the modern-day First Republic of France. Alexis de Tocqueville, the observer of the American republic, though he admired the Americans, warned in 1835, "When I see that the right and the means of absolute command are conferred on any power whatever, be it called a people or a king, an aristocracy or a democracy, a monarchy, or a republic, I say there is the germ of tyranny, and I seek to live elsewhere."[1] Alexis de Tocqueville never went on to say that the American experiment was too democratic, but he must have felt we might not be immune to it, any more than France. To what extent is democracy over emphasized or under emphasized in the history of republics?

Historically, even so-called free societies were naturally formed around a few with all the power, and they left the masses as powerless peasants or quasi slaves. Aristotle's "rule by the many" really didn't imply democracy in any modern sense of the term. Ancient Greeks and Romans never extended the right to vote to women. Slavery was common in Greece and Rome and was not seriously challenged in any republic until the 19th century AD. In the 19th century, Western Civilizations would abolish slavery and turn to universal manhood suffrage, but would not extend the right to vote to even half the population, which of course was female. As a rule, even if the masses gain the upper hand by violence, it only lasts a short time, as they always remain dependent on those who lead and who manipulate them for their own interests.[2] Therefore the law must be sovereign, and it must, in some fashion, create checks and balances between interests that will help maintain freedom on the broadest terms possible. Even the Mosaic Covenant allowed the continuation of slavery among noncitizens, and gross inequality between men and women. Mankind in his natural state of nature is not capable of utopia.

Neither the Hebrew republic nor the American republic was really based on the right to vote as the absolute arbiter of all matters between members of society. The wisdom in this certainly did not come from man, and is often misunderstood today. Our own most fundamental document of freedom, the Declaration of Independence, teaches us that liberty first rests on every man's right to private property. It does not even mention the right to vote. It extolls that:

---

1. Alexis de Tocqueville, 94.

2. Consider the Iranian Revolution of 1979 AD that overthrew the monarchy and ended up a totalitarian theocracy. I wonder what will come of the Egyptian Revolution of 2011?

... all men are created equal and are endowed by their Creator with certain unalienable rights, among which are the right to life, liberty, and *property*;[3] [and that] governments are instituted by men to secure these rights, and that government derives its just powers from the consent of the governed; [and that whenever governments] seek to alter or abolish these rights, it is the right and duty of man to abolish such government.

Our very pursuit of happiness depends on our recognition that God's ideal republic is one that limits the authority of government so that it may not take our life to fight its wars without our consent;[4] that it may not govern us in any manner without our consent; and that it does not own our resources upon which we depend to sustain our personal economy. Most significantly, government should not use its power to tax in any manner that steals our life, our liberty, or our property. Thus, our early republic did not allow direct taxation of its people. All taxes were to be indirect sales taxes, which were imposed on the wealth created by private property. Only free trade in a free marketplace creates true wealth without stealing it from one man to give it to another. However, two taxes America has submitted to in more recent times, that have made our government our master rather than our servant, have been the direct taxation of income and property.[5]

To maintain freedom, a nation must start with private property rights that extend to all citizens, not just a protected "noble" class. No one should be promised an equal outcome in life, but everyone should enjoy equal opportunity. The result will be economic growth that sustains a dominant middle class, rather than a majority of people living in poverty. Then, to protect the majority middle class, the nation must divide power in a federal system and between branches of government. Freedom depends less on gaining power over the state and more on limiting the power given to any who hold the reigns of government. The right of private property available to all citizens may be more important to sustained liberty of the people than even the right to vote. A republic is first of all about civil liberties that check the tyranny of man; and only secondarily about the right to vote. Our founders understood the best civil government (or republic) first means limited and divided power for those who hold office, second, limited liberty (or democracy), and third, no universality of authority granted to any institutions of society.

If a society makes elections the only path to freedom, without first establishing a legal protection of private-sector religious and economic civil liberty, it will soon use elections to create some kind of tyranny. We have witnessed in our own time how easily elections become a contest between interests to seize power. They often produce the best government that taxes and promises can buy. In 1848, Karl Marx confused free government with what he called a "dictatorship of the proletariat."[6] Marx believed if one class of society took power another had to give up power. He believed class warfare was a natural requirement in any evolution toward power by the masses. Ac-

---

3. Thomas Jefferson inserted the words "pursuit of happiness" for the word *property*, but everyone understood he was referencing his ideas directly from John Locke's *Second Treatise on Civil Government* published in 1690. An essay that claims civil society was created for the protection of life, liberty, and property.

4. From both the Biblical record in the Book of Judges, and the American colonial practice of drawing men of arms from volunteer and local militias we witness the deeper meaning behind government by consent of the governed.

5. "Fair Tax" advocates today are for returning to indirect taxes and abolishing at least the income tax. Their main concern is with protecting the private sector's ability to make wealth for everyone's benefit, as opposed to stealing wealth from one to give to another.

6. Marx openly promoted absolute democracy, as do socialists today, who encourage the vote be used by the "have-nots" to take from the "haves" by various redistribution-of-wealth schemes.

cording to Marx, a revolution to seize the property of the business class would produce a socialist utopia. Government ownership of all property was the communist road to justice. Marx was wrong, because all communist nations just replaced the private ownership of property with governmental bureaucratic ownership by a new privileged elite. The law must be supreme and both protect the poor from injustice and those that create the most wealth from gaining centralized control. Also the law must limit the power of the majority so that they cannot use the power of the vote to steal from the makers of wealth.

The downfall of the Roman Republic was its inability to keep the patrician class in check and give due process to the plebeian class. The Romans did not maintain enough democracy, and ended up placating the lower classes with bribes of "bread and circuses." The trend in the American republic toward a welfare state of lower-class entitlements, won by a governmental redistribution of wealth, could evolve into the downfall of our republic. The key to a successful republic is the right balance of power under the law, allowing all to rise by their own hard work and abilities to at least a comfortable middle-class status, if not higher. What is needed is a rule of law that protects both minority rights and majority rule. Poor people will always be part of any nation, and should be provided voluntary economic aid through the charity of those blessed with wealth. A Christian nation should make it a duty to give to charities. On the other hand, if the poor are made dependents of the state in growing numbers by involuntary taxing policies of the state, then the poor will assume they are entitled to the care of others and not responsible for their own welfare. If the poor are encouraged to glean for themselves what godly men of wealthier means make available, and both the rich and the poor look to God as the source of their comfort, the numbers that live in poverty will be minimized. All these principles of government have their roots in the Mosaic Covenant and constitution of Scripture.[7]

In both the Hebrew and American experience, however, there were difficulties that caused corruption in their systems. The central problem is found in the nature of man. Man is not inclined to be good, and is desperately in need of salvation. Therefore, only a people willing to be obedient to divine guidance and rehabilitation are capable of self-government in a free republic. Because of this, John Adams admitted, "Our Constitution was made only for a moral and religious people. It is wholly inadequate for the government of any other."[8]

Having made a case against absolute-democracy, let me make a case as well for the value of increased democracy in our own republic's history. Democracy in the American experiment did not come on day one. Actually, the secret ballot and women's suffrage are a positive revolution of our own modern times. We should not assume that standard existed in colonial times. I certainly do not condemn the growth of democracy in our republic, especially in expanding the right to vote and the abolition of slavery.

But I do think it is easy to lose sight of the danger of a generation willing to pervert its concept of democracy by demanding the license to make up its own code of morality, contrary to the Law of God, while all the time calling it liberty. This can be accomplished by means of absolute majority rule as well as by turning to an absolute, so-called, "benevolent-despot." A good republic should have elements of extensive yet limited democracy. Even the American republic, in my opinion, was not

---

7. Deuteronomy 28: 1-14 contrasted with Deuteronomy 24: 14 and 17-22.

8. John Adams, *War on Religious Freedom* (Virginia Beach, Virginia: Freedom Council, 1984), 1. (In these founding years of America, the term religion always referred to all the Christian denominations, and was not used to refer to Islam or other non-Christian religions.)

democratic enough at its founding. However, the fault of many modern republics has been the trend toward absolute democracy and the demand of everyone to do what is right in his own eyes.

So what was an election like in the early colonial days? I will take my example from what I learned by visiting Williamsburg, Virginia. I'm sure you are aware that Williamsburg is a theme park where buildings and people are remade in the image of the 17th century, and everyone and everything represent life in pre-Revolutionary American history. Williamsburg became the capital of colonial Virginia in 1689. This was the time of the "Glorious Revolution" of England. The English dual monarchy of William and Mary was constitutionally limited and would from that day forward rule equally with parliament. The English government then functioned under an equal separation of powers among the monarchy, the House of Lords, and the House of Commons. The House of Commons was elected and could not be dissolved by the monarchy, except to call for new elections. But, even then, this British Republic was not a democracy in any modern sense of the term. It was, however, a constitutional monarchial republic.

In the colonial republic of Virginia, there were lifetime terms for members of the House of Burgesses, and the king, in England, appointed the upper house and the governor. The legislature met every year for as long as needed. The governor called for elections to the lower house when someone died, resigned, or was impeached for some crime. Every white male 21 and older who owned more than 100 acres of land without a house, or 25 acres with a house, had the right to vote. The method of voting was to stand in line and, upon reaching the table of the clerk recording the vote, to then audibly declare both your name and the candidate's name you wished to support. The candidates were present and offered gifts of food and drink to those standing in line to vote. The elections were not about parties or policies, but rather about choosing the most admired members of the gentry. Personal respectability, not promises, was the issue at every election. By the way, James Madison argued early in his political career to eliminate gift-giving at elections and was ignominiously defeated in that election. Later, when terms of office were established and election of the whole House of Burgesses came due on the same day, the election date became a holiday. It became a time for fairs, races, balls, theatrical performances, and gaming of all sorts. How would you compare this system with our own today? Of course, it was far from what we would call democratic.

The Greek city-states were the birthplace of male, citizen, democracy; and the earliest standard for all developing representative systems of government started with the Hebrew republic. But the former would not pass modern standards for democracy, and while the latter was God's template for maintaining human freedom under the law, it was most assuredly not a democracy. The human experiment of free government has been built on both foundations right up to our own time. As the historical record reveals however, neither the Hebrews nor the Greeks were able to maintain their liberty indefinitely. But both their contributions to the idea of free government and the lessons to be learned from their inability to maintain it have become great educational gifts to the rest of mankind.

I have tried to show how American government was born, uniquely, out of a conscious effort to learn from the Biblical history of Israel, and how English common law regarding the best way to govern a free nation also was drawn from the Bible. All republics, even those of ancient Greece and Rome, in some way find their roots in the Mosaic constitution. However, the American experiment has been the most conscious effort to apply Biblical principles to governing. But it now seems that we are denying the truth regarding our roots and our founding history. It is my hope that this book will help us rediscover the roots of the national liberty that was America's foundational strength, in order to prevent any natural decline in our freedoms.

Thankfully, God's judgment of nations comes only after his grace affords them a time of repentance. Israel, when disobedient to God, was given many opportunities for revival. Asking for a king was a national sin, but note how God still worked to rehabilitate the nation. Saul was picked as Israel's king because the people demanded it. It was not God's will that Israel be ruled by a king, but the Lord found "a man after his own heart" in David, the second king of Israel. Still God told Samuel to submit to the people's demands and required that the king submit to a contract limiting his powers. Are you beginning to grasp the unique way the Judeo-Christian God works in the lives of nations and, yes, even individuals? Truly, he ordained a model for good governing and expected other nations to copy it. This model was based on consensual submission to his law. If our nation today elects someone to lead us who proposes, in disobedience to God, policy that in effect rejects God as king, we would be wise to apply the same evaluation as applied in the case of Saul. That evaluative lesson is that we should always be aware of how our choices are a test of accountability, as well as a blessing. God can humble the proudest of men to accomplish his will. But if our leaders fail the test, God sometimes chooses to give a people what they want even if it is not what they need; and God always desires for his people to see history as an object lesson. That is why so much of the Bible is written as a history book and with an emphasis on cause and effect .

David symbolized a time, yet to come, when the Messiah will finally rule from the "New Jerusalem" as a perfect king. For men to govern, however, the better plan is that of a republic, as under Moses' constitution. The Davidic Covenant was not an endorsement of monarchy, but a promise of one to come who would descend from David as the God/Man who alone is worthy to rule as king. Rulers of free nations must exercise power as ministers of God and as servants of the people. Like the federal republic of Israel, power must be decentralized within the state. Ambition checking ambition keeps rulers humble.

The great fault of the British republic was that it evolved from war to war into a centralized United Kingdom dominated by England over Scotland, Wales, and Ireland.[9] First under kings, and then under a national Reformation parliament, union was achieved by force. The evil side of Oliver Cromwell is a matter of recorded history, especially in his attempted ethnic cleansing of the Irish Catholics. Even after establishing the British parliamentary republic, all power was centralized in London. Only recently, in the 20th century, have the British attempted to increase independent decision-making powers of significance in Scotland, Wales, and Northern Ireland. I submit, democratically elected authority that comes from the top down does not maintain liberty as perfectly as a federal system.

On the other hand, the American system evolved in a peaceful manner, from local government to chartered colonial government (the basis for later State government), then finally to very limited Constitutional national government. This was a pattern of development similar to that of the ancient Hebrew republic. Note that this same pattern of authority from the bottom up was built into the Northwest Ordinance of 1787, which was passed by the Continental Congress for the development of new States in the western territories.

---

9. During the reign of Edward I of England, (1272-1307), Wales was forced under English rule and Scotland led by William Wallace rebelled against English rule. From Edward I to Queen Anne, Scottish rebellions came and went until the Act of Union in 1706. Ireland was militarily engaged with England between 1534 and 1691 and again between 1888 and 1912, when most of the island won its independence.

First the settlement of villages around homesteaders was required, as well as the protection of their private-property rights. Land was to be surveyed into one-mile square sections, and sold to those that had developed it. Those land-titled settlers were required to form townships that provided local government services, and later as several township governments together reached a required population they were allowed to apply for territorial status, with an elected governor. As the population finally increased in a territory it could apply for full Statehood. Drawing up their own State Constitution by electing delegates to a convention, they would then ask to be accepted into the national union of States. Alexis de Tocqueville, the French observer of the American scene in the early 1800s wrote, "every village [in America] forms a sort of republic accustomed to conducting its own affairs in America."[10] The American republic always grew from the bottom up in a peaceful and legal manner.

The United States supreme court of the 19th century again and again protected the great powers reserved to the States and their local governments, as opposed to the few but significant delegated powers assigned to the national government. Those powers reserved to lower levels of governments were categorized as the responsibility for public safety, health, welfare, and morals. To this day, almost all police power (public safety) in America is the responsibility of local units of government first, and State governments second. Police power at the national level is small and very specialized, by comparison. The national government, by original intent, was to govern only with regard to the general welfare, not to regulate the health and welfare of specific interests in the various States.[11] The courts understood the public morals to mean the whole realm of criminal law. These most fundamental powers of government were really reserved only to the States. Today, as a result, most criminal law is State law and varies across this nation.

However, in the 20th century, a "progressive" reform effort informally amended our Constitution through supreme court decisions. Over time, and court-case by court-case, national authority expanded until there was little authority prohibited to the central government.[12] All presidents, before the 20th century, presided over only five departments; the number of U.S. departments has grown to 15 today, and there are numerous Boards and Commissions with power to make administrative rules and regulations. The result has been that State and local governments often find themselves administering programs, not of their own creation, but of national or State origin. Such programs may even come as unfunded mandates, hindering the ability of local governments to fund their own programs. Centralization of all power is never a friend of liberty. We once referred to our union as *these* United States of America; now it has become more appropriate to refer to *the* United States of America.

Also, like Europe, the United States has in recent times begun to abandon her Christian heritage in favor of an absolute democratic secular society. Perhaps this weakness to which America has succumbed is the experience of most republics. That is, the tendency to shift sovereignty from the proven wisdom found in the law to the wisdom found in popular opinion. The gateway to our decline in this matter, I'm afraid, has arisen out of an unintended interpretation of our own greatly acclaimed national Constitution. The first three words in the preamble read "We The People . . . do ordain and

---

10. Alexis de Tocqueville, 16.

11. In the 19th century, so called "earmarks" passed today to benefit only one senator's State would have been unconstitutional.

12. The Progressive Party movement began early in the 20th century and resulted in changing legal education so that original intent no longer decided what was constitutional; lawyers now view our system as a *living constitution.*

establish this Constitution for the United States of America." Most of the State Constitutions, both preceding and following the writing of our national Constitution, open with a similar line, but with one significant difference: the mention of God. For example, the Michigan Constitution's preamble reads, "We the people, grateful to Almighty God for the blessings of liberty, and earnestly desiring to secure these blessings undiminished to ourselves and our posterity, do ordain and establish this Constitution." The States were mindful of the source of their prosperity and freedom. Like Israel, at its best, they trusted in God and not in their own goodness.

In colonial times there was a common cry in the press and in speeches, "We have no king but King Jesus!" Years later, King Jesus has been cast aside, and the people have become lord and master of their own accomplishments and destiny. Today it is taught in the temples of higher learning that we were never a Christian nation and all of our due process of law and freedoms were of our own invention and interpretation. Many of our university professors are thus false prophets who exercise their free speech to mock and destroy the truth of God's Word. Today, freedom of the individual, no matter how ungodly or unrighteous under God's law, may be sovereign in America.

Moses had advice that could be applied to America regarding this national sin. The chilling warning given in chapter 13 of the Book of Deuteronomy concerns the danger of turning from the clear word of God to the word of false prophets. Here one can see how God views so-called wise men whose view of freedom runs counter to his. If we were to put this part of God's law in our modern setting, we would probably agree to less severe methods of punishment, but the admonition should be the same. The principles underlying this passage are clearly: 1) one should not tolerate free speech intended to corrupt your soul; 2) freedom should not be a license to tempt national disobedience to God's laws; 3) the wages of sin is death, and national sins will produce national death; and 4) true freedom of speech must be separated from the right to lie. Truth is not a matter of opinion.

It may surprise some, but limited government applies to even the power of the people, not only to rulers. Despite that, judges today have ruled that speech condoning sinful acts of human lust, promiscuity, and even witchcraft are protected under the First Amendment. Ironically, these are the same First Amendment rights that were born out of the English Reformation to protect freedom of religion in the form of prayer, preaching, publishing, and assembling. But of course, if the people are sovereign, and not God's law, what else can we expect will be the effect. As in the days of the judges in Israel's history, when many did what was right in their own eyes, so today in America we have adopted the same philosophy. Whether the state has all authority over every act of the people, or the state grants every individual absolute freedom to do as he pleases, both lead to tyranny. The former is called authoritarianism, and the latter is called anarchy.

Only government under the Law of God will keep a nation free. Where are God's prophets today to protect the people from tyranny? We need preachers like the Rev. Richard Price, who in 1789 gave an election sermon after the election of our first president of the United States. His sermon was not directed so much at Washington as it was a warning regarding the French Revolution that had just broken out abroad. A few of his words were these,

> The tendency of every government is to despotism, and in this the best constituted governments must end, if the people are not vigilant, ready to take alarm, and determined to resist abuses as soon as they begin.... Whenever public attention to this is with-

drawn ... then servants will soon become our masters.[13]

How far we have moved from the true meaning of limited government, separation of powers, and decentralized government. At the national legislative level, through the 17th Amendment to our Constitution, we have eroded the power of State governments by making U.S. senators independent of the State legislatures. Also, at the judicial level, we have exchanged the supreme law of the land (a written Constitution) for a "living constitution" that is anything the judges say it is.

When one looks at nations, a natural tendency is to evaluate them by the acts of their central leaders. This approach of evaluating Israel's national character by concentrating on her national judges, most of whom offend us, makes us miss the whole point of the Book of Judges. In like manner, our evaluation of the American republic is always one of examining the use of power by our presidents. Neither Israel nor America was ever great because it needed and had strong central leaders. The lesson of Judges, remember, is not that Israel needed a king, but the fact that the people successfully ruled themselves without the need for dominate central leaders. Likewise, America's real character is in how we have the capacity to govern ourselves well, despite some of our elected leaders. Israel, like America, was given strong leaders when needed, but national authority mostly was very limited and restrained. The presidency of the American republic should not be considered her strength, but rather the fact that our nation, in submission to Christianity, was able to govern herself with governors of the individual States, and through her elected local governmental officials. The more we have increased the power of the national Presidency the more our freedom has declined. A part-time national government, with very few bureaucratic departments, and limited and strict construction of its delegated powers was the greatness of both the American republic and the ancient Hebrew republic.

How can we maintain the separation of the three branches of government if each branch is not strictly under written limitations in the Constitution? Montesquieu, an early Enlightenment writer, who it is said still held Biblical views, took the idea of separation of powers right from Isaiah 33: 22. "For the Lord is our judge, the Lord is our lawgiver, the Lord is our king; he will save us." Since God is perfect and infallible, he can possess all three powers and still be just and fair, but not sinful men. Today our greatest hope for holding back any kind of tyranny is that Christian men and women will always control and influence at least one branch of the government. Preferably Christians will "leaven" the whole of society and politics, and we will continue to be known as a Christian nation.

Another influence affecting our founders regarding their belief in the separation of powers into three branches of government was the Reformation's development of church government. The Protestant movement produced three distinct different patterns of church government. The Episcopalians, mostly found in southern colonies, emphasized rule from one head bishop. The Presbyterians, mostly found in the middle colonies, emphasized the rule of an aristocracy of elders. Then the Congregationalists, mostly found in New England, emphasized the rule of all those making up the congregation, with authority over their ministerial clergy. Thus it was a natural means of bringing the nation together under a central government that included all three approaches to government. James Madison made a similar analogy when he wrote that, the Constitutional Convention looked to the "essential qualities of a monarchy (unity, vigor, and secrecy) to enable the president to execute the laws with

---

13. Ellis Sandoz, *Political Sermons of the Founding Era*, (Indianapolis, IN: Liberty Fund, 1998), Vol 2, 1019.

energy and dispatch." Then, the founders established an unelected supreme court and U.S. senate in order to give, "to this part of the system all the advantages of an aristocracy (wisdom, experience, and consistency of measures)." Finally, elements of democracy were established in the House of Representatives, which would be elected directly by the people every two years. The best republic must guard against any form of absolutism, even that of absolute democracy.

According to Stephen K. McDowell, of the Providence Foundation, America's decline has not occurred simply because the secularists have denied our Biblical founding ideas. Rather, some fault must also be laid at the feet of the church in America for generally abdicating its role and responsibility. Today, too many Christians live as if politics and public institutions are outside the interests of believers. We, the church, are acting as if we can lead dual lives: one life in the world of work, education, and governmental affairs, which we leave to the secularists; and one life in the church, which is our only Christian domain. But our Calvinist founding fathers believed that the church was charged to take cultural dominion by being an influence in all parts of a society. God has a place for his disciples in the arts, in education, in the business sector, in politics, and in all other walks of life. When it becomes evident that many Christians only walk the walk on Sunday, and not every day of the week, how can we expect nonbelievers to take us seriously? Different from our founders, we seem to have abdicated our responsibility as the church to make reformation within the nation. Our founders understood this was their calling. Now, with our children raised in two dominions, their hearts are pulled in two directions, one worldly and one heavenly. Many are being won by secularism. Thus the church is less vigorous and, at times, worldly itself.

It is time for a new "Great Awakening" within the church of America.[14] Will our end be any different than Israel's? The church and its ministers of God must rise up in the role of prophets, like in ancient Israel, and lead us back to our roots; and God's people who are called by his name must repent and turn from their wicked ways so that God can heal our land and revive our God-given destiny to defend freedom as properly defined under Biblical principles of the law.

The key verse of Scripture in this writing, referenced in the center of the Liberty Time Wheel found in Appendix 1 is *"Where the Spirit of the Lord is, there is liberty."* We Christians are not at liberty to do whatever is right in our own eyes. This definition of freedom is really better described as licentiousness. The Law of Moses is a schoolmaster that condemns our ungodly and sinful nature. Disobedience to the law of God causes slavery and tyranny, but where the Spirit of the Lord dwells, there is true freedom. If the Spirit indwells a man, that man is as one being transformed with an ever-increasing glory that comes from the Lord. *"You my brothers were called to be free. But do not use your freedom to indulge the sinful nature, rather serve one another in love. The entire Law is summed up in a single command: Love your neighbor as yourself."*[15] Unrestrained, the community of believers, the true church, can and should impact a whole nation.

Please do not equate my notion of a Christian nation with that of making the state a theocracy. To do that would cause people to put faith in the state for our salvation. Actually, the "Kingdom of God" should be a nation within all nations whose godly conduct of self-control and brotherly love

---

14. See Appendix 10. There I review how religion in America has always played a role in shaping society. The influence reviewed in the timeline period labeled E is our own time, and I wonder if it has been less powerful than earlier Christian reform movements were.

15. Galatians 5: 13-14.

helps build and sustain freedom. A people who are ruled by their sinful passions will be held in check only by the excessive police power of the state. When the need for more and more police power becomes apparent in a nation, freedom is in jeopardy. However, as a citizen, a Christian filled with the Holy Spirit should be a restraining influence against all the forces of evil. God's people, who are called by his name, must not only pray for their rulers, but vote, and be actively promoting Christian values in politics. In addition, church members should not leave to the government issues of social justice for the poor and vulnerable, but should tithe so that through the church (not the state) the nation will provide for the widow, the orphan, and the homeless and destitute. Outside of this decentralized Biblical template, the state becomes absolute and liberty cannot be sustained.

To maintain our national liberty, we must take control of our schools again and promote the teaching of Judeo-Christian cultural "exceptionalism" in the building of civilization. We must not neglect our Christian responsibility to be active citizens, as applicable to our own times, and we must again vote in mass to elect those who think like our founders did.

Chapter 11

Maintaining National Unity

In all past societies religion has been the source of national unity. But, interestingly modern societies in the West are trying to build national unity around a diversity of separate cultures. Today, America is being tutored, by various educational and media sources, into accepting a state authorized "politically correct" diverse cultural (or moral) mandate. The Biblical model of the Hebrew republic, of course, wrapped its national unity around the absolute moral law of God. In a similar way, the church, not government, used to be America's culture maker. This modern turn of events where the state is trying to take on the role of culture maker is not natural. Especially in a republic, politics should reflect society's religious moral moorings as a representative system, and not try to impose culture on society. The fraternity of nationalism precedes the building of government. The ideal government is a representative republic that serves the brotherhood of a people united in their values and faith.

Throughout history the king was also the high priest, and religion and government were inseparable. But uniquely, the national unity of the first republic, Israel, was in its Judeo religion based on the books of Moses. The high priest and chief civil magistrate of Israel were kept as separate spheres of authority. Even though our American founders looked to the Mosaic constitution for a template from which to build our own government, the national unity of the American republic took a slightly different form. The authority of the state was defined in a written Constitution, and (like ancient Israel) the moral foundation was kept sacrosanct and independent of the state, but undefined in any constitutional-document. The First-Amendment of the Constitution says, "Congress shall make no law respecting an establishment of religion [nationally], or prohibiting the free exercise thereof," in the States of the union. Religion was not a delegated power given to the national government of our republic. All powers over morality (criminal law and religious establishments) were reserved to the State republics or to the many local churches. The churches of America are protected independent spheres of authority within the private sector. Furthermore, when our founders referred to our nation as a Christian nation, it reflected their understanding that the mention of religion in the Constitution meant our unity was to be found in the common values of all Christian denominations.

Significant division over cultural foundational morality will cause the fall of governments or might have to be resolved by civil war. But today, in so-called "enlightened" secular republics, there is no claim of national unity in religious values. Secular republics today are encouraging such wide pluralism in society that they are trying to hold together, as one people, Christian, Muslim, Buddhist, and other variant religious groups as well as openly hedonistic organized interests. Therefore, they place their national unity in central government. In a secular republic, the only thing sustaining its national unity is its "anything goes" definition of freedom. Liberty, thus, is defined, as unrestrained tolerance of all value systems. But this is not liberty at all; it's an open door to anarchy. Again I remind you, without national moral unity, a republic will face civil strife or even civil war that ironically endangers everyone's liberty.

It is also true that, all republics, to a greater or lesser extent, must deal with the threat of civil division just because they encourage some degree of freedom of conscience. But there is a limit to how much a society can be tolerant of foreign value systems. For example, can Western Christian culture allow Islamic Sharia law to govern male and female relations within our nation when the two systems are so morally incompatible? The Hebrew Republic had such a cultural civil war recorded in Judges Chapters 19 through 21. It revolved around the issue of homosexuality, which had pervaded one tribe in direct conflict with the morality of the nation. National unity was maintained, but at a terrible cost.

The American Civil War was the supreme test of our national unity, and helped resolve a long-standing issue of all history. That issue was whether slavery could logically be allowed to coexist within any Christian republic. As pointed out in Part Two, Chapter Five, of this book, Israel's Republic coexisted with slavery. However, slavery was reserved as a temporary means of settling debts or as a punishment for foreign enemies that were a threat to Israel's security. Ironically, ancient Israel both recognized the evil of slavery and allowed it under certain restrictions. A brother Israelite was protected from any lifetime slavery, but aliens living in the Hebrew commonwealth were not protected.[1] Israel's national cry of unity was always, "remember the Lord your God who brought you out of the land of slavery." Obviously, it is important that we too remember and recall the history of our own nation's struggle for national unity, as regards this issue of slavery.

Slavery in Christian modern republics has also been defended and, at the same time, abhorred. But in the end, all slavery was outlawed in Western Christian civilization. However, today we are not always taught the full truth regarding how our nation dealt with the issue of slavery. The very first time Negro slavery was introduced in the English colonies was 1619. But since most U.S. history texts do not go into enough detail, an impression is left that Virginians accepted West Indies style slavery at that time. They did not. Actually, the founding generation in both Plymouth and Virginia were under the government of Puritans. Puritans were those within the Church of England who were trying to reform it along more Biblical lines. Two main players in the London Company that drew up the colonial Charter of Virginia were the Puritans Richard Hakluyt, and his ally in parliament, Edwin Sandy. These two men and those they picked to settle in Jamestown were very much opposed to slavery like that in the West Indies. Puritans in Plymouth, New England had always, without question, opposed the West Indies slave trade. Virginia, on the other hand, would not remain opposed to this type of slavery.

It is important that I define different kinds of slavery before going on with the American historical experience with the West Indies style of slavery. Slavery of some kind seems to have existed through all the history of nations. It actually has never been totally eradicated from our morally depraved human planet. Any type of lifetime slavery is always a dehumanizing thing because it treats human beings as though they were property and had no soul. It can lead to the worst kind of slavery, such as the West Indies type. The slav-

---

1. Read Deuteronomy 24:7. Even a runaway from lifetime slavery, who was escaping the tyranny of nations surrounding Israel, was not to be returned to his master but allowed to live freely among the Hebrews. Read Deut. 23:15.

ery that had its beginning in the West Indies, and later thrived in the American plantation South, was particularly evil. It promoted the idea that some people were less than fully human and were even ordained by God to be the slaves of the rest of humanity. Such slaves were not even allowed the comfort of protected family ties and support. Mothers were often torn from children, and husbands from wives, when sold at the auction block. The West Indies style slavery, introduced by Western Europeans, was the first time in history slavery was totally based on race.

By comparison, sometimes lifetime slavery has been just a little more humane, as when it is based on a class structure and its victims are referred to as serfs. Serfs were believed to have a soul, and in a Christian state were offered all the sacraments of the church. Serfs were considered fully human and their family ties were protected and respected by their masters. In Israeli history, it is clear that slavery at its worst was the serf type experience. However, in its most "humane" form, Hebrew slavery came in the form of what was called indentured servitude. Under the law-of-Moses, there was no mention of the use of jails or prisons; in its place, the Hebrews relied on indentured servitude. This was temporary slavery to pay off a debt to society or to an individual. These "slaves" had rights and were to be reinstated in society with some kind of property for starting over after serving their time. It might have been a better system than our jail system today.[2]

When the Dutch pirate ship landed in Jamestown and sold 20 Africans to the settlers, they were sold as indentured servants, just like many European settlers were sold in colonial history.

The Dutch were part of the West Indies style slaving system, but not these Virginians at this time. Colonial indentured servitude was a temporary slavery with a contract that required their freedom be returned to them in seven years, and that, after serving their time, they be given title to 50 acres of land. This idea came right out of the Bible (see Part Two, Chapter Five). These 20 Africans were all free men by 1626. According to Stephen McDowell, "the early settlers in America had no intention of propagating the West Indies style slavery in Virginia. As late as 1650 there were only about 300 Africans living in Virginia, none treated as West Indies type slaves until 1654."

In the 1640s England had its civil war, and the Puritan, Oliver Cromwell, became the republican head of state. King Charles the First was beheaded, and the monarchy was temporarily ended. Cromwell made it clear he was opposed to the slavery practiced in the English West Indies. But many Cavaliers, soldiers of the king and on the losing end of the civil war in England, immigrated in 1649 to Virginia. This nearly tripled the population of Virginia with members of the Church of England that were not opposed to the West Indies style of slavery. These noblemen were not accustomed to work and they began at that time to promote lifetime West Indies style slavery in Virginia.

Ironically, the first person to force an African into lifetime slavery and all its cruelties inherited from the West Indies was one of the original African indentured servants, who was a free man by then. This man, Anthony Johnson, went to court in 1654 to establish the legality of lifetime slavery in Virginia. The court, reflective of the changing attitude of the colony, ruled that such slavery was legal. The ruling meant that John Castor, America's first lifetime slave, could be sold again and again to others as though he were no different than a horse or a cow. Please do not conclude that Mr. Johnson alone was responsible for the horrid practice being introduced. Those mainly

---

2. Prisoners released from jail today are not even given much of a chance to return to a life-supporting job, let alone feel they are contributing anything in the way of supporting the needs of society while they serve their time. (There are Biblical references to prison in the time of the rule of kings, but not under the republic.)

responsible were white Europeans who had sold their souls out of greed, regardless of the cost to humanity. Those immediately responsible for what happened in Virginia were white members of the jury panel. Please also do not make the mistake of accepting the claim that Christianity was to blame.

The West Indies style slave trade exploded in America between 1670 and 1700. But there was always a tiny minority of free black Americans in the colonies as well. In 1701 the House of Burgesses, with Christian members leading the way, was able to pass a heavy tax on slave ships that arrived in Virginia, in hopes of slowing or stopping the trade. But the English parliament overruled Virginia's law and the slave trade continued without any economic hindrance. Sadly, many Christian churches in Virginia and in other southern American colonies adopted corrupted explanations of Genesis 9:25 to justify slavery, particularly, black slavery.[3] But, of course, not everything done in the name of God is of God. Any reading of the Bible to justify slavery on the basis of race is nothing but heresy. However, the slave traders could sooth their consciences by showing that they had the support of the church. It did not take long for the West Indies style of slave trade to explode in Virginia. According to Stephen McDowell, by 1730 " there were 28,500 lifetime black slaves in Virginia, amounting to one fourth of the population."

History books today usually tell the story of the Constitutional Convention as though it was a pro-slavery document. Once again, this is not true. First of all, the word slavery does not appear in the whole document, in its original form. Curiously, when slaves are actually referenced, as in Article 1 and section two, paragraph three, and in Article 1, section nine, paragraph one, they are referred to as "persons" not as property. In Article 1, section two, the clause is called the "Three Fifths Clause" and it sets forth the means of determining the number of representatives each State is entitled to in the national House of Representatives. Those who claim this is a pro-slavery clause say it makes the slave three fifths of a man or women. But, according to historian David Barton, even Frederick Douglaas, the abolitionist and former slave of our early history, did not agree.[4] In the mind of most of the founders, this clause was not about the worth of persons, but rather about congressional representation. The slave States of the union wanted to count all their slaves when counting the population of their States so as to increase their representation in the house. Fifty percent of some slave States' population was made up of slaves. The "Three Fifths Clause" was forced on the slave States by States opposed to slavery so as to reduce the effect of the unreasonable demand being made. The South got some of its way, but was forced to sign onto a clause calling slaves persons. Under God, all persons are equal before the law. All southern States, agreeing with the northern States, had signed the Declaration of Independence which stated: "All men [persons] are created equal." The founders also placed in the Constitution, Article 1, section nine, a clause that allowed Congress to end the slave trade by 1808. It was Jefferson, therefore, who initiated the end of the slave trade in America in the last year of his presidency. Also in 1787, the Continental Congress, still in power before the adoption of the new Constitution, passed the Northwest-Ordinance, which outlawed slavery in the Northwest Territory and any States to be created out of that territory. The founders of our national republic were anticipating the gradual abolition of slavery.

---

3. See the footnote in the NIV Bible, Genesis 9: 25. This passage concerns the prophetic curse placed on Canaan, son of Ham, son of Noah.

4. Obviously the slave States were not counting slaves as if they would thus be also among those to be represented as equal citizens in this new republic. The goal was to increase white citizen representation disproportionately in slave States as compared to free States.

However, as soon as one generation passes and another generation takes the reigns of leadership the once secure national unity may begin to weaken. The pro-slavery forces in America did not weaken their resolve; but the antislavery forces, which had held the upper hand, began to compromise their principles. To retain liberty, a nation must continually produce new generations that understand and stick to its causes. But between 1820 and 1860 freedom in America was compromised four times by the national government. First, there was the Compromise of 1820, which established that no new State would be admitted into the union unless a slave State also was ready to be admitted. Second, the Compromise of 1850 created the fugitive slave law, which allowed slave owners to pursue runaway slaves into free States and return them to slavery without giving the slave due process of law. Third, the Kansas-Nebraska Act of 1854 allowed a vote of the people of a newly admitted State to decide whether it would be a free State or slave State. Finally, the supreme court ruled in the Dred Scott Decision in 1857 that slaves were property and not persons under the U.S. Constitution. This took away any hope of ending slavery.

The following prophecy of founder George Mason, a Christian statesman from Virginia, would soon come to pass.

> Every master of slaves is born a petty tyrant. They bring the judgment of heaven upon a country. As nations cannot be rewarded or punished in the next world, they must be in this. By an inevitable chain of causes and effects, Providence punishes national sins by national calamities.[5]

Both the Democrat and Whig Parties must take blame for allowing our nation to drift toward civil war. But a new party calling itself the Republican Party was born in 1854 in Jackson, Michigan, and it tried to return the nation to the principles of the founding of our republic. Thinking they were saving the union, the Democrat and Whig Parties actually moved our nation away from the absolute moral principles of God and allowed morality to be defined by a vote of the people. The notion of popular sovereignty, found in the Kansas-Nebraska Act, had moved us from a nation whose rights came from the absolute truth of God's law, plus the consent of the governed, to a nation whose rights would only come from a vote of the people.

In contrast, our founders believed that "All men are created equal and are endowed by their Creator with unalienable rights of life, liberty, and pursuit of happiness." I have demonstrated that the source of this belief was in the Mosaic constitution that is a direct revelation of God. If we make the people totally sovereign rather than God's law, then things like the Kansas-Nebraska Act may, in the name of freedom, actually take another's freedom away. Democracy that is not under God can easily turn into tyranny of the majority.

If the generation that followed the founders' generation in American history had continued by Christian reformation of society to abolish slavery, America could have avoided civil war. But churches in America were split over the issue of the day, and did nothing, out of fear of witnessing the division of the nation. Meanwhile, in Great Britain, a different development was under way. John Wesley and his brother Charles, whose lives overlapped the time of George Washington, founded what became the Methodist Church. The Wesleys spent a short time in the colony of Georgia as missionaries and tried to influence that colony not to allow slavery to get a foothold. They were unsuccessful, but their reformation work in England was much more powerful.

The Methodist movement in England rescued the peasant and labor class from a life of pov-

---

5. Mark A. Beliles and Stephen K. McDowell, *America's Providential History* (Charlottesville, VA: Providence Foundation, 1989), 227.

erty, and ended up affecting legislative reforms that led parliament to abolish the slave trade and slavery itself throughout the British Empire. After a lifetime of working to impact the political life of England, John Wesley died in 1791. But his Methodist Churches in England gathered 229,426 signatures, to be added to another 122,578 signatures gathered by other Christian groups, petitioning parliament to abolish the slave trade. William Wilberforce, their champion in the House of Commons, never let a year go by that he did not introduce legislation to end the slave trade. With the help of God through his people who are called by his name, Wilberforce finally got the votes in the year 1807 to end this wicked business in the British Empire.[6]

The very next year the U.S. republic, under President Thomas Jefferson, ended the slave trade that brought slaves from Africa to America. Smugglers continued to bring in slaves from Africa however, and slave sales of native-born African-Americans continued in the South. Wilberforce was on his deathbed in 1833 when, because of his and the churches' persistence, England became the first nation to abolish slavery throughout its huge colonial empire.

However, President Abraham Lincoln, elected in 1860, had to preside over an American Civil War. The election of Lincoln and his fellow Republicans in Congress was historic. It was the only election in the history of the United States in which a minor party defeated both major parties, in what had always been a two-party system. No party platform in 1860 called for the abolition of slavery, but the Republicans called for repeal of the Kansas-Nebraska Act and the end of the further extension of slavery in the territories. The election produced a split Democrat Party, each schism nominating its own candidate, and the Whig Party and Republican Party each nominating its own candidates. The popular vote was split nationally four ways, and Abraham Lincoln won the plurality with 40% of the vote. He took the majority of electoral votes and, because of his clear personal opposition to slavery the southern States seceded from the union shortly after the election.

Lincoln, wanting first of all to preserve the union, finally did decide to make it a war against slavery. By the time of the South's invasion of the North and the Battle of Gettysburg, Lincoln had concluded that God wanted him to take up the righteous cause of abolition. In his second inaugural address he implied that God in his providential timing had brought on this terrible war as his judgment on both the North and the South for tolerating this evil institution. In 1862, President Lincoln abolished slavery in Washington D.C., and issued the Emancipation Proclamation nationwide in 1863. In 1865, before the war was concluded, Congress put forth the 13th Amendment under the leadership of Republican Lyman Trumbull, making slavery unconstitutional. By then, Whig Party members had joined either the Democrat Party or the new Republican Party, leaving the nation again with a two-party system. Then, sadly, Lincoln was assassinated.

The history of reconstruction following the Civil War is almost always taught from the perspective of finding fault with the Republicans and ignoring what the Democrat Party was doing. Today, the emphasis of textbooks is placed on the carpetbaggers and the heavy hand of the U.S. Army in occupying the South. This is not to say this history of reconstruction is totally in error, but it does leave out important matters. The organization of the Ku Klux Klan (KKK) by Democrats and its activity is perhaps the most basic part of this history left to the imagination. For 10 years,

---

6. The slave trader John Newton was convicted of his sins in this matter in 1779, and joined the abolition movement in England. He wrote the Christian hymn "Amazing Grace" upon his conversion. A recent movie, "Amazing Grace," relates his involvement in the slave trade and his informal alliance with William Wilberforce.

between 1865 and 1875, there was little or no formal white government in the southern States. The occupying Union Army required all rebels who fought in the war to sign an oath of loyalty but most refused and therefore couldn't run for office. Republicans controlled the U.S. Congress, and all southern State Governments, while the Presidency was held by Andrew Johnson the antislavery Democrat who had been Lincoln's Vice President. The southern whites referred to these elected southern State governments as rule by the radical Republicans. Today, rather than cover the history of black Republican rule in the southern States after the war, textbooks usually just refer to the "radical Republicans" of the time, without much explanation.

Congress also required the new southern State governments, controlled by newly elected former slaves, to ratify the 13th, 14th, and 15th Amendments before they could be readmitted to the Union and could send members to congress. Seven highly qualified black Republicans were elected to the congress, and one became Speaker of the House. Federal troops enforced civil rights legislation passed by Republican State governments. Civil rights legislation passed by the Republicans gave federal courts, backed by federal troops, jurisdiction over Klan activities because State judges and juries were letting the Klan get away with murder. Civil rights legislation was also passed against segregated schools. That was almost 100 years before similar present-day civil rights legislation.

Tragically, in the 90 years between 1875 and 1965, the Democrat Party of the South would overturn the above accomplishments of the Republican Party. To help smooth over a corrupt presidential election in 1875, federal troops were removed from the southern States. This, plus Klan activities to prevent black voting, allowed Democrats to again gain complete control of all southern State governments. During these years, the racist Democrats started to gain control of one or both houses of the congress, and at times the Presidency. President Woodrow Wilson, a Democrat in the early 20th century, was a supporter of the KKK, as well as being an open racist. Racial segregation of all life in the South began to return "virtual black slavery." Poll taxes, literacy tests to register to vote, the use of multiple ballots and polling places to confuse voters, Jim Crow laws to take legal rights from blacks, gerrymandering blacks out of election districts, white-only primaries, and even the lynching of Republican black candidates and voters all became commonplace in the South, as white Democrat supremacists took over government once again. In 1900, the Democrat Party actually started a movement to repeal the 14th and 15th Amendments. It failed. Churches in the South were either deaf-and-dumb to what was occurring or were high-jacked by the Klan's "Christian" bigotry.

Despite this condemnation, I do not believe it is fair to say that only the South brought judgment on our nation in the form of the Civil War. The war was God's judgment on this nation, but it was equally poured out on the North and the South. The apathy and willingness of the North, which accepted the tyranny imposed on African-Americans by Southern slavery, called for God's judgment on it as well. The South had won all the battles in the early going of the war. Only after Lincoln made it a war against slavery, did the North begin to win the war. According to Stephen McDowell, President Lincoln in one of his many speeches addressing the war said, "the thunder of cannon on the battlefields causing bloody deaths on both sides is the thunder of God's voice crying, "Let my people go!"[7]

Sadly, it was not until the war that associations of clergymen representing Methodists, Baptists, Episcopalians, Lutherans, Quakers, Congregationalists, United Brethren, mission boards, and

7. Mark A. Beliles and Stephen K. McDowell, 232.

YMCA groups all over the North sent official condemnations of slavery to President Lincoln. Within a few months, 125 remonstrances signed by northern clergymen poured into Congress. Like the petitioners of England in 1791, finally churchmen of America were taking a stand, turning in one petition 200 feet long that bore thousands of signatures of abolitionists. According to Stephen McDowell, Senator, Charles Sumner thanked the ministers, saying, "In the days of the Revolution, John Adams, yearning for independence, said, "Let the pulpits thunder against oppression, and the pulpits thundered. The time has come for them to thunder again."

In a sense America's fourth Great Awakening took place in the 1950s and 60s under the leadership of the Rev. Martin Luther King, Jr., who was able to bring together churches made up of both black and white Americans to undo the nearly 100 years of segregation and racial hatred that had followed the Civil War.[8] Under Republican President, Dwight Eisenhower and the supreme court headed by Chief Justice, Earl Warren public school segregation was ended in 1954. Then, under President, John F. Kennedy an alliance was formed between Rev. King. and the Democrat Party. Except for the followers of some Democrat governors in the southern States, America (Republican and Democrat) began to come together in a great peaceful movement of civil disobedience with the goal of bringing about the integration of the races by law and by a change of heart. King's "I Have a Dream" speech delivered from the Lincoln Memorial steps in Washington D.C. in 1963, would go down in our history as one of the greatest addresses to the nation ever given. But both President Kennedy and Rev. King were assassinated. Thus it became the legacy of succeeding President Lyndon. B. Johnson, with the support of Republicans and a few Democrats, to pass the civil rights legislation as the fruit of this reformation movement in our history. It was the bipartisan influence of a national Christian conscience led by King, however, that made this possible.

Sadly, almost as soon as we ended a system that segregated one group of people, making them outcasts of society, we again, positioned the law against another group. I speak of the U.S. Supreme Court's decision in 1973 that denied the constitutional personhood of babies in the womb.[9] Even republican courts are no guarantee of justice, if unchecked by the law of God. Nor are legislative acts of a republic any real guarantee of justice, if rights depend alone on majority rule, unencumbered by the law of God.

We have ended slavery and we have ended laws of segregation, but many African-Americans still live in dependence, as wards of a welfare state. We have all, white and black, rich and poor, rejected our founding principles and made ourselves dependent on central government for social justice. We are giving up self-government and self-reliance for governmental handouts. Even our State and local governments are becoming dependent on the central government to fund the many social programs now mandated by national law. Private charity organizations in America still do more than any such organizations in other countries, but even they are giving up their important role as the largess of the public treasury more and more takes their place. The new mantra is the claim that the state is the source of our equality and that it can by decree make everything right for those in poverty by redistributing the wealth.

Lastly, since the death of the Rev. Martin Luther King, Jr., others have turned the civil rights movement into a call for cultural pluralism. Equal justice under the law, called for in our Constitution, should be applied to individuals regardless of race or ethnicity, but we are now calling for preferential protection of certain groups that are placed

---

8. See Appendix 10.

9. For obvious reasons, I consider the Roe v. Wade court case our Dred Scott S.C. case of 20th century America.

on affirmative action lists by legislators. Turning our civil rights movement on its head, we now give certain groups more than equal protection. Affirmative action legally discriminates in favor of those groups who can somehow demonstrate that they deserve preferential treatment. Even the poor of other nations seem to be entitled to the fruits of our national wealth. No longer do we call for the integration of foreigners into our Judeo-Christian culture; rather we welcome diversity of cultural influences. Our national unity is again threatened.

Today, the American state encourages hostility toward our past Judeo-Christian culture as though it were the cause of all that has been wrong in our history. Instead of revealing the individual transformation of men and women as Christianity freed them from demonic cultures, our history is taught only stressing our failures and weaknesses. The great strength of our Judeo-Christian culture is in its attention to individual accountability and individual rights regardless of our race, or ethnicity. Instead of giving the down trodden a hand up and the ownership of their own success by putting aside bad habits and adopting godly manners, we are training them to have their hand out and have made them dependents of the state.

In conclusion, I take you back, again, to the ancient Hebrew republic that faced civil war in 930 BC, under the monarchy, over issues of tribal rights vis-à-vis the authority of the central government. Their national unity was destroyed and two states emerged---Israel and Judah. They coexisted, but each fell victim to rejecting the God of their freedom for gods of other nations that made them virtual slaves to sin. What will be the future of the American republic? We are divided by secularism vis-à-vis Christianity, and divided by the immigration of cultures foreign to and sometimes unwilling to assimilate traditional American values.

Cultural unity is necessary if we are to remain strong. Our national unity must rest alone in our uniquely Judeo-Christian Constitution. We seem to have lost any understanding of the cultural moorings of our founding years. Not that we can't continue to be a nation that welcomes all races and peoples wanting to share in our freedom and equality. But we must not equate our diversity with the cause of our freedom. Diverse peoples come to our shores because of the freedom they know exists here; they are not the cause of it. The Lord God loves diversity in race; after all, he created mankind and most of his creatures with a capacity for biological variation. God did not, however, create all human cultures. Most cultures were born out of rebellion against God. Free republics are born out of this Judeo-Christian culture and none other, and cannot survive except within it.

Alexis de Tocqueville recognized in 1835 that our national unity was our common Christian conscience that was promoted by and matured in our many Christian churches. Unless our churches today experience a nationwide revival and once again become the culture makers of manners in America, we will continue to become more and more divided and confused about who we are and what our destiny should be. The churches led in the struggle over the development of national racial integration (unity), but despite this, new issues of national diversity continue to threaten our unity. If we would be a more perfect union, we should expect the state to protect our liberty, but not to define it. The church must again lead in our maintenance of national unity. Our national pledge of allegiance still needs to be: we will strive to be "one nation, under God, *indivisible*, with liberty and justice for all."

Chapter 12

Conclusion

In Matthew 13: 33, there is a parable told by Jesus Christ to his disciples. "The Kingdom of God is like yeast that a woman took and mixed into a large amount of flour, until it worked all through the dough." Of course the Kingdom of God is made up of all believers who are ruled by their king, Jesus. The church universal (believers) needs to think of itself as the yeast mixed into the dough (the world's nations)[1] to leaven the whole loaf. The yeast is of no effect or use sitting in a bowl by itself. It has an effect only as it is placed inside the dough. If the dough is society, the leavening effect works throughout every part of it. Thus the believer is to be involved in politics, economics, education, the arts, and in every aspect of society; the resulting effect will be the raising of all in society to new heights. This is a picture of Christian reformation.

Let me quote again from the early 19th century French observer and writer Alexis de Tocqueville, who visited our nation in its infancy.

> On my arrival in the United States the religious aspect of the country was the first thing that struck my attention; and the longer I stayed there, the more I perceived the great political consequences resulting from this new state of affairs." Continuing in the same vein elsewhere in his writings, de Tocqueville said: "I sought for the greatness and genius of America in her commodious harbors and her ample rivers, and it was not there; in her fertile fields and boundless prairies, and it was not there; in her rich mines and her vast world commerce, and it was not there. Not until I went to the churches of America and heard her pulpits aflame with righteousness did I understand the secret of her genius and power. America is great because she is good and if America ever ceases to be good, America will cease to be great.[2]

Our Personal Responsibility

In a Christian republic we might say the people make the laws, but the church makes the people. Sometimes those elected may not be Christians, but it is the job of the Christians, as much as any others in society, to influence the elected. Ideally you shouldn't be able to enter any field of work or career without seeing that Christian influence. Alexis de Tocqueville's observation was that the Christian church in general had an impact in America wherever he looked. This is what makes a nation a Christian nation. The Christian influence doesn't necessarily have to be a majority of the people, either.

Today the Christian influence in America has many powerful adversaries, which it lacked in most of our earlier history. The United States Supreme Court, in the 1960s, outlawed prayer and the posting of the Ten Commandments in all pub-

---

1. Matthew 28: 18-20.
2. Mark A. Beliles, & Stephen K. McDowell, 115-6.

lic schools. Since that time, secular social policy legislation, devoid of Christian values, has been pushed on the family and educational institutions.

Secular governors and presidents, as well as State legislatures, and the national Congress submitted, in our early history, to pre and post election sermons by clergy of various Christian denominations. No church denomination was to be made the established church of America, but God's "prophets" of various Christian denominations inserted themselves into politics and administration of the law so as to keep elected leaders true to our foundation as a Biblical people. There could be no religious test for election but that did not mean there would be a required submission of the church to the state. Ministers would likewise not run for elected office, but would boldly insert themselves as guardians of the Judeo-Christian foundation of our society and its governors.

In our own time, we have turned this on its head. Yet, at times, we may still find a few contempory ministers who have, like most preachers in our founding years, not hesitated to address political and social matters as spiritual issues of the day. Often religious coalitions try to influence elections today, but they are fighting against already entrenched secular policy supported by many voters who do not share Biblical traditional values. We need more preaching in our Biblically based churches that is critical of government leaders of our time, who have "unconstitutionally" inserted themselves into establishing unBiblical law and have thus led our nation away from God. These secular leaders often force their own definition of morality on all of us, destroying the free exercise of religion as guaranteed by the First Amendment. Bible believing churches often withdraw from the fight only interested in their own members and not the wider effect this has on society.[3]

Actually, when you find some field of work or arena of human activity abandoned by any Christian influence, you in effect are witnessing what happens in society absent the presence of the "kingdom of God." America today is not the America of the 19th century or even the America of most of the 20th century. During both of those earlier centuries, the keeping of the "Sabbath" by closing down businesses on Sunday was evident all across our nation. But in the last half of the 20th century and into this 21st century, commercial activities seem to be open everywhere on Sunday. We may still be a Christian nation in the 21st century, but it is much less evident now that Sunday has become a day like any other day of the week. A very large proportion of our society today is hostile to Christianity and there is a "cultural war" going on over public policy that is Christian in orientation. Many mores that had their origin in Christianity are today being abandoned by much of our nation, or are even now legally discouraged, by acts of our government's lawmakers and courts.

For example, we are now witnessing the effect of what happens in society when marriage is redefined or just plain ignored before giving birth to and raising children. Studies show that 93 percent of children born in the United States in 1964 were born to married parents. In 2007, only 59 percent of all births in the nation occurred to married couples. The same study showed out-of-wedlock child bearing had risen, from 7% to 41%. The negative effect of this trend is directly tied to a rising rate of poverty in our nation. Mothers who have children out of wedlock almost always end up as single parents, and struggle to make a decent living. Although single parents sometimes do a very commendable job of rearing their children, many children raised without a father are much more

---

3. Confusing the issue is the fact that churches today are divided—some have been developing a liberal social gospel, while others remain conservative in their theology. The liberal churches feel they are right to advance secular state policies even if they conflict with the sacred Scriptures. It is my opinion that these liberal churches are led by "false prophets."

susceptible to experiencing a life of crime. Data shows that single parents were six times more likely to be poor than were married couples.[4] The best weapon against poverty and resulting higher crime rates today could very well be a return to the pre-1964 Christian laws regarding marriage, and formerly accepted Christian mores about family responsibilities.

While a Christian presence in society is important, I must add that equally important are the governing laws and constitutions passed on to our own time by our founders. I have demonstrated that these almost always had a Biblical basis. Therefore, so long as they continue without amendment, they help keep this a Christian nation. The most important way to secure our God-given freedoms is to keep our school curriculum honest and faithful in teaching the truth about our Constitutional founding. In Europe today secularization has almost totally taken over. We will follow suit if we do not, once again, promote in our schools a true remembrance of our founding history. This is what motivates me to write this book. We are allowing the secular unbeliever to redefine, and even informally amend, the meaning of our Constitutional protections and rights. In the process we are losing rights and the state is becoming the absolute "moral" (maybe better put, "amoral") authority over our lives.

A part of our history no longer taught in our schools is how we, uniquely, have been subject to what are called great revival movements of the church. Look at the time line of American history I have prepared, which shows the history of our nation in successive "Great Awakenings."[5] In each national revival on that Time Line of Christian Movements in America, new leaders arose in various venues to "leaven" society. Note that these leaders were both church ministers and laymen

---

4. This data was taken from *Backgrounder*, published by The American Heritage Foundation, Sept 16, 2010.

5. See Appendix 10.

of different secular careers. If this is to happen again, it will require a new great spiritual awakening in our country. I pray for that day. God gave us the formula as he dealt with the backsliding of his nation Israel.

In Second Chronicles 7: 13 it is recorded:

If my people, who are called by my name, will humble themselves, and pray, and seek my face and will turn from their wicked ways, then will I hear from heaven and will forgive their sin and will heal their land.

The point is, first our churches must, once again, become the powerful influence for righteousness in America, and then the fire of reformation can spread again throughout all of society. God has not created the world just to abandon it and leave the outcome of history totally to we human-beings. He both has given the church a role and responsibility to make reformation within nations, and at the same time, God has his own sovereign control of the end result of history. The first part of this conclusion is about our human responsibility in a Christian nation. The second part is about God's sovereignty in history.

God's Sovereignty in History

History is a study of human progression throughout time. For most, that movement is usually depicted as nothing more than a power struggle in which empires rise and fall, and of tyrants dreaming of world domination. An endless future cycle of power struggles can be predicted even into the exploration of space and "new worlds." However, the Biblical perspective of history is different. The Judeo-Christian perspective of history is one of providential origin, purpose, and a glorious destiny. God is the creator of all things; man is in rebellion against his creator; and the basic problem in history is that of sin. Sin is systemic in all human institutions. History is the battle of Christ versus antichrist; and man's basic need is salvation through the blood of Jesus Christ, and then life in Christ and willful obedience to God's law. Finally, the promise of Biblical history is a new heaven and earth of perfect righteousness and justice. History outside of Christianity is an endless cyclical struggle of might makes right. History in the mind of the Christian is a linear view of time with a beginning, a guidebook for the journey, and a victorious end.

God's creation is wonderfully balanced and preserved by natural laws he put in place. Otherwise, sinful man would finally totally corrupt the world and, like the antediluvian world, our world would degenerate into utter chaos and violence. God's laws control the physical, or material, world we live in so that planets don't collide with one another, and we can depend on the rising and setting of the sun, and cycle of seasons. This despite the fact we also must contend with a cursed creation (because of the Fall in Eden), with its storms and earthquakes, etc. But we often forget, that just as laws of physics exist, so do laws of economics and politics, also set in place by God. Since my concern has been mostly with the actions of governments and nation-states, I remind you that God ordained the establishment of nation-states so that a balance of power would naturally exist in our world to hold back the possibility of worldwide tyranny. History reveals a continuing rise and fall of evil empires, but this does not, in my opinion, predict a final victorious "Nimrod" who will rule the world.[6] Precisely because of this, I do not expect, nor do I think the Bible predicts, that one day worldwide tyranny under a final Anti-Christ will totally engulf all mankind. The purpose of the "kingdom of God" within the nations is to one day prepare the world for heaven on earth under the King of Kings. When the Christ returns he will judge all mankind, separating the "wheat" from the "tares," and setting up a righteous rule of perfect justice and freedom. The church was instituted of God not to fail but to bring in the "Kingdom of God."

However, the concern of this book is not with eschatology but has been concerned with a single progressive movement in history. That movement has been the journey of specific nations that have contributed to the development of free republics. The thesis has been that man is not the source of freedom, but the source is God, and his blueprint found in the Bible. The printing of Bibles in the common languages during the Reformation of European nations was foundational to the rise of modern republics. As I said at the start of this inquiry the progression of this development of republics was like a fully wound-up clock set down in the laws of Moses for the benefit of God's chosen nation. His chosen people were to be priests to the rest of the nations. As priests, their primary responsibility was to introduce the world to the one true God and all of his attributes. One attribute of God is that of liberty under his sovereignty. God showed his sovereignty in Israel's history by miraculous intervention on its behalf; and he showed his interest in liberty by asking the Hebrews for their free consensual submission to his law. If Israel obeyed God's law it would prosper and be blessed. If it disobeyed the law of God, it would be judged and disciplined. In this warning we have a picture of God's providential laws of social and political cause and effect.

Israel's disobedience over time brought the downfall of her republic, and even more important brought the downfall of her witness to the nations regarding God's open invitation for others to be grafted into his family.[7] God did not want Is-

---

6. Nimrod was the tyrant at Babel whom God put down by instituting the establishment of nation-states each with their own languages. Some anticipate a new "Nimrod" they call the Anti-Christ they say will finally rule the world.

7. Consider the Old Testament Book of Jonah, where God actually forces Jonah to preach to the terribly wicked Assyrians, in Nineveh. It appears most of the city repented of their wickedness. Yet, just 23 years after Jonah died, the Assyrians sacked Samaria. Could history have been changed if Israel had itself remained faithful and had reached out earlier to the many Gentile nations around it?

rael to isolate herself as though God loved it only. When God judged Israel and sent her into captivity, it was not only a disciplinary act, but was also an act of making her a priest to the nations, as with Daniel and Esther.

When a nation rejects the Gospel of Christ, that nation also rejects all the fringe benefits that can accompany it. Throughout the world today, Christianity is the religion with the most followers. As you look at the worldwide influence of Christianity, it has done more to change people's lives, for the better, than any religion. All people within nations unaffected by a powerful Christian influence are still lands of tyranny and oppression. Yes, republics in history have arisen out of pagan cultures, or in a modern setting out of secular cultures, but they have always been inferior. Furthermore, it is questionable whether any people would have discovered the necessary ingredients in law for truly free societies without some exposure to God's revelation to Moses. In addition, I suggest, no republic today will long exist in a nation that has no Judeo-Christian foundation. It is born out of that religious heritage and can only survive in it. When Jesus Christ came into history, his "great commission" to his disciples was to go into all nations and make more disciples. One eventual fringe benefit of that "great commission" has been a gradual "winding up the liberty time wheel" again resulting in the development of modern free republics.

Wherever the church has not yet produced national republics it has prepared the soil, so to speak, by freeing men and women from the power of sin in their individual lives. Today the Christian church, in all its diversity, is rapidly growing in "third-world" nations and, as a result, they too may experience reformation politically, in the future. Regardless of the outcome of events occurring in the less developed world today, it is not too late for America to rededicate itself to its original founding principles. Our American republic was openly born out of a conscious effort to apply Biblical principles of governing found in the laws of Moses. We cannot know the future state of our union, but I hope it stays on the tracks of the providential "train engineer" for a ride right into his "promised land."

Let me take you back again to the era of our early colonial founding. A doctrinal expression of the nature of God that explains the manner in which God is sovereign and yet man is free was made in what is called the Westminster Confession of 1646. The Westminster Assembly that drew up this confession of faith was embraced by the Presbyterians of Scotland and in America. The Puritans of that day also embraced this confession. Of course, this Westminster Assembly met during the English Civil War when the Kingdoms of Scotland, England, Wales, and Ireland all ended up under the rule of a Puritan commonwealth. I quote Article Three, sections 1 and 2:

> God from all eternity, did, by the most wise and holy counsel of his own will, freely, and unchangeably ordain whatsoever comes to pass: yet so, as thereby neither is God the author of sin, nor is violence offered to the will of the creatures, nor is the liberty or contingency of second causes taken away, but rather established. Although God knows whatsoever may or can come to pass upon all supposed conditions; yet hath he not decreed anything because he foresaw it as future, as that which would come to pass, upon such conditions.[8]

Here in this Article of the Westminster Confession, which is designed to explain the doctrine of God's sovereignty, we have a clear admission that it in no way takes away the doctrine of the free will of man. This supports the Christian belief of a sovereign God in history and yet a God of

---

8. The Westminster Confession of Faith (1646), www.newtowncrommelin.com/wp-content/uploads/westminster-confession-of-faith.pdf/Westminster_conf_faith.html.

liberty without in any manner diminishing either attribute. It also supports the notion I have developed in this book, that a free nation can be under God and at the same time under the consent of the governed. This is God's law of cause and effect. God is the first cause of everything, but man is created capable of creating second causes. However, God's ultimate effect stemming from his sovereignty cannot be averted by man's second causes. Man is free in the sense that he can make choices not in God's will, but man is also therefore accountable for such choices. Under God's sovereignty man faces consequences, of which he is forewarned under God's law. Moses' Book of Deuteronomy ends with a listing of choices that will bring judgment, and choices that will bring grace. However, man cannot save himself by the effect of his choices, and is totally dependent on God's grace. If man is faithful to the law of God he can reach a place of limited ideal existence in history, but only as a taste of what will ultimately be on eternity's side.

Not everything that has occurred in history was God's will. Not everything we do as individuals is God's will. But God will not be mocked. Nothing can undo his first causes in creation, or the ultimate effect his will has on the future. The Christian view of humanity is that we are free moral agents. If we are wise, we will trust and obey God and join the movement of history that is his providential plan and purpose. In the kingdoms of this world man is required to submit to the state. That submission is forced and is slavery. In the "Kingdom of God" one is drawn by the Spirit to freely submit. Submission to God is an act of freedom. The "Kingdom of God" is maintained and spread by a loving obedience of the heart. A Christian nation moves in the providence of God by revival, followed by backsliding, followed by revival. The movement may have its ups and downs, but like the stock market, should over time be a steady climb and not a steady decline. In the words of Jesus, ". . . upon this rock I will build my church and the gates of hell shall not prevail against it."[9]

This book is not intended to make anyone despair. However, it is written to bring a great awakening so as to preserve our children in the power of the Gospel unto eternal life, and freedom in the remainder our given time in history. God is still looking for the church to make reformation in the world. We should not be surrendering to the spirit of antichrist as though God has failed. The state should not replace the role of God. If it does, it will only produce tyranny. However, the state, under God, produces freedom and justice in a fallen world. That was God's will and purpose in ordaining the establishment of the state.

> *Let every soul be subject unto the higher powers. For there is no power but of God. [Existing] powers ... are ordained of God....For rulers are not supposed to be a terror to good works, but to the evil.... For he is the minister of God to thee for good; but if thou do that which is evil, be afraid, for he beareth not the sword in vain.*[10]

God has never dealt with any nation as closely and fully as he has with Israel. He, nevertheless, is directly concerned with every nation as a governmental entity. He has even determined their geographical boundaries and the time each would rise and fall. All governmental authority comes from God, and rulers are to be ministers of God over the people for good and not for evil. But, ultimately governments usually become instruments for evil and not for good. At that moment the people cry out to God for deliverance.[11] Government is there to enforce justice when the people take up criminal ways; and the church must be there to uphold God's Law when the government promotes un-

---

9. Matthew 16: 18.
10. Romans 13: 1–7.
11. Acts 17:24–27.

godly ways. There should not be a religious test to run for public office; but likewise the government should make no law prohibiting free exercise of "true-religion". The role of the governor is to be a minister of God, upholding the Law of God.

The lawgiver, Moses, said to Israel, *"What nation is there so great, that hath statutes and judgments so righteous as all this law, which I set before you."*[12] Any modern-day government would do well to emulate the Hebrew republic. Without question, our American founders tried to do just that. Many have said of America, what nation is so great as this governmental system in America under its Judeo-Christian culture and written Constitution! Like the Hebrew psalmist, we can boast, "I will walk in freedom for I have sought out your precepts [O Lord]."[13]

Sadly, however, modern political and judicial practices in America are departing from this divine standard. The philosophies of evolution (a living constitution) and relativism (pluralism) dominate our schools of law today. Principles of righteousness and justice, rooted in the nature of God and in his revelation have been largely replaced by legislation based on "stateism" and human licentiousness. Even the Ten Commandments are banned from our schools, despite the fact that they are engraved in the supreme court building itself.

It is not the intent of this book to create a battle plan to save America from those who despise the founding of our nation, and who desire to create a "new America". I will, of course, join that effort in every way I can, but my purpose here is only to reveal the glory and reality of the Biblical roots of our republic. I have accomplished that goal.[14]

---

12. Deuteronomy 4:8.

13. Psalms 119:45.

14. Both Democrat and Republican Parties are today infected with the European "Enlightenment" worldview of stateism as opposed to the "Reformation" worldview that promoted limited delegated powers for central government. Republicans do more lip service to limited government, but are not doing much to educate and return us to our founding Constitutional system. I appeal to all true Biblical believers, Democrat or Republican to get serious about helping create a "reconstructionist" reformation in American today. See my epilogue for a definition of "reconstructionism."

Epilogue

It is always good for the reader to have some understanding of the presuppositions guiding the arguments developed in an author's writings.

For example, the Enlightenment philosophes referred to in Part One of my book did not start with a belief that there was a God that was involved in and directing history. If they believed in God at all, they were deists. That is, they believed that after God created the world he withdrew from it and left its fate totally in the hands of man. Without any aid to be found in the Scriptures, man developed his own ideas and societies. To them, man alone is responsible for the future of the world. Today the disciples of the French Revolution rightfully call themselves progressives. To them, one should not look back for wisdom, but one should progressively look ahead, as if there were no absolute truths stemming from earlier times that are applicable to all of time. To them, the journey is one of evolution, or a struggle to escape old superstitions and to instead build a man-made utopia.

In contrast, the Reformationists referred to in Part One of my book believed that a sovereign God created the world and that he providentially cares about the creation and is involved in the outcomes of history. The future of the world is entirely in God's hands, and mankind has been given only limited authority and dominion over his fate. Through special-revelation, God gave man a moral code and a template for governing one another justly. If humankind ignores God's revelation, it suffers under tyranny. If humankind applies God's wisdom in establishing all his governing institutions, it enjoys God's blessing and freedom from tyranny. The Christian religion is an historical faith. This worldview requires one to be a conservative. A conservative looks for the wisdom of the past. He preserves the lessons of cause and effect so that his children do not repeat the mistakes of the past. He holds on to the proven paths of good and just societies. When his nation backslides into old destructive paths, he works to reconstruct it according to the wisdom of his nation's founders. He knows man is an imperfect being and in need of salvation, and he thus looks to God for guidance, trusting in God's future promises of a "heavenly" utopia on earth.

Obviously, as the author of this book, I have tried to demonstrate the truth of the "Reformation Man's" presuppositions. Christians whose writings I have cited mostly classify themselves as believers in Christian Reconstructionism. This means that they believe that the American founders were drawing on Biblical revelation regarding Israel's Mosaic constitution as the best guide to construct a new national republic. The beliefs characteristic of Christian Reconstructionism include: 1) a strong faith in progressive individual regeneration by the Holy Spirit, which makes one capable of self government, and, of necessity, precedes all successful national republican development; 2) not a belief in theocracy, but rather a belief in something called theonomy; 3) a belief in the Christian eschatological viewpoint of postmillennialism; and 4) a belief in separate and limited human spheres of law and authority--- minimal state power, free enterprise economics, and an independent sphere of authority for the church.

First, as regards individualism, it is about individual submission to God's law, not by force, but by the voluntary will. It is opposed to collectivism that forces, either through a church or through the state, submission to a moral code. True believers in Christ should be free to bring their values into all parts of society, the best they can accomplish it. No society in history was more successful at this than has been the American republic. All individuals are equally responsible to God, family and country, regardless of race or ethnicity. Individual virtue and integrity are the only sure foundation upon which to build a free country. Let the true church compete for the heart and soul of society one convert at a time, and it will eventually win against all adversaries.

Second, as regards theonomy, it is about widespread individual submission to God's law, and not about collective consensus building to make the law. In a Christian nation, no civil law should ever contradict the law of God. There is no place for one single established religion, but no prohibition regarding the free exercise of religion, either. Biblical law must be equally applied to all people, regardless of their beliefs. Civil law established under Biblical law should not regulate beliefs, but only actions. Judeo-Christian mores will govern everyone, but other religious rites of worship may exist so long as they are tolerant of Christian laws of behavior.[1] All law, whether secular or religious, is enacted morality. The source of the law is the god of the society. In secular societies god is man himself. Either one is under God's Law or under man's law. There is no neutral position for any system under the law. In a theonomy, open hostility to God's law should not be tolerated. God's law is there to subvert sin. Compare that to a pluralistic freedom for all to determine what is right in their own eyes, and the resulting tolerance of sin with its corrosive effect on society.

Third, as regards the postmillennial future of the world, it is a belief that God cannot fail. Reconstruction may take many wrong turns, but ultimately the gates of hell shall not prevail against the church.[2] The only satisfactory goal is that America become and remain a Christian nation. If America cannot maintain that status, the church will make disciples in other nations who will conform to the task. Nations will rise and fall over time until those that survive until Christ's return will each be somewhere on the reconstructionist road to freedom and true justice.[3] God's salvation not only rescues individuals, but has its positive effect, as well, on society as a whole.

For the times any Christian individual actually lived through, it most likely always appeared that evil was triumphal. But consider whether the following sweeping review of history actually confirms that the opposite is true, thus, confirming the postmillennial viewpoint that Christ will come again after a long growing victory of the church in history.[4] The antediluvian world had fallen under the evil dominion of the "way of Cain." Because the whole world of man was filled with violence and had turned against God and would have worshiped the Devil and come under his dominion in one world government, the judgment of God came down upon man in the form of a literal global Biblical Flood. Only Noah found grace in the eyes of the Lord God. Noah and his family were saved, by the building of the Ark, and after the Great Flood his sons would repopulate the earth. But after a few generations, Nimrod

---

1. Contrary to a theonomy, sometimes in Western society today the civil law directly, or indirectly as well, forces Christians to be tolerant of behavior that is hostile to their values, while at the same time allowing the freedom of Christian religious worship. Law always regulates behavior. Today in America we live under a combination of Christian law and also law that is hostile to Christianity. Our nation is not a theonomy any longer, but neither is it totally secular.

2. Matthew 16: 13-19 and 28: 16-20.

3. Only God knows the hour or the day of Christ's return; but the Church will go on having a positive effect on human societies until he comes.

4. The term millennium should not be interpreted to refer to an actual 1000 years, but rather, as used in ancient literature, be symbolic of a very long time.

arose to unite the world again against God, at Babel. At that moment in history, God ordained the establishment of nation-states by confusing the languages of the people. God put in place a natural balance of power to forever hold back the rise again of a totally global evil empire. Thus, every new "Babylon" is destroyed in history.

A mega worldview of political science appears throughout the Scriptures in the form of a spiritual and worldly battle for the soul of mankind. Behind the scenes it is between God and the Devil, but on a physical level it is also between nation-states striving for world dominance. God is involved in human history to direct the outcome, but at the same time God allows man the free will to choose between good and evil. One way God holds back total world tyranny is through national warfare. A balance of power mechanism evolves throughout history in which evil nation holds back evil nation. However, there eventually arises an evil national leader who gains an advantage over other nations through some new method or technology of warfare. It is no coincidence that the first new "would-be Nimrod" arose out of that land of ancient Babel. This terrifying war machine was called Assyria and no nation seemed able to stop its advance. It is no coincidence that Assyria was allowed to conqueror Israel; that Assyria was swallowed up by Babylon; and Babylon conquered Jerusalem taking captive God's prophet Daniel.

At that point in history all who believed in God could not be blamed for fearing that all was lost and that it would only be a matter of time before the world was ruled by evil again even as it had been before the Great Flood. Daniel's visions of four successively larger empires would leave one thinking God had failed, and the Devil had won. Because the way of man-led tyranny can be so beastly, Daniel pictures each coming empire as some form of animal. Already the symbol of Babylon was a winged lion. The city of Babylon displayed this symbol of its power on blue and gold tiles at the towers of all its gates. The second empire, that overthrows Babylon, was larger than the first. It was the Medo-Persian Empire and was pictured by Daniel as both a bear and a ram. The third empire, that overthrows the Persians, was larger yet, and was pictured as both a four-winged-leopard with four heads, or as a He-goat with four horns.[5] Finally the fourth empire shown to Daniel in his vision was a nondescript beast exceedingly strong, with iron teeth, ten horns, and whose empire is so large it represents a tyranny like none ever witnessed in history. This beast was representative of the Roman Empire. Interestingly, the beast pictured in the Book of Revelation, written by the Apostle John while under Roman imprisonment, is clearly a deeper spiritual revealing of Daniel's fourth beast.

God did not reveal the future to Daniel to make him, and all who would read his prophecy, lose hope. Our problem is that we are finite and can only see the moment in time we have been given. The marvelous nature of the revelation of God, we call the Bible, is that it gives us a true historical perspective. We know it is true because its prophecies have come true, as those of Daniel did. We may not see much to hope about in our lifetime, but we can trust the vision of the future given to us by God in his Word. As I have demonstrated in this book already, Scripture given to us by Moses describes a chosen nation not designed to be a tyranny but a free commonwealth. The chosen nation's government was designed for it by God. Israel was expected to be an influence for freedom and justice. Israel was to be a people whom the rest of the nations would observe and wonder at its just law and constitution. In Daniel's time the chosen-nation had been wiped out,

---

5. This turns out to represent the conquest of Alexander the Great, whose empire divided into four kingdoms under Greek kings after the death of Alexander. The swiftness of a leopard fits the army of Alexander; and the He-goat was the symbol on all Macedonian coins in that era of history.

and its influence seemingly destroyed. Daniel gives his readers a perspective on history that let's us see the rise and fall of tyrannies that seem too mighty to fall; but then reveals a small stone cut out of the "mountain" of human tyranny which strikes and "crushes all those kingdoms, bringing them to an end."[6] Daniel's prophecy ends predicting that a Messiah (the savior of the world) will come out of Israel when it has returned from exile to its homeland.[7]

With the cross of Christ, Satan was cast down from heaven, from where he had continually accused God's chosen ones.[8] Now Christ sits at the right hand of God the Father, pleading the cause of his holy priesthood of believers who are scattered throughout the nations to bring light and hope into the world. More than ever before, since the "year of our Lord's coming," the warfare of history is now a story of mixed evil and good within nations that affects the rise and fall of earthly kingdoms. The progression of history slowly reveals an international growing "Kingdom of God."[9] The combined good and evil that motivated the Crusades in the 11th and 12th centuries checked both the growth of empire in the Middle East and in Eastern Europe. God's judgment came against the evil within both Islam and Christianity in that age. The combined good and evil that motivated the Byzantine, Mongol, and Islamists emperors effectively checked the spread of world-empire in the 13th century. The combined good and evil that motivated the Western European kings in their conquest of the Western Hemisphere, Africa, and the Far East effectively destroyed the last strongholds of ancient idolatry. The new nations born out of those broken European empires also held back world government, while at the same time God was expanding the reach of the "Kingdom of God." Finally, reformation, within Christendom itself, made possible the rise of the United States of America, which was providentially called upon to hold back Nazism and Communism in the 20th century. In our own time, the United Nations, which some have prophesied will produce a final evil and truly world-empire to be ruled by "the Anti-Christ," has actually been a failure. Ironically, the UN is dependent on strong nation-state balance-of- power politics that has held back world tyranny since the first Babylon.

When evil triumphs and large regional empires are formed, mankind often loses heart and develops a defeatist attitude. But God cannot be defeated, and his church is here in the "last days"[10] to bring in the "Kingdom of God." God will give his priesthood of believers the final victory as individual souls are saved one by one. He will also hold back the enemy as needed by use of natural calamities of either man-made military action, or other judgments through acts of God in nature. There will be no final "Anti-Christ" victory through the rise of one man (like Nimrod). In the final analysis, the Devil has never won in this long struggle for world domination. He has lost again and again and again. Never lose sight of that. Postmillennial doctrine is a faith in the mission of the church and all of history reviewed above really confirms it.

Fourth, the Reconstructionists believe that God also provides in his Word the best basis from which man may be governed while awaiting the return of Christ. To them, the constitutional structure of government under God's ideal template will be one of limited freedom, limited and divided governmental authority, and no universality of power by any institution. There is room

---

6. Daniel 2: 44-45.

7. See Appendix 4, Exhibit B.

8. Isaiah14: 12 and Luke 10: 18, and Revelation 12: 7-11.

9. Matthew13: 24-30.

10. "The last days" is a phrase that should be interpreted to mean all of history since the Resurrection of Christ and the establishment of the Church.

only for the universality of the rule of God's revealed law.

> In a Biblically reconstructed society, government needs to be republican. The functions of government need to be limited to providing defense, maintaining order, assuring justice, and punishing criminals. Education needs to be a responsibility solely of parents... Only churches and other private agencies, not the government, should provide relief and welfare to the poor.[11]

These examples of a properly reconstructed society are but a few, and no nation would probably be totally identical to another developed under this template. No nation will ever reach perfection, until the one perfect Lord and Savior reigns and all the "tares" are removed from their place in the Day of Judgment. Let all God's people occupy to that end till he comes. Trust in God. Be not afraid. Be each one faithful to the end.

The tendency of many is to blame leaders who have led us astray down humanistic paths rather than keeping our nation on the path of our founders who sought the wisdom from above.[12] But the crisis that threatens us, the force that could topple our monuments and destroy our foundations, is within ourselves. We must choose whether we will be our own god, or whether we will submit to freedom only found in the one true God. At the same time, we cannot escape the fact that we all live under the effects of God's natural laws that were put in place from the beginning. We have discovered the natural laws of nature, put in place at creation; but have we discovered the moral laws of cause and effect that no society can escape? Nations rise and fall, and freedom within nations rises and falls according to the Creator's laws of moral cause and effect. Free nations must learn not to give their consent to rulers who lead them away from godly wisdom passed on by our forefathers. Ultimately the "buck stops here," with ourselves.

---

11. Gary Scott Smith, *God and Politics, Four Views on the Reformation of Civil Government,* (Phillipsburg, NJ: Presbyterian and Reformed Publishing Company, 1989), 18.

12. For those who may have been looking for a more through development of our recent history under the presidencies of Bill Clinton, George W. Bush, and Barack Obama, that has not been my intended goal in writing this book. There are others who have directly addressed these things. I refer you to Joel McDurmon, *God verses Socialism.* (Powder Springs, GA: American Vision Press, 2009). Our nation today faces serious threats to its liberty, but I cannot cover all that involves in this book.

Appendicies

1	*The Liberty Time Wheel* (with fold-out)	149
2	*The Time-line of Western History (1500–1800 A.D.)*	151
3	*18 Principles of Social Science Undergirding the Hebrew Commonwealth*	152
4 A	*The Hammurabi Code of Law* (sample)	153
4 B	*The Biblical Judeo-Christian Connection*	154
5	*The Mosaic Constitution*	157
6	*The 12 Tribes of Israel & Map*	158
7	*The Time-line of the Hebrew Republic*	160
8	*The National Hebrew States-General*	163
9 A	*King Alfred's Doom Book (Rooted in Mosaic Law)*	164
9 B	*Due Process of Law (Rooted in Deuteronomy)*	165
10	*Great Christian Movements in American History*	166

Appendix 1

THE LIBERTY TIME WHEEL

My thesis is not that the American Republic will eventually turn into an exact copy of the ancient Mosaic Hebrew Republic; but rather that all republics are born out of a Judeo-Christian influence, and cannot survive outside of that Biblical influence. Each republic formed in history also has a tendency to degenerate, due to the fallen nature of man. Hebrew history moved from a Mosaic republic into a continually corrupting form of constitutional monarchy. At times, its kings were held accountable to the law and, at times, they acted as absolute monarchs. The Greek and Roman republics degenerated into destructive class-warfare, because they lacked the discipline created by a constitutional value system found only in *true-religion*. The British common law monarchy degenerated from constitutional monarchy based on *true-religion* into absolute monarchy, and then evolved as a parliamentary republic. The American Republic was born out of true-religion, as the most conscious endeavor to copy the principles of Mosaic republicanism ever attempted in history. Though I don't reflect it in my Liberty Time Wheel, all modern republics of Western Civilization face an uncertain future as they have become divided over whether they will remain nations "under God" or under absolute democracy (socialism). Unquestionably, the *true-religion* of Judeo-Christianity will Providentially continue to make reformation spiritually and socially in history to the glorious end of time, culminating in Christ's return.

The compressed period on the Liberty Time Wheel of 1117 years, between 246 BC and 871 AD was divided as follows:

246 – 49 BC: the last years of the Roman Republic (Punic Wars and Civil Wars)
49 BC – 476 AD: Julius Caesar Dictatorship and a succession of Roman Emperors
476 AD – 871 AD: the rise of Christendom till the English King Alfred

Now if the ministry that brought death, which was engraved in letters on stone, [came with a fading glory] . . . how much more glorious is the ministry that brings righteousness! . . .

Now the Lord is Spirit, and where the Spirit of the Lord is there is freedom. And we, who with unveiled faces all reflect the Lord's glory, are being transformed into his likeness with an ever-increasing glory, which comes from the Lord who is Spirit.

2 CORINTHIANS 3: 7-18

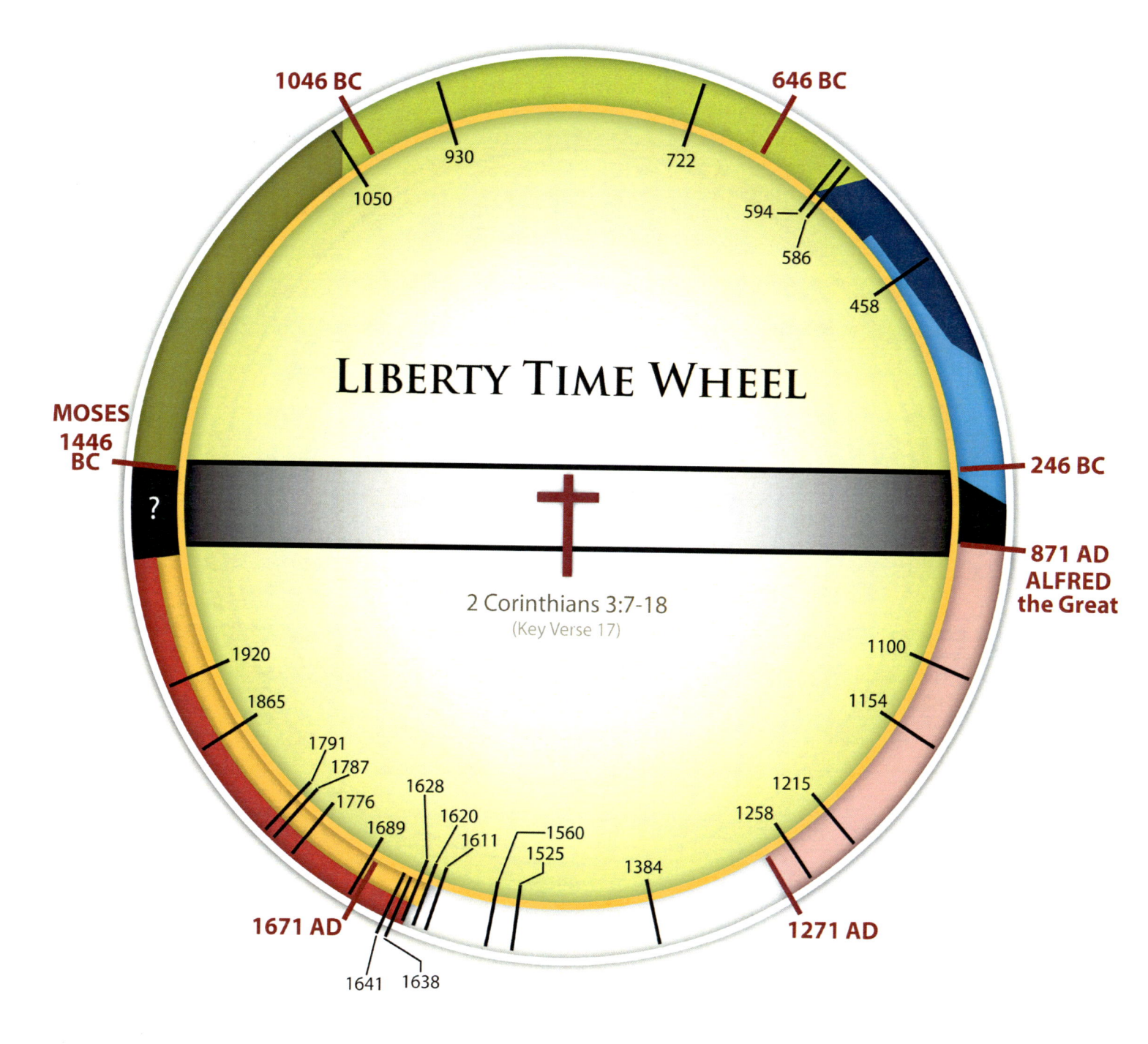

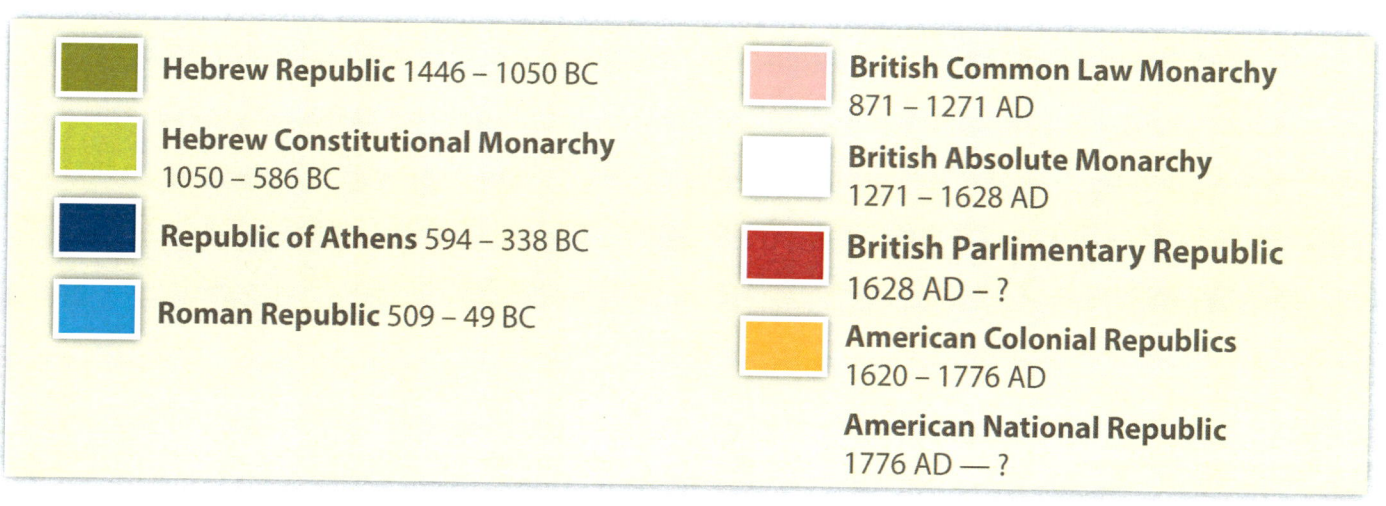

LIBERTY TIME WHEEL

2 Corinthians 3:7-18
(Key Verse 17)

MOSES 1446 BC
1046 BC — 930, 1050
646 BC — 722, 594, 586, 458
246 BC
871 AD ALFRED the Great — 1100, 1154, 1215, 1258, 1384
1271 AD
1671 AD — 1641, 1638, 1689, 1628, 1620, 1611, 1560, 1525
1920, 1865, 1791, 1787, 1776

- **Hebrew Republic** 1446 – 1050 BC
- **Hebrew Constitutional Monarchy** 1050 – 586 BC
- **Republic of Athens** 594 – 338 BC
- **Roman Republic** 509 – 49 BC
- **British Common Law Monarchy** 871 – 1271 AD
- **British Absolute Monarchy** 1271 – 1628 AD
- **British Parliamentary Republic** 1628 AD – ?
- **American Colonial Republics** 1620 – 1776 AD
- **American National Republic** 1776 AD — ?

149

Appendix 2

TIME LINE OF WESTERN HISTORY 1500–1800 A.D.

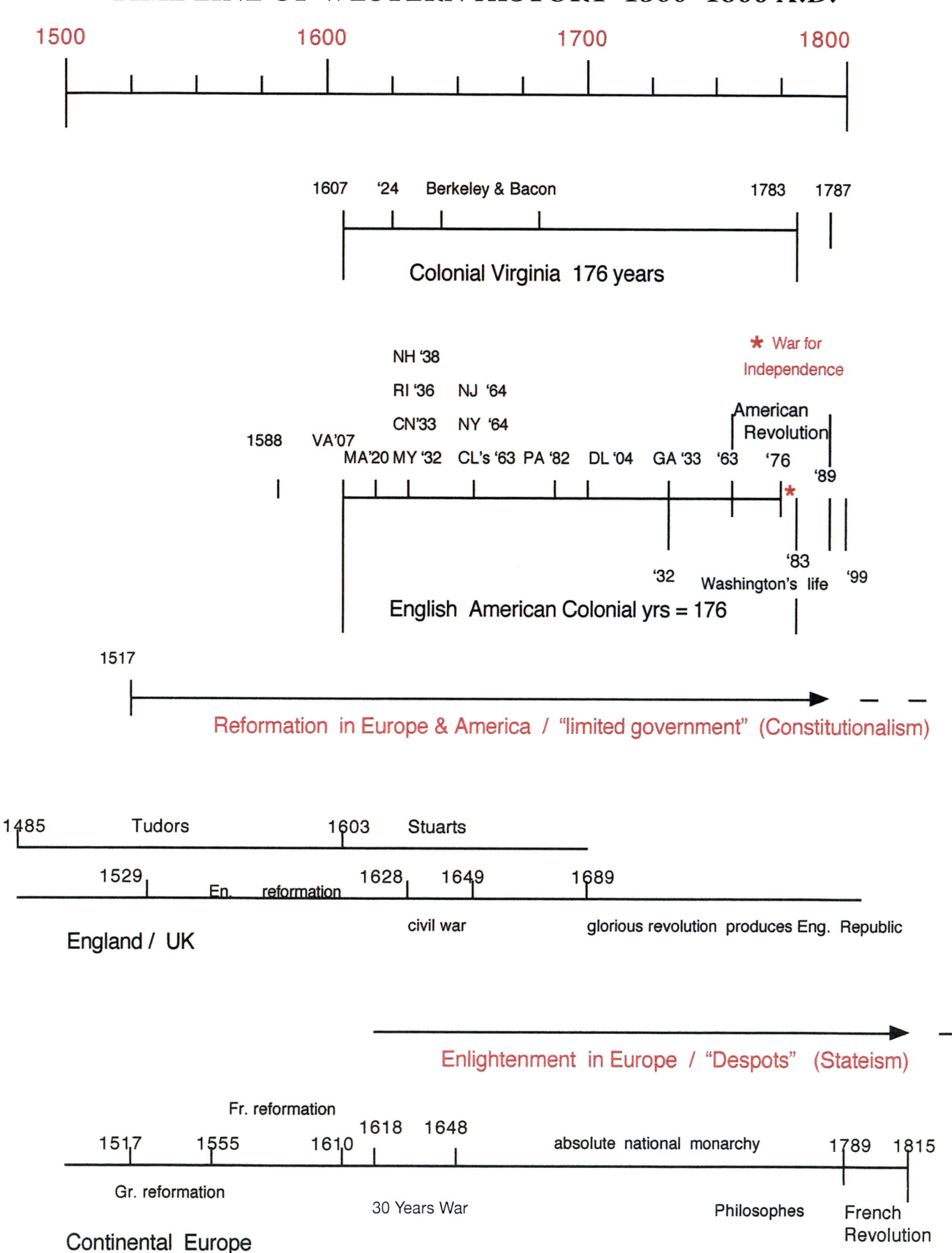

1500 — 1600 — 1700 — 1800

Colonial Virginia 176 years
1607, '24, Berkeley & Bacon, 1783, 1787

English American Colonial yrs = 176
1588; VA '07; MA '20; MY '32; CN '33; RI '36; NH '38; CL's '63; NJ '64; NY '64; PA '82; DL '04; GA '33; '63; American Revolution '76; '83; '89; '99
'32 Washington's life
* War for Independence

Reformation in Europe & America / "limited government" (Constitutionalism) — 1517 →

England / UK
1485 Tudors — 1603 Stuarts
1529 En. reformation — 1628 — 1649 civil war — 1689 glorious revolution produces Eng. Republic

Enlightenment in Europe / "Despots" (Stateism) →

Continental Europe
1517 Gr. reformation — 1555 — Fr. reformation 1610 — 1618 — 1648 30 Years War — absolute national monarchy — Philosophes — 1789 French Revolution — 1815

151

Appendix 3

18 Principles of Social Science Under-girding the Hebrew Commonwealth

According to Rev. E.C. Wines

1. The Unity of God
2. National Unity
3. Civil Liberty
4. Political Equality
5. Elected Magistracy
6. Popular Sovereignty
7. Government Accountability
8. Speedy and Impartial Justice
9. No Standing Army
10. Agrarianism
11. Universal Skills and Industry
12. Private Property Rights
13. Sacredness of the Family
14. Sanctity of Life
15. Universal Literacy Education
16. Checks and Balances
17. Social Union
18. Venerable Public Opinion

Source: *Commentaries On the Laws of the Ancient Hebrews*, by E.C. Wines, page 445.

Appendix 4

EXHIBIT A

Hammurabi Creates a Code of Law in Mesopotamia
1780 BC

Hammurabi's Babylonian empire stretched from the Persian Gulf north throughout the land between the rivers: Euphrates and Tigris. The Greeks called it Mesopotamia, meaning the land between the rivers. King Hammurabi's code of law was probably the first written code, and was chiseled in the ancient cuneiform system of writing on a tall back stone stele preserved down to our own time. The Mosaic Code of Law was more than 300 years younger, but both spoke of justice in terms of phrases like, "an eye for an eye" or "bone for bone" or "a tooth for a tooth." However, this is were their similarity ended. Note below the sharp difference in the law as applied to different and unequal classes of the Babylonian society. Take a look again at Chapter Seven which explains the magnificent system of adversarial justice found in the Mosaic constitution in contrast to Hammurabi's code which is Draconian in comparison.

> If a seignior has destroyed the eye of a member of the aristocracy, they shall destroy his eye.
>
> If he has broken another seignior's bone, they shall break his bone.
>
> If he has destroyed the eye of a commoner or broken the bone of a commoner, he shall pay one mina of silver.
>
> If he has destroyed the eye of a seignior's slave or broken the bone of a seignior's slave, he shall pay one half his value.
>
> If a seignior has knocked out a tooth of a seignior of his own rank, they shall knock out his tooth.
>
> If he has knocked out a commoner's tooth, he shall pay one third mina of silver ... [1]

---

1. James B. Pritchard, *Ancient Near Eastern Texts*, 3rd edition (Princeton, NJ: Princeton University Press, 1969), 164-180.

Appendix 4

EXHIBIT B
The Biblical Judeo-Christian Connection

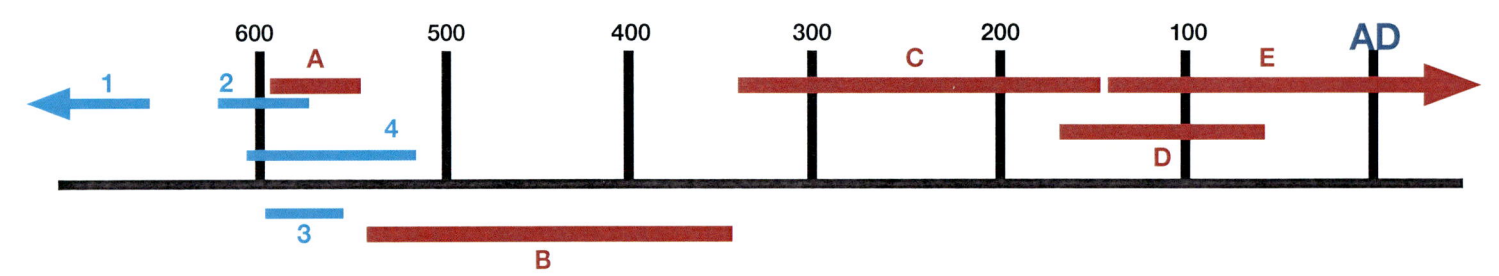

The Kingdom of Israel split in 930 BC; and the northern kingdom thereafter had no trurely good rulers. It befell God's judgement in 722 BC, and its people became subjects of the evil Assyrian Empire. Finally in 609 BC, following the death of Josiah, king of the southern Kingdom of Judah, kings of Jerusalem became vassals of Babylon. In 586 BC Jerusalem was sacked and that was the end of the ancient Jewish state. But, at the close of the Kingdom of Judah there arose **four major prophets** who predicted the transition of God's plan from the old to a **new** covenant. These prophets anticipated the time when all of history would then be divided between time before Christ (Messiah) and time since the *year of our LORD* (anno Domini or A.D.). Since Israel had not fulfilled its responsibility to be a priest to the nations, now a Christian era would fulfill that responsibility. But in preparation for the coming Messiah, the Jews would come under gentile rule and be scattered among the nations. Thus they would be forced to be a priest to the nations. They are unique in history as a people who never lost their national identity, though they lost their homeland. They were also promised the right to return to the homeland, where they would enjoy quasi self government while under a succession of gentile empires.

After the failed reformation led by Kings Hezekiah and Josiah, Judah fell to the Neo-Babylonian Empire (**A**). But those taken into Babylonian exile were given the right to return to Jerusalem and rebuild the temple and walls while under the rule of the Persian Empire (**B**). Then, when Alexander the Great conquered the Persian Empire, the Jews came under Hellenistic rule (**C**). The Persians had allowed them significant self governing rights, but the Greeks tended to persecute the Jews, which resulted in a rebellion and a very unstable time of Jewish independence from 167-63 BC (**D**). However the Hellenistic Empire, in 146 BC, was overthrown by Rome (**E**) and, in 63 BC, Pompey, a Roman General, took over the Neo-Judean state allowing it to keep its religious law and even to build the magnificent Herodian Temple in Jerusalem. It was under the Roman rule that the promised Messiah made His appearance, and the Jews were finally introduced to the **New Covenant**. Rome soon grew hostile to the Jews however, and the temple was destroyed for the last time and the Jews once more scattered over the whole world. Some have become Christians under the **New Covenant** along with gentiles of many nations. Some still waited for God to return them again to Jerusalem (Zion).

Appendix 4

1. Isaiah prophesied in chapter 62: 2,5, and 10-12 (740-681 BC):

The nations will see your righteousness and all kings your glory; & you will be called by a **New Name**, that the mouth of the Lord will bestow . . . As a young man marries a maiden, so will your sons marry you; as a bridegroom rejoices over his bride, so will your God rejoice over you . . . . Pass through, pass through the gates! Prepare the way for the people. Build up, build up the highway! Remove the stones, Raise the banner for the nations. The Lord has made proclamation to the ends of the earth; Say to the Daughter of Zion, See your Savior comes! and His reward is with Him. They will be called the Holy People, the Redeemed of the Lord; and you will be called the Sought After, the City No Longer Deserted.

2. Jeremiah prophesied in chapter 31: 31-33 (626-585 BC):

The time is coming, declares the Lord, when I will make a **New Covenant** with the House of Israel and with the House of Judah. It will not be like the covenant I made with their forefathers when I took them by the hand to lead them out of Egypt, because they broke my covenant, though I was a husband to them. This is the covenant I will make with them after that time, declares the Lord. I will put my law in their minds and write it on their hearts. I will be their God and they will be my people.

3. Ezekiel prophesied in chapter 11: 16-20 (593-571 BC):

This is what the Sovereign Lord says: Although I sent them far away among the nations and scattered them among the countries, yet for a little while I have been a sanctuary for them in the countries where they have gone. Therefore say: This is what the Sovereign Lord says: I will gather you back from the nations and bring you back from the countries where you have been scattered, and I will give you back the land of Israel again. ... I will give them an undivided heart and will put a **New Spirit** in them; I will remove from them their heart of stone and give them a heart of flesh. Then they will follow my decrees and be careful to keep my laws. They will be my people, and I will be their God.

4. Daniel prophesied in chapter 9: 2, 11, and 25 (605-530 Be):

In the first year of Darius the Mede I Daniel understood from the scriptures, according to the word given to Jeremiah.. that the desolation of Jerusalem would last 70 years . . . All Israel has transgressed your law and turned away refusing to obey you. Therefore the curses and sworn judgments written in the Law of Moses, the servant of God have been poured out on us, because we have sinned against you . . . . While I was praying thus, Gabriel stood before me and said, Know this: From the issuing of the decrees to restore and rebuild Jerusalem until **the Anointed One** . . . , there will be seven sevens, and sixty-two sevens. (483 years) . . . (then He) will be cut off . . . .

If one uses the date of the decree of Artaxerxes I, given to Ezra to rebuild the temple (458 BC), as the starting point of Daniel's 483 years, one arrives at 25 AD. The life span of Jesus was about 30 years. It can be demonstrated that our historical calendar is probably off by 5 years—most think Jesus was born in 5 BC. AD 25 would then really be 30 AD. Give or take a little for errors in dating that is remarkably close to the time of the crucifixion. (See I Corinthians 11: 23-26)

Appendix 5

The Hebrew Commonwealth Under the Mosaic Constitution

The LAW, or Covenant, covers it all.
The GOVERNING INSTITUTIONS, under the Law, constitute the constitution.

LAW OF GOD

12 TRIBES of ISRAEL

HIGH PRIEST — Birth Right Office

NATIONAL JUDGE — Called by God

UPPER Council of 70 Elders — Elected Princes + Birth Right Clan Leaders

STATES GENERAL

LOWER Assembly of Congregation — Elected Leaders in Cities

Levitical Cities — Birth right Bureaucracy

Tribal Cities — Elected Leaders

157

Appendix 6

12 TRIBES in Order of Birth

1. Reuben

2. Simeon

3. Levi (not given a Tribal Lot)

4. Judah

5. Dan

6. Naphtali

7. Gad

8. Asher

9. Issachar

10. Zebulun

11. Joseph (given two Tribal Lots)
    a. Manasseh
    b. Ephraim

12. Benjamin

JUDGES DEALINGS & TRIBES

MOSES & JOSHUA true national military leaders

OTHNIEL an adopted alien & son-in-law of Caleb, the former prince of Judah; repelled the Arameans of Damascus & other Kings of Mesopotamia a threat to all Israel. The army led by Othniel was likely made up of men of arms totally from his own tribe of Judah.

EHUD from Tribe of Benjamin; repelled Moabite invasion and took over Moab for a time. only Tribes 11 and 12 are mentioned but probably 1 & 7 had reason to participate.

SHAMGAR adopted alien acting independently against the Philistines; just a contempory of Deborah.

DEBORAH from tribe of Ephraim; only led the tribes: 6, 10, 11 b, 12, & 9 Asher refused to take part against this northern threat which was a proxy war for the Sidonites.

GIDEON from the Tribe of Manasseh; repelled the Midianites with only the support of Tribes: 8, 10, 6, 11 b, & 11 a; but Ephraim resented that the leadership came from Manasseh; Abimelech, one of Gideon's sons made himself king for 3 years.

TOLA from the Tribe of Issachar; no military role.

JAIR from the Tribe of Gad; no military role

JEPHTHAH from the Tribe of Gad; repelled the Ammonites with only the help of transjordanian Tribes: 1, 7, & 11a ; Ephraim tried to overthrow Jephthah refusing to accept him as judge of Israel.

IBSAN from the Tribe of Issachar; no military role

ELON from the Tribe of Zebulun; no military role.

ABDON from the Tribe of Ephraim; no military role

SAMSON (of Tribe of Dan) all exploits done single handedly against Philistines. no Tribes followed him

SAMUEL (from Tribe of Ephraim) turned over all military roles to a king.

Appendix 6

Map of Canaan — Twelve Tribes Portions

Appendix 7

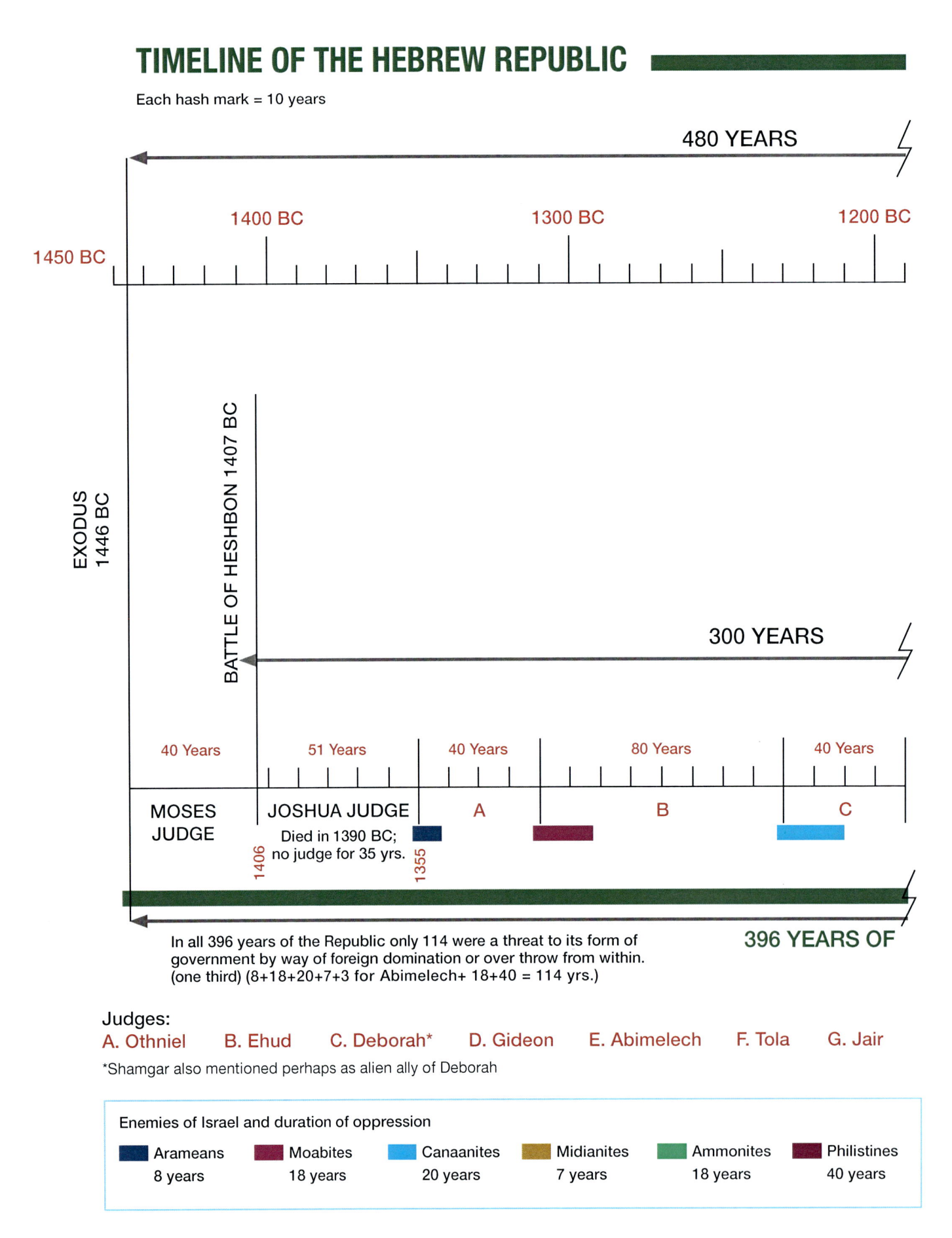

TIMELINE OF THE HEBREW REPUBLIC

Each hash mark = 10 years

480 YEARS

1450 BC — 1400 BC — 1300 BC — 1200 BC

EXODUS 1446 BC

BATTLE OF HESHBON 1407 BC

300 YEARS

40 Years	51 Years	40 Years	80 Years	40 Years
MOSES JUDGE	JOSHUA JUDGE — Died in 1390 BC; no judge for 35 yrs.	A	B	C

1406   1355

396 YEARS OF

In all 396 years of the Republic only 114 were a threat to its form of government by way of foreign domination or over throw from within. (one third) (8+18+20+7+3 for Abimelech+ 18+40 = 114 yrs.)

Judges:
A. Othniel   B. Ehud   C. Deborah*   D. Gideon   E. Abimelech   F. Tola   G. Jair

*Shamgar also mentioned perhaps as alien ally of Deborah

Enemies of Israel and duration of oppression

Arameans	Moabites	Canaanites	Midianites	Ammonites	Philistines
8 years	18 years	20 years	7 years	18 years	40 years

Appendix 7

1 KINGS 6:1 ⟶ 966 BC

1100 BC — 1000 BC

- Life of Eli (1174–1076)
- Life of Samuel (1107–1015)
- Life of Samson (1096–1056)

JUDGES 11:26 ⟶ 1107

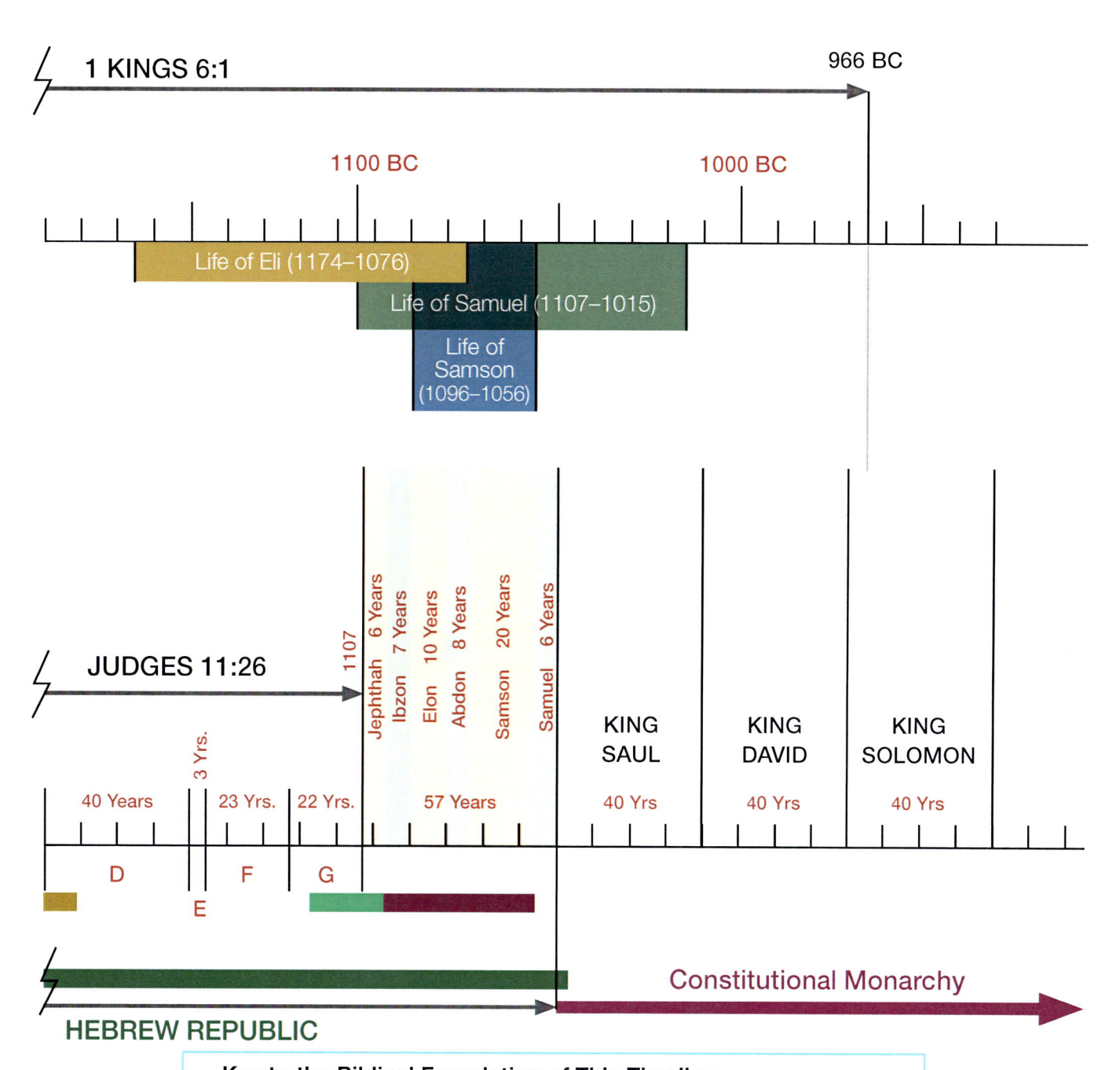

- Jephthah 6 Years
- Ibzon 7 Years
- Elon 10 Years
- Abdon 8 Years
- Samson 20 Years
- Samuel 6 Years

| 40 Years | 3 Yrs. | 23 Yrs. | 22 Yrs. | 57 Years | KING SAUL 40 Yrs | KING DAVID 40 Yrs | KING SOLOMON 40 Yrs |

D, E, F, G

HEBREW REPUBLIC → **Constitutional Monarchy**

Key to the Biblical Foundation of This Timeline:

I Kings 6:1 NIV	966 + 480 = 1446 BC Exodus
Deut 1: 3-4 NIV	1446 - 39 = 1407 BC Battle Heshbon
Judges 11:26	1407 - 300 = 1107 BC enter Jephthah

- Moses from the Exodus to his death (1406 BC) is the Republic's first Judge
- 7 Judges in texts to right = 248 years   (Judges 3:11, 30; 5:31; 8:28; 9:22; 10:2, 3)
- From Jephthah 1107 + 248 = 1355 BC
- From Moses' death 1406 to 1355 BC = 51 years / 2nd Judge Joshua plus the time of the Elders of that generation that out lived him.

- 5 Judges in texts to right = 51 years   (Judges 12:7, 9, 11, 14; 15:20)
- From Jephthah 1107 - 51 = 1056 BC
- From 1056 - 1050 = 6 years for Samuel's Judgeship before Saul

Acts 13: 17-22 1 Kings 2:1-4, 10

Appendix 8

The National Hebrew States General

GOD IS KING of this Federal Republic

PRESIDING: NATIONAL JUDGE over COUNCIL of 70

Reuben	Simeon	Judah	Issachar	Zebulun	Ephriam
Prince & 4 Leaders of 1000s	Prince & 5 Leaders of 1000s	Prince & 5 Leaders of 1000s	Prince & 4 Leaders of 1000s	Prince & 3 Leaders of 1000s	Prince & 4 Leaders of 1000s
Manasseh	Benjamin	Dan	Asher	Gad	Naphtali
Prince & 8 + 1* Leaders of 1000s	Prince & 7 Leaders of 1000s	Prince & 1 Leader of 1000s	Prince & 5 Leaders of 1000s	Prince & 7 Leaders of 1000s	Prince & 4 Leaders of 1000s

*See Numbers 26 – 27 adding 1 to Manasseh

LOWER ASSEMBLY OF THE CONGREGATION

City elected Judges and Rulers of 100s, 50s, and 10s

FOR NATIONAL LEGISLATIVE PURPOSES

It may have been just the locally elected judges from every city that made up the lower house of the "Whole Assembly" of Israel. It would be difficult to guess the size of this body because there was no set number of judges and officers to be elected in each city. Attendance in the lower house by every city was mandatory.

See Deuteronomy 1:13–15, and 16:18

As near as I can tell, a national meeting of the lower house never occurred in isolation. Especially in military matters, but perhaps in any case, attendance in the lower house by every city was mandatory. The Council of 70 apparently met often, by itself, without the lower house. The Council met as a court and otherwise to discuss national policy. Also, the Levite tribe served as staff and bureaucrats from their various cities, scattered throughout the other tribal lands.

Appendix 9

EXHIBIT A
English Common Law Roots in the Law of Moses
From King Alfred's Doom Book

1. "Mind that you hallow the rest-day. You must work six days; but on the seventh you must rest. For six days Christ made Heavens and Earth, the seas, and all the shapen things in them; but He rested on the seventh day."
Exodus 20: 8

2. "If anyone buys a Christian slave, let him be bonded for six years — but the seventh, he must be freely unbought. With such cloths as he went in, with such must he go forth. If he had a wife she must go out with him."

"He that steals a Freeman and sells him, and it be proved against him, so shall he suffer death."
Exodus 21 : 2-6

3. "Don't let a woman live who is wont to receive enchanters and conjurers and witches."
Exodus 22: 18

4. "The man who intentionally slays another man — let him suffer death. He, however, who slays another out of necessity, or unwillingly, or involuntarily — and did not lay in wait for him — he is worthy of his living and must be given asylum; but if one presumptuously and willfully slays his neighbor through guile-drag him from My altar, so that he should suffer death."
Numbers 35: 11-33

5. "If anyone, while fighting, hurt a pregnant woman—let him pay a fine for the hurt, as the evaluators determine. If she die — let him pay soul for soul."
Exodus 21: 22-23

6. "If a thief breaks into a man's house at night, and he be slain there — the slayer is not guilty of manslaughter. If he does this after sun rise, he is guilty of manslaughter, and he himself shall die — unless he slew out of necessity. If a thief be caught red-handed with what he stole — let him pay two fold for it.
Exodus 22: 2-4

7. "Do not listen to the words of a liar; nor permit his judgments against another; nor speak to anyone who gives testimony in his favour." — Exodus 23: 1

8. "Do not act in any way uncouthly toward the stranger from abroad nor oppress him with any unrighteousness."
Exodus 22: 21

Google: *King Alfred the Great and our Common Law*, Rev. Dr. F.N. Lee

Appendix 9

EXHIBIT B

The Roots of Western Due Process of Law in Deuteronomy

1. Elected Representative government. (How else do the people "bring in men of wisdom" ... if not by popular election?)
Deut 1 : 13-15

2. A Judicial system with equal justice under the law.
Deut. 1: 16-17 Not to take bribes Deut 16: 18-20

3. Cities of Refuge to protect the accidental slayer of life from the death penalty. (Make the penalty fit the crime.)
Deut 4: 42 and Deut. 19: 4-6

4. Accountability to your fellow man protecting his inalienable rights.
Deut. 5: 16-21

5. Accountability to the most helpless even the alien in your midst.
Deut. 10: 17-19 and Deut 24: 19-22

6. Every Seven years an adjustment for eradication of the debtor class to avoid the natural development of a dominate class and even permanent slavery. Here rests the first use of the concept of bankruptcy, and probably the origin of such by the Greeks in Athens under Solon. Deut 15: 1-8 plus verses 12-15 Probably the basis for an indentured servant system during English colonialism. Also see Deut 23: 15-16

7. Grand jury inquiry and requirement of more than one witness to bring down the death penalty and when the matter cannot be settled as to guilt even a right of appeal before the Levite experts in the law.
Deut 17: 2-9 and Deut 19: 15-18

8. Chief Executive of the nation shall be under the law as much as the lowest citizen.
Deut 17: 14-20

9. Private property rights and responsibilities.
Deut 19: 14 and Deut 24: 14-15 and 25: 13-15

10. If a slave has taken refuge with you, do not hand him over to his master. Let him live among you where ever he likes. Do not oppress him.
Deut. 23: 15

11. A father shall not exercise capital punishment over his son except as he stands accused before a jury. (Why the inquiry if guilt is assumed?)
Deut 21: 18-21 and Deut 22: 13-30 and 24: 16

Appendix 10

Great Christian Movements in American History
and the Interconnection Between Great Preachers and Lay-leaders of Reform

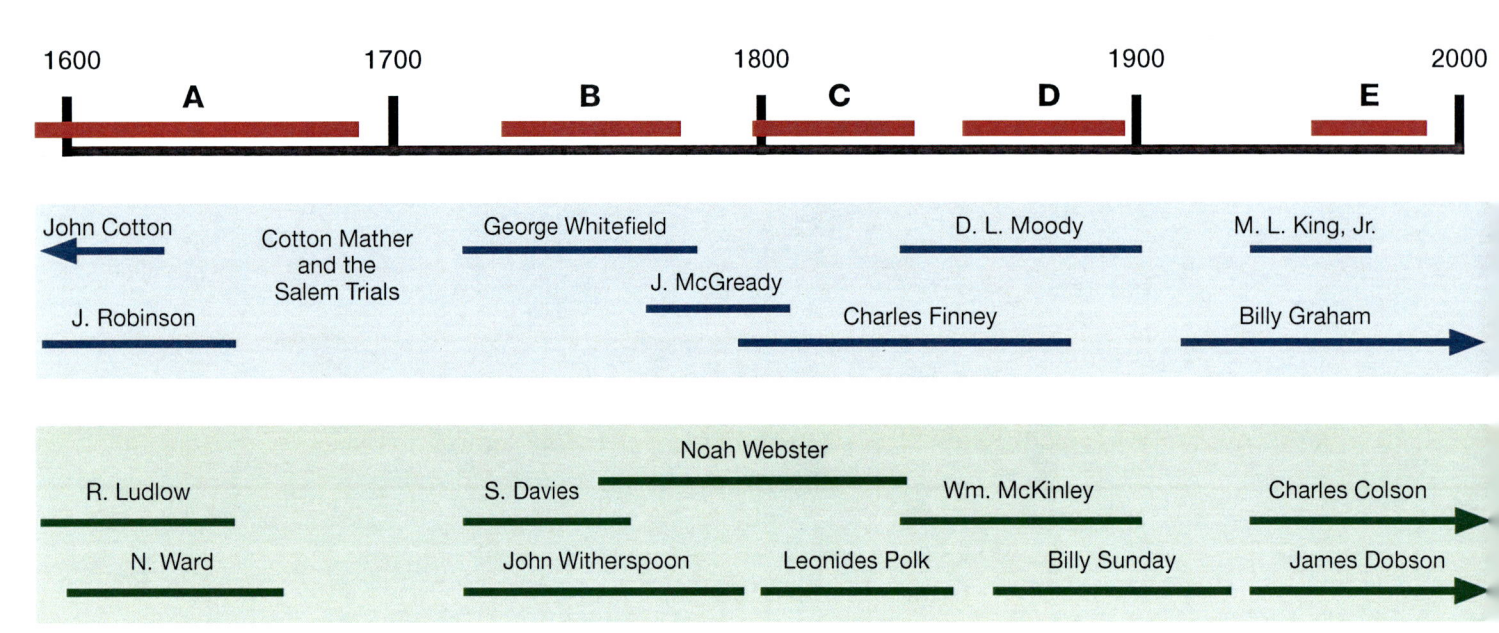

```
1600        1700            1800        1900          2000
     A              B         C          D         E
```

Preachers: John Cotton, J. Robinson, Cotton Mather and the Salem Trials, George Whitefield, J. McGready, D. L. Moody, Charles Finney, M. L. King, Jr., Billy Graham

Lay-leaders: R. Ludlow, N. Ward, S. Davies, John Witherspoon, Noah Webster, Leonides Polk, Wm. McKinley, Billy Sunday, Charles Colson, James Dobson

A. The English Reformation, Civil War, and Glorious Revolution

John Robinson (1575-1625) was an English Puritan minister at the time of King James I. The King drove his congregation out of Scooby, England and they went to Leiden, Holland. There he became the spiritual leader of what became the Pilgrim Fathers who settled in Plymouth, New England in 1620 under William Bradford. Finally, in the 1640's, Civil War broke out in England between the Stuart King Charles I and the Puritan leader Oliver Cromwell and his allies in Presbyterian Scotland. During this turmoil many more Puritans were migrating to America. A direct connection between the development of republican government in England and in the colonies emerged, under preachers like **John Cotton** (1585-1652) of New England. (For more detail see pages 105–106 in part four.)

As a result **Roger Ludlow** a lawyer developed the first written constitution of history, called *The Fundamental Orders of Connecticut.* Also, a lawyer, **Nathaniel Ward** in Massachusetts Bay Colony, drawing from the Old Testament and the book of Deuteronomy drew up a constitution for his colony called *The Body of Liberties.*

B. The First Great Awakening Revival Impacts the American Revolution

George Whitefield (1714-1770) is known as the father of camp meeting evangelicalism. He was a minister of a Methodist Church in Georgia, but spent most of his life traveling and preaching out of doors to thousands at a time. His preaching changed the lives of great and small both in England and in America. He helped bring the colonies together as a Christian nation.

One of those influenced was the lawyer, **Samuel Davies**, whose testimony helped lead Patrick Henry to a like Christian public service. Davies also served as President of Princeton College. A man also impacted by the First Great Awakening was **John Witherspoon**, signer of the Declaration of Independence and a later President of Princeton. He helped provide a Christian education for James Madison, a Vice President, three Supreme Court Judges, ten early Cabinet members, twelve Governors and sixty Congressmen.

Appendix 10

C. The Second Great Awakening Revival Impacts the Civil War Era

James McGready led a gathering of all local churches for a mass communion service at Cane Ridge, Kentucky near Lexington in 1801. It turned into what became known as America's Pentecost. Estimates were that for several days more than 10,000 people witnessed an out pouring of the Holy Spirit that led to maybe 3000 conversions. Social issues like slavery and equal rights for women in American society became great concerns of the churches in America in the first half of the 19th century.

The chief evangelist of the Second Great Awakening was **Charles Finney** (1792-1875). He encouraged women's participation in church and he denounced slavery from the pulpit. He became President of Oberlin College, in Ohio, the first college to coeducate blacks and women and white men. His camp meetings drew thousands as he went from state to state holding revivals.

Noah Webster an educator of this time who greatly influenced elementary public education in early America promoted Christian moralistic education in his popular speller used for 100 years in some schools. He produced the first American Dictionary and translated the first American language Bible. There was no attempt in that America to separate Christian influence in public matters. Webster called on teachers to encourage students to learn to vote for Christian men for public office when they came of voting age. During the Civil War **General Robert E. Lee** and **General Leonides Polk** both actively led in prayer before their troops. General Polk led three Generals to salvation in the Confederate Army. Imagine a great awakening going on right during a Civil War.

D. The Third Great Awakening Revival Shapes America

Dwight L. Moody (1837-1899) may be the American Evangelist that is most known as part of this spiritual awakening in United States history. But he was not alone. This was also the time of William Booth who started the Salvation Army, and of great foreign missions movements usually centered in England, but always impacting churches in America. Moody is known for Moody Bible Institute today in Chicago.

William McKinley, saved at a revival meeting during the second great awakening, worked his way from local offices all the way up to winning election as the 25th President of the United States. He took the oath of office on a Bible open to Solomon's prayer for wisdom. When the Philippines were taken in the Spanish American War, he decided to annex the islands and encouraged American missionaries to help win them to Christ.

Another man impacted by the third great awakening was **Billy Sunday**, a preaching professional baseball player of this era. God is always looking for bold witnesses in all professions of life.

E. The Born-Again Revival Crusades Shape America

Billy Graham (1918-?). His impact on American history has been in a time when we are the super power of the world. His Crusades thus have impacted the world much like our country has in every other venue of life. He was able to have an audience with every President since Truman. He especially took a stand against communism and against racial discrimination in all its forms. **Martin Luther King, Jr.** (1929-68) as a Southern Baptist minister made a huge impact on ending the segregation laws keeping Black-Americans from equal protection under the law. Sadly, an assassin took his life; but his cause did not die with him.

In part because of America's large evangelical Christian population kept active by these preachers, men like the next two have had a large impact in venues outside of the Church. **Chuck Colson**, a lawyer involved in the President Nixon scandal that sent him to prison for three years, found God and started a prison ministry and has written books that have addressed many issues in our culture that are pulling our nation away from its Biblical foundation. Another man, **James Dobson**, a medical and psychological Doctor, in this same vein, has given his life to addressing issues of abortion, child abuse, and homosexuality. In America's cultural war today, again it has been Christian leaders who have led the fight for justice; some from the pulpit and some from secular postitions in society.

BIBLIOGRAPHY

Barton, David. *Celebrate Liberty / Famous Patriotic Speeches.* Aledo, TX: Wall Builders Press, 2003.

Beliles, Mark, and McDowell, Stephen K. *American Providential History.* Charlottesville, VA: Providence Foundation, 1989.

Brendlinger, Irv A. *Social Justice through the Eyes of Wesley.* Ontario, Canada: Joshua Press Inc., 2006.

Eidsmoe, John. *Christianity and the Constitution.* Grand Rapids, MI: Backer Books, 1987.

Hamilton, Alexander, James Madison, & John Jay. *The Federalist Papers.* Ed. Benjamin F. Wright. New York: Barnes and Noble Books, 1961.

Hall, David W. *Calvin in the Public Square.* Phillipsburg, NJ: P & R Publishing, 2009.

Johnson, Robert Bowie, Jr. *The Parthenon Code.* Annapolis, MD: Solving Light Books, 2004.

Jones, Dr. Floyd Nolen. *Chronology of the Old Testament.* Green Forest, AR: Master Books, 1993.

Jordan, James B. *Judges/ A Practical and Theological Commentary.* Eugene, OR: Wipf & Stock Publishers, 1985.

Lillback, Peter. *Goerge Washington's Sacred Fire.* Bryn Mawr, PA: Providence Forum Press, 2006.

McDowell, Stephen. *The American Dream / Jamestown & the Planting of the American Christian Republic.* Charlottesville, VA: Providence Foundation, 2007.

Morris, Dr Henry M. *God and the Nations.* Green Forest, AR: Master Books, 2002.

Royal, Robert. *The God That Did Not Fail.* New York: Encounter Books, 2006.

Rushdoony, Rousas I. *Institutes of Biblical Law.* Phillipsburg, NJ: The Presbyterian and Reformed Publishing Co., 1973.

_____. *This Independent Republic.* Fairfax, VA: Thoburn Press, 1964.

Sandoz, Ellis. *Political Sermons of the American Founding Era.* Volume 1 and 2. Indianapolis, IN: Liberty Fund, 1998.

Sidney, Algernon. *Discourses Concerning Government.* Liberty Classics, 1990.

Smith, Gary Scott, *God and Politics,* Presbyterian & Reformed Publishing Co., Phillipsburg, N.J., 1989.

Bibliography

Stark, Rodney, *The Victory of Reason – How Christianity Led to Freedom, Capitalism, and Western Success.* New York: Random House Trade Paperback, 2006.

Stacey, Robert D. *Sir William Blackstone and the Common Law.* Powder Springs, GA: American Visioin Press, 2008.

Steinsaltz, Adin. *The Essential Talmud.* London: Weidenfeld and Nicolson, 1976.

Tocqueville, Alexis de. *Democracy in America.* New York: Washington Square Press, 1964 (Orig. 1835).

The Holy Bible: *The 1599 Geneva Bible.* Powder Springs, GA: Tolle Lege Press, 2007 (Reprint).

The Holy Bible: *The NIV Study Bible.* Grand Rapids, MI: Zondervan Publishing House, 2000.

Wines, Rev. E.C. *Commentaries On the Laws of the Ancient Hebrews.* Powder Springs, GA: American Vision Press, 2009 (Orig.1853).

Woods, Thomas E. Jr. and Gutzman, Kevin R.C., *Who Killed the Constitution?* New York: Crown Forum, 2008.

About the Author

John W. Zull is now 70 years old. He comes from a family of eight siblings, of which he is the second oldest. His father was a Baptist minister. John surrendered to the call of the Holy Spirit for salvation at a very young age. He graduated with a BA in education from Western Michigan University, in Kalamazoo, Michigan in 1963. In the first four years of his public school teaching career he earned his MA degree from the same university, majoring in political science. He has viewed his 37 years of public school teaching as a vocation, to which he was called by God. He has been married 49 years to the same wonderful love of his life, Arlene. They have two children and four grandchildren. Most of his career he taught U.S. History, World History, and Government classes in Portage Northern High School. He retired in June of 2001. While working John was elected, and reelected, City Councilman in Portage City from 1987 to 2000; and upon retirement he ran for Kalamazoo County Commissioner, where he still servers the citizens of his county. His belief in Christian service to society, as unto the Lord, that fills the pages of this book, is something he has tried to live out in his life. In his retirement years, John has been helped immensely by attending worldview conferences led by organizations like American Vision and Vision Forum. At these conferences many of the greatest contemporary apologists for biblically based nation building inspire those attending to once again take "dominion" for Christianity in America. Such organizations are now the leaders in modern day "reformation" efforts in Western Civilization's twenty first century.

John wishes to dedicate this book as as a spiritual and cultural legacy to his children and grandchildren: Richard and Julie Soderquist, Hannah and Rachael, Jon and Karen Zull, Jacob and Sarah. He acknowledges a debt of gratitude he owes to his wife, Arlene, and to friends who encouraged and advised him in its preparation.